coastal kitchen

coastal kitchen

Nourishing Seafood Recipes for Everyday Cooking

JENNY SHEA RAWN

Globe
Pequot

Essex, Connecticut

Globe
Pequot

An imprint of Globe Pequot, the trade division of
The Rowman & Littlefield Publishing Group, Inc.
4501 Forbes Blvd., Ste. 200
Lanham, MD 20706
www.rowman.com

Distributed by NATIONAL BOOK NETWORK

Copyright © 2023 by Jenny Shea Rawn

Photography by Jenny Shea Rawn unless otherwise noted

British Library Cataloguing in Publication Information available

Library of Congress Cataloging-in-Publication Data

Names: Rawn, Jenny Shea, author.
Title: Coastal kitchen : nourishing seafood recipes for everyday cooking / Jenny Shea Rawn.
Description: Essex, Connecticut : Globe Pequot, 2023. | Includes index.
Identifiers: LCCN 2022047382 (print) | LCCN 2022047383 (ebook) | ISBN 9781493073115 (cloth)
   | ISBN 9781493073122 (ebook)
Subjects: LCSH: Cooking (Seafood) | LCGFT: Cookbooks.
Classification: LCC TX747 .R39 2022 (print) | LCC TX747 (ebook) | DDC 641.6/92—dc23/
   eng/20221114
LC record available at https://lccn.loc.gov/2022047382
LC ebook record available at https://lccn.loc.gov/2022047383

This book is dedicated to:

My husband, Adrian, who is my rock, no. 1 taste-tester,
loyal fan, partner, and biggest supporter.

My unconditionally supportive, loving, and encouraging parents,
Mimi and Peter Shea, who instilled in me a love of the ocean and its
offerings and the New England coastline from a very young age.

My precious "beach babies," Lucca and Lexi, who bring me joy every day and
who love the beach, ocean, and creatures of the sea just as much as I do.

Jenny, age 5, with a box of lobsters

Disclaimer

This book is for informational, educational, and entertainment use only and is not intended to prevent, treat, or cure any disease. Although the author has taken great care in writing this book, we make no warranty about the accuracy and completeness of its content and, to the maximum extent permitted, disclaim all liability arising indirectly or directly from its use and the application of any of the contents within this book. The recommendations, recipes, and information in this book are not intended to replace the advice of a qualified health professional, including a registered dietitian nutritionist. The nutrition information provided within these pages are estimates, not exacts, and should be interpreted as such. The nutrition information will vary based on cooking methods, brands used, interpretation of the recipes, etc. The nutrition highlights provided are based upon 3-ounce servings of cooked fish or shellfish. Always speak with your health-care professional prior to making any diet or lifestyle changes.

Contents

Foreword

by Linda Cornish, President & Founder of Seafood Nutrition Partnership

Seafood is one of the best foods we can add to our diets that can support our personal health and at the same time our planet's health. As president and founder of the nonprofit Seafood Nutrition Partnership (SNP), I have had the honor of working on an important mission to inspire a healthier America through partnerships and outreach to raise awareness about the health benefits of eating seafood at least twice a week.

The public health benefits of eating more seafood include improved brain health, heart health, and overall wellness. Yet only 20 percent of Americans follow the USDA Dietary Guidelines' recommendation to eat seafood at least twice per week. That is why I am so happy to see Jenny Shea Rawn create this gorgeous book, *Coastal Kitchen*. Jenny is a registered dietitian with a master's degree in nutrition and a master's degree in public health, a seafood lover and enthusiast, food photographer, recipe developer, and mother of two young kids. Jenny has always been supportive of SNP's mission by sharing simple yet elegant seafood recipes with beautiful imagery that motivate her audience to try seafood. Jenny's food photography and recipes help make seafood shine—after all, we eat with our eyes first.

Coastal Kitchen is a wonderful resource for those looking to incorporate more seafood into their diet—and those looking for new seafood recipes and inspiration. And it's a stunning coffee-table book—every single recipe has a beautiful image accompanying it! It contains simple yet elevated and nourishing recipes perfect for everyday cooking—and also some extraordinary seafood dishes that are perfect for entertaining.

In *Coastal Kitchen* Jenny covers the basics of seafood cookery, answers the most common questions she gets about seafood, discusses sustainable seafood, talks through tips to eat more seafood on a budget, highlights the nutritional benefits of seafood, and more. Best of all, Jenny helps make seafood more approachable, more familiar, and less intimidating. *Coastal Kitchen* will help more Americans move one step closer to eating seafood at least two times a week. It has become one of my favorite seafood cookbooks, and I know it will become a favorite of yours as well.

To Your Health,
Linda Cornish
President & Founder
Seafood Nutrition Partnership

Acknowledgments

A special thanks to:

- Our friend and nanny, Linda Sullivan, a.k.a. "Ninna," for working many long days watching Lucca and Lexi while this book was being written.
- The Clam Man in Falmouth, Massachusetts, for being our go-to for the best fresh fish and shellfish case around.
- Eating with the Ecosystem and Red's Best for raising my awareness about and appreciation for the wealth of local seafood available right off our coast.
- Seafood Nutrition Partnership for being a great resource for seafood health information and for helping Americans meet the goal of eating seafood twice a week.
- The Merl family of F/V *Isabel and Lilee* for inviting me on board and teaching me the ins and outs of sea scallops and scalloping.
- Scott Rushnak of Black Gold Fisheries for having me on board F/V *Mussla* and showing me how mussels are harvested.
- Sea State for the tour of their oyster farm and lesson on oysters.
- Cape Cod Select for the cranberry bog tours they've invited me on over the years.
- Boston University nutrition students: graduate student Tianran Ye and undergraduate Sarah Liao for doing the nutritional analysis for the recipes in this book.

Introduction

"Live in the sunshine, swim the sea, drink the wild air."

—*Ralph Waldo Emerson*

This quote hangs in my office on a little bronze plaque, given to me by my mom many years ago. These words have always spoken to me, as I am most at home by the sea. It's always been a source of inspiration, calm, and peace for me. And it's the same for my kids now, as they are true beach babies. For them, a day isn't complete without one or two trips to the beach, a short quarter-mile walk down the road.

As a child in the 1980s, my family vacationed on Cape Cod every year, usually in Chatham. In many of those years, we stayed in a tiny little sand-covered beach shack with little cot beds and a path right to the ocean. My sisters, cousins, and I would play on the beach all day and search for sand dollars, then go to the nearby marina docks to search for starfish and seahorses (I haven't spotted any of those creatures on the Cape since those childhood years). For dinner, we would boil lobsters or visit Kream 'N Kone for the best fried seafood (especially those deep-fried scallops and clams) that you could smell from miles away. That is where my love for seafood started.

When I met my husband, Adrian, we bonded over the fact that we both grew up summering on the Cape with our families and visiting Duck Pond, a little-known small kettle pond in Wellfleet. That pond wasn't easy to find back then and is still a relatively unknown secret spot. It had (and has) pristine water, a tiny beach, and is the perfect spot for kids to swim and explore. I had not met anyone who knew about Duck Pond other than my family and extended family. I knew then that he was a keeper, as he was a lover of Cape Cod, seafood, and the coast just like I was.

When we were first dating, we would often borrow Adrian's parents' sailboat for long weekends and sail from Essex, Connecticut, to Sag Harbor, New York. We'd grill the local fish or lobsters and local corn on a grill off the back of the boat while watching the sunset. Those were good times.

We got married, barefoot, on Martha's Vineyard at Edgartown Lighthouse in 2012 with just our family and close friends in tow. Our wedding dinner featured all the freshest local seafood and produce that the island had to offer.

Adrian and I moved from Boston to the Cape (Falmouth) full-time in 2014, when we were pregnant with our first child, Lucca. We weren't sure how we would adjust to the move from city to sea, but we fell in love with living on the Cape year-round. We have breathtaking beaches that our family utilizes every day of the year, incredible restaurants, good schools, and the *best* seafood—much of which is caught just off the coast. We also have the greatest seafood market I've ever come across—right in town, 7 minutes away. It's a family-owned-and-operated business called The Clam Man, and they have the freshest seafood you'll find, unless you catch it yourself. They sell all the local seafood but also source domestic and international crowd favorites like salmon, shrimp, mahimahi, and the like. We get most of our fresh seafood there.

But we don't *only* buy fresh seafood and we don't *only* buy local seafood. I believe it's critical to support our local fishermen and our local economy by purchasing local and domestic whenever we can, but I also acknowledge that some of the offerings we love aren't in our local waters—salmon being one of them (salmon is one of my daughter Lexi's favorite foods). As long as we are purchasing sustainably grown and harvested fish, I feel good about that.

And we are big fans of tinned (canned) seafood, flash-frozen seafood (especially shrimp and tuna steaks), and dried seafood (two of our favorite snacks are tuna jerky and dried seaweed snacks). You'll find a list of some of our favorite seafood pantry items and seafood essentials on page 249. The fact is, not everyone has access to the same fresh seafood we do, but there are abundant seafood options for *all* of us, no matter where in the country you live—whether that's fresh, flash-frozen (frozen seafood has come a long way!), tinned, dried, or other seafood. Options abound, regardless of geography, budget, taste preferences, time constraints, or skill level in the kitchen.

Most of us (including you, I imagine?) want to eat more seafood. It's tasty (that's no. 1), it's convenient, and it's nutrient-dense (packed with protein and a variety of other nutrients, depending on the species, including brain- and heart-health-promoting omega-3 fatty acids, vitamin D, calcium, vitamin A, B vitamins, zinc, selenium, iodine, iron, magnesium, and phosphorous, to name just a few). In fact, leading health organizations recommend that Americans include seafood on their plate at least twice per week (two servings, about 4 ounces each, especially fatty fish) for better health *across the lifespan*.

According to Seafood Nutrition Partnership, eating seafood twice a week:

- Leads to improved brain and eye development in infants, children, and adults
- Helps to reduce the risk of heart disease
- Is beneficial for both pregnant women and their babies
- Influences your mental health in a positive way, including reducing risk for depression and anxiety

Even though seafood is a star when it comes to taste, convenience, and nutrition, I acknowledge that for many, it is an intimidating protein to cook for several reasons, and that's one of the reasons I wrote this book: to help make seafood more accessible and familiar. There is a misconception that seafood is difficult and complicated to cook, but actually it is one of the simplest and quickest proteins to cook (with the exception of whole lobsters and crabs—but even those are simple, just time-consuming, once you have a few under your belt).

This cookbook aims to take the guesswork out of seafood—to make it easier for you to select, prepare, and cook seafood so that you can create simple yet elevated and healthy seafood meals in your own kitchen. Throughout these pages, I'll be sharing seafood tips and tricks, 120+ simple recipes for everyday cooking, and some new and unique ways of serving up seafood (hello, seacuterie boards!). Plus, I'll be answering the most common questions I get about seafood, including how to make sure you are purchasing sustainable seafood, how to cook lobster, how to sear scallops, and more. I'll also bring you along on a few New England–based food tours (a scallop boat, a mussel-fishing vessel, an oyster farm, and a cranberry harvest) so you can see the food at its source.

The recipes on these pages lean healthy, and you'll notice veggies pair heavily with seafood throughout. I do use butter and salt in moderation, because a little goes a long way in adding flavor. We need flavor for enjoyment. If you need to adjust the recipes to meet your dietary needs, please do so.

My hope is that this book inspires you to cook more seafood at home in your kitchen and helps answer some of the questions you have about selecting, purchasing, and cooking seafood more often.

Why did I write a cookbook featuring seafood?

- No other protein offers such variety—there are endless fish, shellfish, and seaweed options to enjoy.
- Seafood is tasty.
- Seafood is convenient.
- Seafood is nutrient-dense and is one of the healthiest types of food we can eat, mainly because of the omega-3 fatty acids. Seafood—especially fatty fish—is brain food.
- Seafood has a lower carbon footprint than other animal proteins and can be part of a climate-friendly diet.
- Seafood shines with simplicity—it's one of the few foods that requires little more than salt, pepper, and lemon to taste good.
- Seafood requires little cooking time.
- Seafood requires minimal marinating time, if any.
- Consuming seafood supports local and domestic fishermen and women.
- Seafood is fascinating—I hope you'll agree!

Thanks for picking up *Coastal Kitchen*. I hope you enjoy it enough to share with those whom you love.

Best,
Jenny Shea Rawn

Lobster

Lobster. The seafood king of summer and perhaps the greatest crustacean to come out of the sea. It wasn't always that way though. Lobster used to be known as poor man's food and prison food because of its overabundance. Lobster is sweet, succulent, and briny—and paired with butter and lemon definitely stands as one of my top three favorite foods.

Nothing says summer to me more than a classic lobster roll—I prefer Connecticut style (warm and tossed with melted butter on a toasted bun) over Maine-style (chilled and tossed with mayo on a toasted buttered bun), but really, I wouldn't mind one of each, side by side. And how can you beat a traditional New England–style lobster dinner served with a whole steamed lobster, steamers, corn, potatoes, coleslaw, butter, and lemon wedges?

In this chapter we discuss how to steam lobster and we celebrate lobster with the best lobster roll. Then we go less traditional with a lobster BLT platter, lobster tacos, lobster bites, grilled lobster, and more.

Jenny holding a small lobster (this one was thrown back) in Camden, Maine

Lobster 101

Choosing and Storing Lobster

- Lobsters should be *alive* when you purchase them. Do not purchase lobsters that are not moving—choose the feisty ones.
- There are *new-shell* lobsters and *hard-shell* lobsters. New-shell lobsters have recently shed their old shell; their new shell had formed underneath and is softer and larger than the old shell. This shedding often happens between June/July and October/November but can vary. Seawater fills in the space between the new shell and the lobster body, and the resulting meat is tender and sweet. New-shell lobsters are much easier to crack. Hard-shell lobsters have thicker and harder shells, as they have not recently shed their shell. Hard-shells contain more meat, and the meat is a bit denser and firmer. You will need lobster crackers to break their shells. The cooking time for hard shells is longer than the cooking time for new shells.
- Ideally, cook your lobsters on the day of purchase. If you need to store them for a day prior to cooking, keep them in the coldest part of the fridge (not the freezer), which is typically the bottom shelf in the back. You can cover them in damp (not wet) newspaper. Do not put lobsters in a plastic bag or closed container—they will suffocate. Do not put your lobsters in fresh water or on ice, this will also kill them.
- When you're ready to cook your lobsters, place them in the freezer for 10 to 15 minutes prior to cooking to sedate them.
- Not feeling up to cooking your own lobsters? Go lazy man's lobster–style. Have your fish market or supermarket steam and crack the lobster for you, if they are able to (some may or may not be able to due to the summer rush). Or order frozen lobster tails or lobster meat.
- If you purchase frozen lobster tails or meat, purchase product free of any ice crystals or frost, indicating the lobster may have thawed and then refrozen or may have been stored for a long period of time, which can affect the quality. Thaw frozen lobster in the refrigerator overnight. Alternatively, you can place the tails or meat in a sealed plastic bag and run cold water over it until thawed or in a bowl of cold water that's changed every 30 minutes.
- Don't leave frozen lobster or any seafood out on the counter at room temperature to thaw.
- Lobster carcasses make your trash very stinky, so it's not a bad idea to plan your lobster meal around trash pickup day.

Cooking Lobster

Steaming vs. Boiling

For whole lobster, we typically steam it (versus boiling) in a steamer basket inside a large pot because:

- Steaming is a gentler cooking process than boiling it, therefore it's more forgiving. That means if the lobster steams for a few extra minutes, it's less likely to be overcooked.
- Steaming makes for a less messy meat-plucking process. That means less lobster juice squirting all over the place and less lobster smell in my house.
- Steaming provides less chance of burning yourself with scalding hot water and having the water boil over.

How do you steam lobster?

- Place a few inches of salt water (use either seawater or salted water) inside a large pot (pot needs to be large enough to fit all the lobsters, unless you're cooking in batches). Add a steaming basket. Bring water to a rolling boil. Carefully add the lobsters head first into the pot and cover with a lid.
- For 1½-pound lobsters, we steam them for about 17 to 18 minutes (for hard-shell lobsters). Open the pot about halfway through cooking time to move the lobsters around with long tongs or heatproof gloves to ensure even cooking.
- We use timing guidance (for steaming and boiling) from the folks at Maine Lobster (see below)—timing is based on the size of the lobsters as well as cooking method and shell type.
- Hard-shell lobsters will take longer to cook than new-shell. Add approximately 3 additional minutes to the cooking time for hard-shell lobsters.
- Remove lobsters from pot with long tongs or heatproof gloves. Be careful of the hot steam.
- Serve lobsters with lobster crackers for cracking shells and cocktail forks for pulling out the meat.

How long do you steam lobsters?

According to the Maine Lobster Marketing Collaborative (lobsterfrommaine.com), steam lobster according to this chart:

- 1 pound lobster → 10 minutes
- 1¼ pounds → 12 minutes
- 1½ pounds → 14 minutes
- 1¾ pounds → 16 minutes
- 2 pounds → 18 minutes
- 2½ pounds → 22 minutes
- 3 pounds → 25–30 minutes

Note: Find the cooking time based on the size of the lobsters you purchased—if you purchase 4 (1½-pound) lobsters, choose the time for 1½-pound lobster *not* for 6 pounds.

If you are looking to boil your lobsters, visit LobsterFromMaine.com/howtoboil for a great tutorial.

How do you know the lobsters are cooked through?

- An instant-read thermometer in the underside of the tail closest to the body should read about 140°F to 145°F after removing from heat. The temperature will continue to rise to a safe internal temperature of 145°F.
- The "head" will separate easily from the tail and the tail meat will be opaque and white, no longer translucent.
- The green stuff, a.k.a. the tomalley (liver and pancreas), will be firm-ish and green.
- The firm red stuff is the eggs (roe) of the female lobster. If the lobster is not cooked through, the roe will be black and gelatin-like.
- The small walking legs will pull away from the body easily.
- The antennae will easily pull out.
- The lobsters will turn bright red when cooked (from a dark blue-green or greenish brown/black), but that doesn't necessarily mean they are done.

The Best Lobster Roll

Toasted and buttered split-top buns stuffed with baby crispy green-leaf lettuce, warm lobster, melted butter, lemon zest, and chives. These will be the best lobster rolls you'll eat. If you don't want to steam your own lobsters, buy fresh-cooked lobster meat from your local fish market or grocer.

Serves: 4
Course: Main course
Total time: About 45 minutes

INGREDIENTS

2 (1½-lb)	hard-shell lobsters
5 tbsp	salted butter, divided
	Zest of 1 lemon
½ oz	thinly sliced chives
	Kosher salt, to taste
	Freshly ground black pepper, to taste
4	split-top hot dog buns
2 cups	baby green-leaf lettuce

For serving:

	Lemon wedges (from zested lemon above)
	Cape Cod Potato Chips (optional)

INSTRUCTIONS

Place lobsters in the freezer (in the paper bag you purchased them in) for 10–15 minutes to sedate them.

Add a few inches of water to a large pot (pot needs to be large enough to fit the 2 lobsters comfortably, with lid fitting securely). Add ¼ cup of salt to the water and bring to a rapid boil over high heat. Alternatively, you could use seawater, if you live close to the beach. Insert steamer basket.

Once water is boiling, remove lobsters from freezer and place one at a time head first into the steamer basket. (We remove the rubber bands from the claws, but you don't need to. If you do remove them, be careful—those claws pinch!). Bring water back to a rapid boil.

Steam lobsters for 17–18 minutes, or until cooked through. (1½-pound new/soft-shell lobsters should cook in about 14 minutes, so add 3–4 minutes for hard-shell).

Remove lobsters from steamer basket carefully with tongs or protective gloves. Twist off tail and claws from lobster body. Using a lobster cracker and seafood fork, remove meat from the knuckles, claws, and tail (and the small walking legs as well if you'd like—I usually don't bother, especially for lobster rolls). Remove the tomalley (green stuff), roe, and black vein from the tail portion. Rinse the tail if needed. Chop meat roughly, into larger bite-sized pieces.

Melt 4 tablespoons butter. Toss lobster with melted butter, lemon zest, and chives. Season with salt and pepper.

Spread buns with remaining tablespoon butter on both outer sides. Heat a nonstick pan over medium high heat. Add buns and toast on both sides until lightly browned.

Add lettuce to the bottom of each bun. Stuff with lobster meat.

Serve lobster rolls with lemon wedges and potato chips.

Nutrition Facts per Serving **Calories:** 330 / **Total fat:** 16.9g (22% DV) / **Saturated fat:** 9.7g (48% DV) / **Trans fat:** 0.6g / **Cholesterol:** 167mg (56% DV) / **Sodium:** 762mg (33% DV) / **Total carbohydrate:** 22.2g (8% DV) / **Dietary fiber:** 1.1g (4% DV) / **Total sugars:** 3.3g / **Added sugar:** 3.0g (6% DV) / **Protein:** 21.5g / **Vitamin D:** 0.1mcg (0% DV) / **Calcium:** 161mg (12% DV) / **Iron:** 1.9mg (11% DV) / **Potassium:** 306mg (7% DV)

Here's what the best lobster roll includes:

- Big lobster chunks tossed in warm (real) butter.
- Lobster chunks sit atop crisp lettuce—not too much lettuce, but not too little.
- Buttered and toasted split-top hot dog bun (they have the flat sides that are buttered easily).
- Served with lemon wedges (extra wedges, please).
- Served with Cape Cod Potato Chips.
- Served alongside a bottle of rosé or any dry bubbly.
- Eaten outside.

Though I haven't met many lobster rolls I haven't liked, there are a few big no-no's for me:

- **Too much mayo.** I am not a huge mayo fan. If there's a small amount, I am OK with that. If the lobster is drowning in mayo, I'm out.
- **The forgotten roll.** Too many times I've had lobster stuffed into a hot dog bun that hasn't been toasted and buttered. If you are going to have amazingness inside the bun (lobster!), take a few extra minutes to butter and toast the bun. Otherwise, skip the roll and just give me the lobster . . . and the butter.
- **Tossed in oil.** One time we went to a restaurant on the Cape and they served lobster with a side of butter-flavored oil for dipping. Just no!
- **Veggies mixed in with the lobster.** No celery or onion or carrot (things one might put in tuna salad), please. I am a huge fan of veggies, but this is the one time where less is more. The lettuce adds great crunch and freshness, but I draw the line there.
- **Served without lemon.** I always like lemon wedges with my lobster roll, regardless of whether it's a mayo- or butter-tossed lobster. It adds freshness, brightness, and acidity to the rich lobster-mayo-butter.

Grilled Lobster

Lobster on the grill is a relatively simple way to cook lobster, but it does require you to split the lobster in half prior to placing it on the grill. The end result is incredibly delicious. You'll brush the lobster with a garlic herb butter prior to removing it from the grill.

Serves: 2
Course: Main course
Total time: About 25 minutes

INGREDIENTS

2 (1½-lb)	hard-shell lobsters
½ tsp	extra-virgin olive oil
4–6 tbsp	garlic herb compound butter (see page 202), divided
1	lemon, cut into wedges

INSTRUCTIONS

Preheat grill to high heat. Clean and oil grates.

Place the lobsters in the freezer for 10–15 minutes to sedate them.

Place the tip of a large chef's knife between the lobster's eyes and top of the head. Using a quick stroke, cut the lobster down the middle all the way through, head to tail.

Twist the arms off the body and separate the tail halves from the head/body halves—discard the head/body halves. Remove the dark digestive track running down the tail pieces and any roe. Using a lobster cracker or mallet, crack the claws, but don't pull out the meat. Cracking the claws now will help them cook more evenly on the grill, will allow steam to escape, and will make them easier to crack fully once you pull them from the grill.

Brush the lobster tail halves with olive oil. Reduce heat to medium high.

Place the lobster tail halves on the grill, flesh side up, then the claws.

Grill for 5–6 minutes, then add ½ teaspoon compound butter to each tail half. Be careful, as this could cause flare-ups on the grill. Grill for another few minutes until the tail flesh has turned from translucent to opaque. Remove tails from heat.

Remove one claw from the grill and carefully crack it fully open to check if it's done. If done, pull off the other claws. If the meat is still translucent, put the claws back on for a few minutes more. Cooking time will vary depending on the size of the claws.

Melt the remaining compound butter for a few seconds in the microwave. Serve the grilled lobsters with the melted butter and lemon wedges.

Nutrition Facts per Serving **Calories:** 377 / **Total fat:** 25.7g (33% DV) / **Saturated fat:** 15.1g (76% DV) / **Trans fat:** 1.0g / **Cholesterol:** 319mg (106% DV) / **Sodium:** 1,043mg (45% DV) / **Total carbohydrate:** 1.9g (1% DV) / **Dietary fiber:** 0.6g (2% DV) / **Total sugars:** 0.5g / **Added sugar:** 0.0g (0% DV) / **Protein:** 34.1g / **Vitamin D:** 0.1mcg (1% DV) / **Calcium:** 182mg (14% DV) / **Iron:** 0.6mg (4% DV) / **Potassium:** 442mg (9% DV)

Serves: 4
Course: Salad or appetizer
Total time: 5 minutes

INGREDIENTS

12 oz   cooked lobster meat (approximately the amount of meat from two 1¼-lb lobsters), roughly chopped

3 cups   halved grape tomatoes

8 oz   fresh mozzarella pearls

5 large   slivered basil leaves

3 tbsp   extra-virgin olive oil

2 tbsp   white wine vinegar

Kosher salt, to taste

Freshly ground black pepper, to taste

Lobster Caprese Salad

Tender chunks of lobster meat tossed with heirloom tomatoes, creamy mozzarella, fresh basil, extra-virgin olive oil, and white wine vinegar. This simple lobster caprese salad is *the* perfect end-of-summer salad, ready in 5 minutes, as long as you're using cooked lobster meat. For a tutorial on how to steam lobsters, turn to page 3.

INSTRUCTIONS

Combine all ingredients together. Toss and serve.

Nutrition Facts per Serving **Calories:** 413 / **Total fat:** 23g (29% DV) / **Saturated fat:** 7.5g (38% DV) / **Trans fat:** 0g / **Cholesterol:** 123mg (41% DV) / **Sodium:** 832mg (36% DV) / **Total carbohydrate:** 30g (11% DV) / **Dietary fiber:** 5g (19% DV) / **Total sugars:** 5g / **Added sugar:** 1g (2% DV) / **Protein:** 23.5g / **Vitamin D:** 0.5mcg (2% DV) / **Calcium:** 231mg (18% DV) / **Iron:** 2.5mg (14% DV) / **Potassium:** 629mg (13% DV)

Lobster Avocado Bites

Whole-grain tortilla scoops stuffed with lobster and avocado that's been tossed with mayo, white wine vinegar, chives, and lemon–then topped with pea shoots and freshly ground black pepper. This recipe stretches a little bit of lobster a long way–great to serve for a crowd.

Serves: 10-12
Course: Appetizer
Total time: 10 minutes

INGREDIENTS

12 oz	cooked, roughly chopped lobster meat
2 tbsp	mayonnaise
2 tbsp	thinly sliced chives
1 tbsp	white wine vinegar
	Juice and zest of 1 lemon
¼ tsp	kosher salt
¼ tsp	freshly ground black pepper
1	avocado, thinly sliced, then slices cut in half
½ bag	whole-grain scoop tortilla chips
	Pea shoots (optional)

For serving:

	Lemon wedges

INSTRUCTIONS

Combine lobster, mayonnaise, chives, vinegar, lemon juice and zest, and salt and pepper.

Place chips on a large serving platter. Add ½ slice of avocado to each chip, then top with lobster salad and more freshly ground black pepper. Garnish with pea shoots (optional). Serve with lemon wedges.

Nutrition Facts per Serving **Calories:** 177 / **Total fat:** 9.5g (12% DV) / **Saturated fat:** 1g (6% DV) / **Trans fat:** 0g / **Cholesterol:** 42mg (14% DV) / **Sodium:** 294mg (13% DV) / **Total carbohydrate:** 16g (6% DV) / **Dietary fiber:** 2.5g (9% DV) / **Total sugars:** 1g / **Added sugar:** 0.5g (1% DV) / **Protein:** 7.5g / **Vitamin D:** 0mcg (0% DV) / **Calcium:** 34mg (3% DV) / **Iron:** 0.5mg (4% DV) / **Potassium:** 192mg (4% DV)

Buttered Lobster Avocado Toast

The king of toasts. Buttered whole-grain toast topped with smashed avocado and sliced radishes, then loaded with fresh lobster meat drizzled with melted butter and sprinkled with chives and freshly ground pepper. We love making this for special occasions like Father's Day, Mother's Day, or Christmas brunch. It's also a great way to use any leftover lobster you may have from steaming or grilling lobster the day prior.

Serves: 1
Course: Breakfast or brunch
Total time: 5 minutes

INGREDIENTS

1 thick slice toasted whole-grain bread

2 tsp salted butter, softened

4 oz cooked, roughly chopped lobster meat

½ avocado, smashed

1 thinly sliced radish

1 tsp sliced fresh chives

Freshly ground black pepper

For serving:

Lemon wedges

INSTRUCTIONS

Spread toast with 1 teaspoon butter. Melt the other teaspoon of butter in a microwave-safe dish.

Toss lobster meat with melted butter.

Spread avocado on toast and top with radish slices. Add lobster meat. Sprinkle with chives and freshly ground black pepper. Serve with lemon wedges.

Nutrition Facts per Serving **Calories:** 392 / **Total fat:** 20.5g (26% DV) / **Saturated fat:** 7g (34% DV) / **Trans fat:** 0g / **Cholesterol:** 186mg (62% DV) / **Sodium:** 814mg (35% DV) / **Total carbohydrate:** 24.5g (9% DV) / **Dietary fiber:** 7g (26% DV) / **Total sugars:** 2g / **Added sugar:** 2g (4% DV) / **Protein:** 28.5g / **Vitamin D:** 0mcg (0% DV) / **Calcium:** 191mg (15% DV) / **Iron:** 2mg (10% DV) / **Potassium:** 726mg (15% DV)

Lobster Nutrition Highlights

Lobster is rich in protein and is an excellent source of vitamin B3, vitamin B12, zinc, selenium, and copper.

Air Fryer Lobster Tail

Lobster tails stuffed with panko crumbs that have been tossed in butter and white wine, then air-fried and sprinkled with chives, lemon zest, parsley, and sea salt. These air-fried lobster tails are sweet, tender, juicy, and delicious. And they are ready in less than 15 minutes!

Serves: 2
Course: Main course
Total time: 15 minutes

INGREDIENTS

4 tbsp	salted butter
1 tbsp	dry white wine, such as Pinot Grigio
¼ tsp	kosher salt
⅛ tsp	black pepper
¼ cup	plain panko crumbs
2 (5–6-oz)	Maine (or New England) cold-water lobster tails (if frozen, thawed)
	Sea salt, for garnish
	Zest of 1 lemon, and cut lemon into wedges
1 tbsp	sliced chives
	Parsley, for garnish (optional)

INSTRUCTIONS

Preheat air fryer to 390°F.

In a small saucepan over medium heat, melt the butter. Add the white wine, salt, and pepper. Remove from heat and pour half the butter into a small serving bowl—reserve this for serving.

Add the panko crumbs to the saucepan with the remaining butter mixture. Stir to combine.

Using kitchen shears, cut down the center of the top shell of the lobster tails (between the meat and the shell) to split the shell in half. Stop cutting once you get to the tail fin. Naturally you will cut through some of the lobster meat while cutting through the shell—this is fine. If there is a long, thin vein running down the center of the tail, remove that with your fingers or a paring knife.

Using your hands, gently separate the two sides of the tail, allowing more access to the lobster meat (the bottom shell will crack a bit when you are doing this). You don't want to completely split the shell apart, you just want to make room for the panko stuffing that you'll add later. Using a culinary brush and the reserved butter, brush the lobster with melted butter (don't double-dip the brush, one dip is sufficient—you don't want to contaminate the raw lobster juices into the butter that you'll use for the cooked lobster).

Spray or wipe the air-fryer basket with cooking oil. Add the tails to the basket (cut side up) and set the timer for 4 minutes. Open the basket and carefully (air fryer and lobster are hot!) spoon the panko mixture into the butterflied lobster. Close the basket and cook for an additional 2–3 minutes, until the lobster is cooked through. Lobster is fully cooked when it is white and opaque throughout (not transparent) and the shell turns bright red. For these lobster tails, the easiest way to tell they are done is by inserting a meat thermometer into the thickest part of the tail. It should read about 140°F—the meat will continue cooking once removed from heat to a safe internal temperature of 145°F. Cooking time will vary depending on your air fryer and the size of your lobster tails.

Remove lobster tails from air fryer. Sprinkle with sea salt, lemon zest, chives, and parsley (optional). Serve with reserved melted butter and lemon wedges.

RECIPE NOTE: Recipe can easily be doubled to serve 4 people.

Nutrition Facts per Serving **Calories:** 356 / **Total fat:** 24.5g (31% DV) / **Saturated fat:** 14.5g (73% DV) / **Trans fat:** 1g / **Cholesterol:** 251mg (84% DV) / **Sodium:** 970mg (42% DV) / **Total carbohydrate:** 7g (3% DV) / **Dietary fiber:** 1g (4% DV) / **Total sugars:** 1g / **Added sugar:** 0g (1% DV) / **Protein:** 26g / **Vitamin D:** 0mcg (1% DV) / **Calcium:** 153mg (12% DV) / **Iron:** 1mg (5% DV) / **Potassium:** 369mg (8% DV)

Lobster Tacos

Flour tortillas topped with smashed avocado, red cabbage, fresh corn, buttery sweet lobster meat, pickled red onion, and cilantro. These seafood tacos are fresh and crisp and packed with lobster goodness.

Serves: 4
Course: Main course
Total time: 20 minutes

INGREDIENTS

4 ears	corn, shucked (or about 2½ cups frozen cooked corn)
8	street-sized flour tortillas, warmed
4 tbsp	salted butter
¾ lb	cooked lobster meat, roughly chopped
½ cup	low-fat sour cream
1 tsp	Old Bay Seasoning
½	red cabbage, thinly sliced
1	avocado, mashed
½ cup	chopped cilantro
¼ cup	pickled red onion (see page 208)

For serving:

1	lime, cut into wedges

INSTRUCTIONS

Bring a large pot of water to a boil. Add corn and boil for 3–4 minutes. Remove from pot. Let cool slightly, then cut kernels off cob.

Heat tortillas.

Add butter to a medium nonstick skillet over medium low heat. When melted, add lobster meat. Heat for 2–3 minutes, just until lobster meat is warmed through. Remove from heat.

Combine sour cream and Old Bay Seasoning; stir to combine.

Assemble tacos by adding thinly sliced red cabbage, avocado, corn, lobster meat, cilantro, pickled red onion, and Old Bay–sour cream mixture to the warmed tortillas. Serve with lime wedges.

RECIPE NOTE: To heat tortillas, place a cast-iron skillet over medium heat. Add tortillas and heat 30-60 seconds, flip, then heat an additional 30-60 seconds or until tortilla puffs a bit and develops a bit of color and light char. Repeat with all tortillas and keep warm in a clean dish towel. Alternatively, you can carefully heat tortillas one at a time directly over a gas flame, flipping tortillas with tongs and keeping a very close watch so they don't catch fire. Or heat a stack of tortillas in a kitchen towel for 30 seconds in the microwave.

Nutrition Facts per Serving **Calories:** 542 / **Total fat:** 24g (31% DV) / **Saturated fat:** 11g (55% DV) / **Trans fat:** 0.5g / **Cholesterol:** 165mg (55% DV) / **Sodium:** 981mg (43% DV) / **Total carbohydrate:** 59g (22% DV) / **Dietary fiber:** 9g (32% DV) / **Total sugars:** 13.5g / **Added sugar:** 0g (0% DV) / **Protein:** 27g / **Vitamin D:** 0mcg (0% DV) / **Calcium:** 255g (20% DV) / **Iron:** 3.5mg (20% DV) / **Potassium:** 1,018mg (22% DV)

Lobster Grilled Cheese

Hearty buttered bread stuffed with fresh sweet lobster meat, shredded cheddar, and spicy baby arugula. This is the simplest yet most extraordinary grilled cheese sandwich there is. This grilled cheese, my friends, is not for the kids. True seafoodie comfort food!

Serves: 1
Course: Sandwich
Total time: 5 minutes

INGREDIENTS

2 medium-thick slices	hearty bakery-style bread
½ tsp	salted butter, softened
1–2 oz	cooked, roughly chopped lobster meat
½ cup	baby arugula
2 thick slices	cheddar cheese
	Freshly ground black pepper

INSTRUCTIONS

Butter one side of each slice of bread.

Place one slice, buttered side down, in a nonstick pan over medium low heat.

Layer on lobster, arugula, cheddar, and black pepper.

Top with remaining slice of bread, buttered side up.

Heat until bread is lightly toasted, cheese is melted, and lobster is heated through, flipping after a few minutes.

Slice in half and serve.

Nutrition Facts per Serving **Calories:** 563 / **Total fat:** 24.5g (31% DV) / **Saturated fat:** 12.5g (63% DV) / **Trans fat:** 0.5g / **Cholesterol:** 102mg (34% DV) / **Sodium:** 1,060mg (46% DV) / **Total carbohydrate:** 56.5g (21% DV) / **Dietary fiber:** 3g (11% DV) / **Total sugars:** 6.5g / **Added sugar:** 6g (12% DV) / **Protein:** 28g / **Vitamin D:** 0mcg (2% DV) / **Calcium:** 600mg (46% DV) / **Iron:** 4mg (24% DV) / **Potassium:** 285mg (6% DV)

Lobster Omelet with Dill Havarti

A three-egg omelet stuffed with fresh sweet lobster meat and dill Havarti cheese, then topped with shredded cheddar, more lobster meat, and fresh chopped dill. Perfect for breakfast or brunch on any celebratory occasion.

Serves: 1
Course: Breakfast or brunch
Total time: 10 minutes

INGREDIENTS

3	eggs, beaten
1 oz	dill Havarti cheese, thinly sliced
2 oz	cooked chopped lobster meat
½ oz	shredded reduced-fat cheddar cheese

For serving:

1 tsp	chopped fresh dill
	Microgreens (optional, for garnish)
	Freshly ground black pepper

INSTRUCTIONS

Spray a nonstick skillet with cooking oil. Heat pan over medium low heat. Once hot, add eggs. Use a spatula to allow the runny egg to flow under the cooked egg. Once the eggs are almost cooked through, add the Havarti and lobster meat.

Fold one side of the omelet over to the other side. Top with shredded cheddar. Remove from heat. Sprinkle with fresh dill, microgreens, and black pepper.

Serve omelet with toast and side salad, if desired.

Nutrition Facts per Serving **Calories:** 416 / **Total fat:** 28g (36% DV) / **Saturated fat:** 13g (64% DV) / **Trans fat:** 0.5g / **Cholesterol:** 615mg (205% DV) / **Sodium:** 735mg (32% DV) / **Total carbohydrate:** 2g (1% DV) / **Dietary fiber:** 0g (0% DV) / **Total sugars:** 2g / **Added sugar:** 0g (0% DV) / **Protein:** 36.5g / **Vitamin D:** 3mcg (15% DV) / **Calcium:** 384mg (30% DV) / **Iron:** 2mg (10% DV) / **Potassium:** 316mg (7% DV)

Jenny bay scalloping on Nantucket

Scallops (Sea and Bay)

Scallops are bivalve mollusks, which means that the scallop has two shells and between those shells is an adductor muscle—this is the small white circular muscle that we eat. This muscle opens and closes the scallop shell, allowing it to move through the water by opening and closing its shell quickly. Scallops are one of my favorite shellfish. I love that they are sweet, delicate, and cook in just a couple minutes. Even raw, their flavor and texture are incredible. Prior to cooking, be sure to remove the small tough side muscle that's attached to the adductor muscle. We are lucky to live near New Bedford, Massachusetts, the scallop capital of the world and a global seafood hub. For the past twenty years, this fishing port has been America's most valuable fishing port, processing and distributing hundreds of millions of sea scallops each year.

I was invited on board Fishing Vessel (F/V) *Isabel and Lilee* for a fascinating lesson on all things sea scallops and scallop shucking. Captain Chris Merl, his wife, Denice, and the whole Merl family run their scalloping business on the Cape. Chris has been scalloping for over thirty years and will go out on the water year-round, regardless of temperature, which makes scalloping a sometimes pretty treacherous occupation. Denice is a critical part of the business, keeping all the behind-the-scenes operations running, including quality control, virtual cooking classes, farmers' markets, pop-ups, reports, data, paperwork, social media, and more. This fishing family is an example of some of the incredible and passionate fishermen and women who work hard each day to bring us the freshest seafood available.

Captain Chris Merl showing Jenny how to shuck a scallop

F/V *Isabel and Lilee* in Wellfleet, MA

The Merls aboard their scallop boat F/V *Isabel and Lilee*

Jenny shucking a scallop aboard the F/V *Isabel and Lilee*

Scallops 101

Choosing and Storing Scallops

- Always purchase from a knowledgeable reputable source that you trust. You should feel comfortable asking any question at the seafood counter about the item(s) you are purchasing.
- Fresh bay and sea scallops will have a white, off-white, light orange, or even slightly pinkish color with a moist sheen.
- Scallops should smell clean like the ocean and should not smell fishy or have any ammonia odors, indicating spoilage.
- Use scallops the day that you purchase them. If you're planning to use them in 1–2 days, keep them in the coldest part of your fridge, which is typically the bottom shelf in the back. We often place ice packs under and over the container to keep them extra cold in the fridge and preserve their freshness. If you're planning to store them beyond that, freeze them.
- Where you purchase your scallops may also determine how fresh they are and how long they've been sitting at the fish counter. Ask your fishmonger if the scallops were previously frozen, how long they have been in the case, and how soon you need to use them after purchase. If they've been sitting for quite a few days or if the scallops were previously frozen, you may choose to purchase flash-frozen scallops instead.
- If you purchase frozen scallops, avoid bags with ice crystals or frost, which could indicate the scallops have thawed then refrozen or may have been stored a long time, in which case the quality will suffer.
- Thaw scallops in the refrigerator overnight prior to cooking. Or you could place them in a sealed plastic bag and immerse in cold water (changing it every 30 minutes) or run cold water over them until thawed, then use immediately.
- Never thaw on the counter at room temperature.
- I don't recommend cooking scallops straight from frozen, as the texture suffers.

Cooking Scallops

- Scallops should be cooked to a safe internal temperature of 145°F, as measured by a food thermometer in the thickest part of the scallop. But keep in mind, once you pull the scallops off the heat, they will continue to rise in temperature, so pull them off around 140°F. That being said, I don't regularly use a thermometer on scallops, instead I rely on the flesh turning relatively firm and opaque (versus translucent).
- In our house we prefer our scallops slightly undercooked in the center—this is personal preference. If someone in your family or a guest has a compromised immune system, is pregnant, a young child, or an elderly adult, always cook seafood fully through.

Dry vs. Wet Packed Scallops

- When purchasing scallops, make sure you buy dry packed scallops, which have not been treated with any chemicals—there should be nothing added to the scallops you buy. Wet packed scallops have often been treated with a solution that makes the scallops appear white and preserves them, causing them to release water when they cook, which will make it impossible to ever get a good sear on them.
- Purchase domestic bay or sea scallops, if possible.

What's the difference between sea scallops and bay scallops?

- Sea scallops are much larger than bay scallops. They are meatier but still rich, luxurious, and delicate with a clean taste, just like the sea.
- Bay scallops are smaller, sweeter, more tender, and a bit more delicate than sea scallops. They are basically sea candy. Typically available in New England from November through late winter/early spring, these scallops are pricey but worth the spend for a treat.

Scallop Fun Fact

- A scallop has up to 200 eyes that line its shell and allow the scallop to detect light and dark and motion.

Seared Scallop Salad

Seared scallops over a sweet corn, creamy avocado, and fresh herb salad all topped with crunchy chickpeas. This is the perfect salad to celebrate fresh corn, fresh seafood, and all things summer. We eat this salad at least once a week in the summertime.

Serves: 4
Course: Main course
Total time: 20 minutes

INGREDIENTS

For the salad:

5 ears	fresh corn, shucked
1 bunch	scallions, thinly sliced, white and green parts
½ cup	loosely packed basil leaves, slivered
¼ cup	loosely packed flat-leaf parsley leaves, roughly chopped
¼ cup	loosely packed cilantro leaves and stems, thick stems removed, roughly chopped
¾ cup	crumbled feta cheese
¼ cup	extra-virgin olive oil
	Juice of 1 lime
2 tbsp	seasoned rice vinegar
1	avocado, cut into chunks
½ cup	crunchy chickpeas, any flavor

For the scallops:

1 lb	sea scallops, tough side muscle removed, patted dry
¼ tsp	kosher salt
¼ tsp	freshly ground black pepper
1 tsp	extra-virgin olive oil
1 tsp	butter

For serving:

	Lime wedges

INSTRUCTIONS

Heat a large pot filled halfway with water over high heat until boiling. Add corn, cover, reduce heat, and lightly boil for 3–5 minutes. Remove corn from pot and let cool slightly. Once able to handle, slice the corn off the cobs into a large bowl.

Add scallions, herbs, feta, extra-virgin olive oil, lime juice, and rice vinegar to the bowl with the corn and toss. Top with avocado and crushed chickpeas.

Dry scallops very well and season on both sides with salt and pepper. Heat a medium sauté pan with olive oil and butter over medium high heat until glistening. Swirl oil in the pan and add scallops. Don't crowd the scallops—cook in two batches if need be. Sear scallops for a minute or two (until desired doneness) on each side until a nice golden crust forms. Don't move the scallops while cooking, other than to flip them. Remove from heat.

Add scallops to corn salad. Serve with lime wedges.

Nutrition Facts per Serving **Calories:** 507 / **Total fat:** 30.5g (39% DV) / **Saturated fat:** 8g (39% DV) / **Trans fat:** 0.5g / **Cholesterol:** 51mg (17% DV) / **Sodium:** 911mg (40% DV) / **Total carbohydrate:** 43g (16% DV) / **Dietary fiber:** 8g (28% DV) / **Total sugars:** 9g / **Added sugar:** 0g (0% DV) / **Protein:** 23g / **Vitamin D:** 0mcg (1% DV) / **Calcium:** 192mg (15% DV) / **Iron:** 2.5mg (14% DV) / **Potassium:** 798mg (17% DV)

What's the secret to the best pan-seared scallops?

- **Purchase dry versus wet** packed scallops.
- **Make sure you pat them very dry** with a paper towel or clean dish towel. This is key to getting a good sear and a nice crust.
- **Do not crowd the pan.** Cook your scallops in batches if need be. If you crowd them, they will steam vs. sear and will not develop that nice crust.

- **Make sure the pan with your butter or oil (or both) is hot before adding the scallops.** You want to hear that sizzle. I heat my nonstick or cast-iron pan over medium high heat, add a drizzle of neutral oil and a pat of butter, then swirl the mixture and wait until the butter begins to foam a bit before adding the scallops. Season the scallops right before going in the pan with salt and pepper, then sear them for about 1 to 2 minutes on each side, depending on their size and your preferred doneness. After you add the scallops to the pan, don't touch them again until you go to flip them. Stay by their side, as they overcook easily. Don't multitask!
- **Serve scallops right away.** Have every other part of the meal ready, and cook the scallops last, so when they're ready, you're putting them on plates and eating them right away. They cool quickly, so get them on the table fast.

Scallop Tacos with Corn Salsa and Basil Oil

Sea scallops seared then served in warm flour tortillas with a corn, tomato, and chive salsa and avocado–then drizzled with a simple basil oil. This beautiful dish lets those scallops shine, while celebrating all the fresh flavors of summer.

Serves: 4
Course: Main course
Total time: 20 minutes

INGREDIENTS

For the corn salsa:

4 ears	fresh corn, shucked
1 medium	yellow tomato, diced
½ bunch	chives, thinly sliced
	Juice of ½ lemon
	Kosher salt, to taste
	Freshly ground black pepper, to taste

For the basil oil:

1 cup	packed basil leaves (about 1 large bunch)
½ cup	extra-virgin olive oil
1 clove	garlic
	Juice of ½ lemon
¼ tsp	kosher salt
⅛ tsp	freshly ground black pepper

For the scallops:

1 tsp	salted butter
1 tsp	avocado or canola oil
1 lb	sea scallops, tough side muscle removed, patted dry
⅛ tsp	freshly ground black pepper

For assembly:

	Flour or corn tortillas, warmed
1	avocado, thinly sliced

INSTRUCTIONS

For the corn salsa: Heat a large pot filled halfway with water over high heat until boiling. Add corn, cover, bring back to a boil, then lightly boil for 3–5 minutes. Remove corn from pot with tongs and let cool slightly. Once corn is cool enough to handle, slice the corn off the cobs into a medium bowl.

Toss corn with tomato, chives, lemon juice, salt, and pepper.

For the basil oil: In a food processor, combine basil, extra-virgin olive oil, garlic, juice of ½ lemon, salt, and pepper. Process until smooth. Poor into a small bowl.

For the scallops: Heat a nonstick skillet over medium high heat until very hot. Add butter and oil and swirl to melt and coat pan. When hot, add the scallops. Do not crowd the scallops; you may need to work in batches. Let scallops cook on the first side for about 2 minutes. Once the underside forms a nice golden crust, flip scallops and cook an additional 1–2 minutes, or until desired doneness. We like our scallops a bit undercooked in the center. Remove from heat.

To assemble: Assemble tacos by adding avocado slices to each tortilla. Top with a spoonful of salsa. Add 1–2 scallops per taco. Drizzle with basil oil and serve immediately.

Scallop Nutrition Highlights

Scallops are rich in protein and are an excellent source of vitamin B3, vitamin B12, selenium, and phosphorous.

RECIPE NOTES:

• If you don't have time to make the basil oil, toss some torn basil leaves into the corn salsa.

• If you have really fresh, sweet corn, you can cut the kernels off the corn and toss right into the salsa, without cooking.

• You can also use 2 cups of frozen cooked and cooled corn instead of 4 fresh ears.

• You want hot scallops, so have everything else all set and ready to serve–even the tacos assembled almost fully (just without the scallops). Then cook the scallops, add to the tacos, and serve right away.

• Store any leftover basil oil in a jar in the fridge for a few days. Use it as a dip for warmed crusty bread.

Nutrition Facts per Serving **Calories:** 641 / **Total fat:** 40.5g (52% DV) / **Saturated fat:** 7g (35% DV) / **Trans fat:** 0g / **Cholesterol:** 26mg (9% DV) / **Sodium:** 982mg (43% DV) / **Total carbohydrate:** 55g (20% DV) / **Dietary fiber:** 7g (26% DV) / **Total sugars:** 8g / **Added sugar:** 0g (0% DV) / **Protein:** 21g / **Vitamin D:** 0mcg (0% DV) / **Calcium:** 114mg (9% DV) / **Iron:** 3.5mg (20% DV) / **Potassium:** 826mg (18% DV)

Lemon Herb Scallop and Steak Kebabs

Lemon- and herb-marinated scallops are coupled with steak and veggies, grilled to perfection, then sprinkled with sea salt and more fresh herbs. We love this surf-and-turf recipe–it's bright, fresh, and so satisfying. It's a must for the summertime!

Serves: 4
Course: Main course
Total time: 2 hours, 30 minutes (includes marinate time)

INGREDIENTS

¾ lb	sirloin tip steak, cut into 1-inch cubes
½ tsp	salt
¾ lb	sea scallops, tough side muscle removed, patted dry
1	summer squash, cut into ½-inch rounds, then halved (you can keep the small rounds whole)
½	red onion, cut into quarters, separated into pieces

For the marinade:

	Juice and zest of 2 lemons
½ cup	extra-virgin olive oil
¼ cup	parsley leaves
¼ cup	oregano leaves
2 cloves	garlic
1	shallot, halved
½ tsp	kosher salt
¼ tsp	freshly ground black pepper

For serving:

	Sea salt
	Oregano and parsley leaves (optional)
1	lemon, cut into wedges

INSTRUCTIONS

Add steak cubes to a plate. Sprinkle ½ teaspoon salt over both sides of the meat. Let sit for at least 10 minutes.

Combine all marinade ingredients in a high-speed blender. Pulse a few times.

Add the steak cubes to a large plastic bag. Pour in half of the marinade. Marinate in the fridge for at least 2 hours.

Preheat grill to high heat. Clean and oil grates.

While grill is preheating, add sea scallops, summer squash, and red onion to another resealable bag or glass bowl with remaining marinade. Let marinate for 10–15 minutes.

Thread steak, scallops, squash, and red onion pieces onto metal skewers.

Place onto the grill and reduce heat to medium high. Grill for 3–4 minutes on each side, or until desired doneness. USDA Food Safety states that steaks should be cooked to a minimum of 145°F with a 3-minute rest.

Sprinkle kebabs with sea salt and additional fresh herbs.

Serve skewers with lemon wedges, a green salad, and chunks of warm, crusty bread, if desired.

Nutrition Facts per Serving **Calories:** 456 / **Total fat:** 33.6g (43% DV) / **Saturated fat:** 6.1g (31% DV) / **Trans fat:** 0.3g / **Cholesterol:** 75mg (25% DV) / **Sodium:** 901mg (39% DV) / **Total carbohydrate:** 12.3g (4% DV) / **Dietary fiber:** 3.6g (13% DV) / **Total sugars:** 2.8g / **Added sugar:** 0.0g (0% DV) / **Protein:** 29.9g / **Vitamin D:** 0.1mcg (1% DV) / **Calcium:** 119mg (9% DV) / **Iron:** 4.5mg (25% DV) / **Potassium:** 578mg (12% DV)

Baked Scallops with Panko

Sea scallops topped with buttery, crunchy seasoned panko crumbs and lemon zest, then baked in white wine until the topping is crispy and the scallops are just perfectly cooked.

Serves: 4
Course: Main course
Total time: 20 minutes

INGREDIENTS

½ cup	seasoned panko crumbs
2 tbsp	salted butter, softened
1 tbsp	extra-virgin olive oil
½ tsp	dried parsley
	Zest of 1 lemon (cut the lemon into wedges afterwards for serving)
⅛ tsp	freshly ground black pepper
1 lb	fresh sea scallops, tough side muscle removed, patted very dry
¼ cup	dry white or rosé wine

For serving:

	Sea salt
	Lemon wedges (from above)

INSTRUCTIONS

Preheat oven to 400°F.

Spray a medium-sized 9 x 9 x 2–inch baking dish with cooking spray. Alternatively, you could use 2 9-inch oval baking dishes.

To a small bowl, add panko crumbs, butter, extra-virgin olive oil, parsley, lemon zest, and black pepper. Combine well with your fingers.

Add scallops to the baking dish. Spoon panko topping atop scallops. Pour wine into the base of the baking dish (not over top of the scallops). Bake for 11–13 minutes, or until scallops are just opaque, broiling for the last minute or two to toast the panko crumbs (keep a close eye so the panko crumbs don't burn). Bake time will vary depending on the size of your scallops. I test for doneness by pulling out the baking dish at 10–11 minutes and slicing a smaller-sized scallop in half to test for doneness. It's better to slightly undercook—you can always pop them back into the oven.

Remove scallops from oven. Sprinkle with sea salt, if desired. Serve with lemon wedges.

RECIPE NOTE: This panko crumb mixture is also delicious on cod, haddock, or any white flaky fish.

Nutrition Facts per Serving **Calories:** 182 / **Total fat:** 10g (13% DV) / **Saturated fat:** 4g (22% DV) / **Trans fat:** 0g / **Cholesterol:** 38mg (13% DV) / **Sodium:** 560mg (24% DV) / **Total carbohydrate:** 15g (5% DV) / **Dietary fiber:** 1g (4% DV) / **Total sugars:** 1g / **Added sugar:** 0g (1% DV) / **Protein:** 13g / **Vitamin D:** 0mcg (0% DV) / **Calcium:** 23mg (2% DV) / **Iron:** 1mg (4% DV) / **Potassium:** 221mg (5% DV)

Bay Scallop Tacos

Seared Cape bay scallops sit over top of flour tortillas with roasted butternut squash, crispy kale, queso fresco, bacon, and fresh parsley. These tacos are fall-inspired with the perfect combination of savory, saltiness, and sweet.

Serves: 4
Course: Main course
Total time: 55 minutes

INGREDIENTS

1	butternut squash, peeled, cubed (or use pre-cubed squash)
3 tbsp	extra-virgin olive oil, divided
½ tsp	ground black pepper, divided
¼ tsp	kosher salt, divided
1 (10-oz)	bag chopped kale, tough stems removed
1 tsp	unsalted butter
½ lb	fresh bay scallops, rinsed, patted dry, side muscle removed
8	flour tortillas, warmed
2 oz	queso fresco cheese, crumbled
4 strips	reduced-sodium bacon, cooked, crumbled
1 tbsp	roughly chopped fresh parsley

For serving:

	Lemon wedges

INSTRUCTIONS

Preheat oven to 425°F.

Line two baking sheets with tinfoil. Toss butternut squash with 2 tablespoons extra-virgin olive oil, ¼ teaspoon black pepper, and ⅛ teaspoon salt, and place onto baking sheets. Roast squash for 40–45 minutes, or until lightly browned and caramelized, flipping halfway through cooking time. Place butternut squash in a bowl and set aside.

Place the chopped kale onto the foil-lined baking sheets (the same ones you used to roast the squash). Drizzle with 2 teaspoons extra-virgin olive oil and sprinkle with ⅛ teaspoon pepper. Place in the oven and roast for 10 minutes, stirring halfway through cooking time.

Meanwhile, heat remaining 1 teaspoon extra-virgin olive oil and butter in a medium nonstick skillet over medium high heat. Pat scallops dry and season with remaining ⅛ teaspoon salt and ⅛ teaspoon pepper. Add scallops to the hot pan and reduce heat to medium. Sauté about 1 minute until a nice sear forms, then flip and sauté until desired doneness (we like ours with just a brief sear). Don't crowd the scallops, as you don't want to steam them. Cook in batches, if needed.

Assemble tacos by adding kale and butternut squash to warmed flour tortillas. Top with a few bay scallops, queso fresco, bacon, and parsley.

Serve tacos with lemon wedges.

Nutrition Facts per Serving **Calories:** 475 / **Total fat:** 22g (28% DV) / **Saturated fat:** 6g (31% DV) / **Trans fat:** 0g / **Cholesterol:** 30mg (10% DV) / **Sodium:** 913mg (46% DV) / **Total carbohydrate:** 55.5g (20% DV) / **Dietary fiber:** 12.5g (45% DV) / **Total sugars:** 8g / **Added sugar:** 0g (1% DV) / **Protein:** 19g / **Vitamin D:** 0.5mcg (2% DV) / **Calcium:** 440mg (34% DV) / **Iron:** 5mg (27% DV) / **Potassium:** 1,155mg (25% DV)

Caesar Salad Scallop Roll

Seared sea scallops are stuffed into toasted buns with crispy lettuce, croutons, shaved Parmesan, and Caesar dressing. This sandwich is a really fun and easy way to serve up scallops.

Serves: 4
Course: Sandwich
Total time: 15 minutes

INGREDIENTS

4	New England split-top hot dog buns
2 tbsp	salted butter, divided
1 tbsp	extra-virgin olive oil
1 lb	sea scallops, patted very dry, tough side muscle removed
2 cups	crispy baby green-leaf lettuce
¼ cup	reduced-fat Caesar dressing
¼ cup	Caesar croutons, crushed
2 tbsp	shaved Parmesan cheese
	Freshly ground black pepper

For serving:

	Lemon wedges

INSTRUCTIONS

Spread the hot dog roll sides with 1 tablespoon butter and toast them in a skillet on medium heat until golden brown.

Heat olive oil and remaining butter in the same skillet over medium high heat until glistening. Swirl the oil and butter in the pan and add the scallops.

Sear for 1–2 minutes on each side until a nice golden crust forms, or until desired doneness. Remove from heat.

Stuff buns with a few leaves of lettuce then a few scallops. Drizzle with Caesar dressing, then sprinkle with crushed croutons, shaved Parmesan, and freshly ground black pepper.

Serve with lemon wedges.

Nutrition Facts per Serving **Calories:** 322 / **Total fat:** 15.5g (20% DV) / **Saturated fat:** 6g (28% DV) / **Trans fat:** 0g / **Cholesterol:** 41mg (14% DV) / **Sodium:** 869mg (38% DV) / **Total carbohydrate:** 27g (10% DV) / **Dietary fiber:** 1.5g (5% DV) / **Total sugars:** 4g / **Added sugar:** 3g (6% DV) / **Protein:** 18g / **Vitamin D:** 0mcg (0% DV) / **Calcium:** 122mg (9% DV) / **Iron:** 2mg (12% DV) / **Potassium:** 288mg (6% DV)

Seared Scallop Cobb Salad

Sea scallops are served on Bibb lettuce, bacon, blue cheese, tomatoes, red onion, and avocado with an apple cider vinaigrette. This is your favorite Cobb salad, just elevated with one of our favorite seafoods of all time.

Serves: 2
Course: Main course
Total time: 15 minutes

INGREDIENTS

For the salad:

½ **head**	Bibb lettuce, chopped
1	avocado, thinly sliced
10	cherry tomatoes, halved
3 strips	reduced-sodium bacon, cooked, crumbled
2	hard-boiled eggs, sliced
¼	red onion, finely diced
2 tbsp	blue cheese crumbles

For the vinaigrette:

2 tbsp	extra-virgin olive oil
2 tbsp	apple cider vinegar
1 tsp	Dijon mustard
½ tsp	brown sugar
⅛ tsp	freshly ground black pepper

For the scallops:

½ lb	sea scallops, patted dry, tough side muscle removed
⅛ tsp	freshly ground black pepper
½ tbsp	salted butter
½ tsp	olive oil

For serving:

	Lemon wedges

INSTRUCTIONS

Divide salad ingredients evenly between two salad plates or bowls.

Whisk vinaigrette ingredients together.

Season scallops with black pepper. Heat butter and olive oil in a nonstick skillet over medium high heat until glistening. Swirl the oil and butter in the pan and add the scallops.

Sear for 2 minutes, flip, and sear another 1–2 minutes until a nice golden crust forms, or until desired doneness. Remove from heat and place atop salads.

Drizzle vinaigrette over salads. Serve with lemon wedges.

Nutrition Facts per Serving **Calories:** 510 / **Total fat:** 39g (50% DV) / **Saturated fat:** 9.5g (48% DV) / **Trans fat:** 0g / **Cholesterol:** 210mg (70% DV) / **Sodium:** 832mg (36% DV) / **Total carbohydrate:** 17g (6% DV) / **Dietary fiber:** 6.5g (23% DV) / **Total sugars:** 5g / **Added sugar:** 1g (2% DV) / **Protein:** 25g / **Vitamin D:** 1mcg (6% DV) / **Calcium:** 115mg (9% DV) / **Iron:** 2.5mg (13% DV) / **Potassium:** 988mg (21% DV)

Scallop Tostadas with Herb Vinaigrette

Crisp corn tortillas topped with avocado, black beans, arugula, red cabbage, *cotija* or feta cheese, and sautéed bay or sea scallops, then drizzled with a simple herb vinaigrette made with chopped cilantro, scallions, extra-virgin olive oil, and lime juice. This is a stunning small plate that celebrates fresh, local bay or sea scallops.

Serves: 4
Course: Appetizer or light main course
Total time: 25 minutes

INGREDIENTS

For the corn tortillas:

8 small	corn tortillas
1 tsp	olive oil

For the cilantro scallion vinaigrette:

½ cup	cilantro, divided (you'll use half in assembly below)
4	scallions, divided (you'll use half in assembly below)
¼ cup + **2 tbsp**	extra-virgin olive oil
	Juice of 1 lime
⅛ tsp	kosher salt

For the scallops:

1 lb	bay or sea scallops, tough side muscle removed
⅛ tsp	freshly ground black pepper
1 tsp	canola or avocado oil
1 tsp	salted butter

INSTRUCTIONS

For the corn tortillas: Preheat oven to 350°F.

Place tortillas on baking sheet. Brush lightly with olive oil on both sides. Bake for 6–8 minutes on each side, or until crispy and lightly browned. Remove from oven.

For the vinaigrette: Finely chop ¼ cup cilantro and 2 scallions. Add to a small bowl with extra-virgin olive oil , lime juice, and salt. Whisk well. Alternatively, you can add the ingredients to a food processor and pulse a few times to combine well.

For the scallops: Pat scallops very dry. Season scallops with pepper on both sides. Heat a nonstick skillet over medium high heat. Add oil and butter. Swirl fat when pan is hot. Add scallops to pan. Cook on one side until a nice crust develops, about 2 minutes. Flip and cook another 1–2 minutes. Cooking time will vary depending on the size of scallop, type of scallop, and your preference.

To assemble: Lay the corn tortillas flat, then top with avocado, arugula, red cabbage, black beans, *cotija* or feta, scallops, cilantro, and scallions. Drizzle with vinaigrette.

Serve tostadas with lime wedges.

RECIPE NOTES:

• We have made this recipe with both bay and sea scallops. Use whichever scallops you prefer or whichever you can get your hands on (bay scallops have a limited season) for these tostadas.

• As a time-saving step, use pre-shredded red cabbage.

• To make these tostadas into tacos, skip the step of baking the corn tortillas and just lightly char them in a dry skillet on the stovetop.

For assembly:

1	avocado, sliced or cut into chunks
2 cups	arugula
1 cup	shredded red cabbage
1 (15.5-oz)	can low-sodium black beans, drained and rinsed
2 oz	*cotija* (an aged Mexican cheese) or feta cheese, crumbled
	Cilantro, roughly chopped, reserved from above
	Scallions, thinly sliced, reserved from above

For serving:

| 1 | lime, cut into wedges |

Nutrition Facts per Serving **Calories:** 597 / **Total fat:** 35.5g (45% DV) / **Saturated fat:** 7.5g (37% DV) / **Trans fat:** 0g / **Cholesterol:** 40mg (13% DV) / **Sodium:** 768mg (58% DV) / **Total carbohydrate:** 48g (17% DV) / **Dietary fiber:** 16g (56% DV) / **Total sugars:** 2.5g / **Added sugar:** 0g (0% DV) / **Protein:** 26g / **Vitamin D:** 0mcg (1% DV) / **Calcium:** 238mg (18% DV) / **Iron:** 4mg (22% DV) / **Potassium:** 947mg (20% DV)

Scallops with Corn, Tomato, and Basil Salad

Simply seared scallops are served over an easy fresh corn, tomato, basil, and mozzarella salad. Summertime bliss in a bowl. This is an elegant yet *very* simple dish. And one of our favorite summer meals.

Serves: 4
Course: Main course
Total time: 20 minutes

INGREDIENTS

For the corn salad:

5 ears	fresh corn, shucked
1 cup	grape or cherry tomatoes, halved
8 oz	pearl mozzarella balls, or use mini marinated mozzarella balls
½ cup	basil, slivered
¼ cup	seasoned rice vinegar
3 tbsp	extra-virgin olive oil
	Kosher salt, to taste
	Freshly ground black pepper, to taste

For the scallops:

1 lb	sea scallops, tough side muscle removed, patted dry
¼ tsp	freshly ground black pepper
1 tsp	salted butter
1 tsp	avocado or canola oil

INSTRUCTIONS

For the corn salad: Heat a large pot filled halfway with water over high heat until boiling. Add corn, cover, reduce heat, and lightly boil for 3–5 minutes. Remove corn from pot and let cool slightly. Once able to handle, slice the corn off the cobs into a large bowl.

Add tomatoes, mozzarella, basil, rice vinegar, and olive oil to the bowl with the corn. Toss to combine. Season with salt and pepper. Set aside.

For the scallops: Season scallops on both sides with pepper. Heat a medium skillet with butter and oil over medium high heat until butter is melted and pan is hot. Swirl pan and add scallops. Don't crowd the scallops—cook in two batches if need be. Sear scallops for 2 minutes, flip, then cook another 1–2 minutes (until desired doneness) until a nice golden crust forms. Do not move scallops until you flip them. Remove from heat.

To assemble: Place scallops atop the salads. Serve with a nice crusty baguette, if desired.

RECIPE NOTE: Salad can be made a day in advance. If making ahead of time, sear scallops and add basil just prior to serving.

Nutrition Facts per Serving **Calories:** 472 / **Total fat:** 26g (33% DV) / **Saturated fat:** 9g (45% DV) / **Trans fat:** 0.5g / **Cholesterol:** 62mg (21% DV) / **Sodium:** 949mg (41% DV) / **Total carbohydrate:** 35g (13% DV) / **Dietary fiber:** 4g (13% DV) / **Total sugars:** 8g / **Added sugar:** 0g (0% DV) / **Protein:** 30g / **Vitamin D:** 0mcg (1% DV) / **Calcium:** 421mg (32% DV) / **Iron:** 1.5mg (8% DV) / **Potassium:** 647mg (14% DV)

Scallop Salad with Bacon Vinaigrette

Seared sea scallops served over top of crispy green-leaf lettuce, crunchy bacon, and white beans–all drizzled with a warm bacon vinaigrette. This is the salad to top all salads. It's rich and decadent, while still being fresh and crisp.

Serves: 4
Course: Main course
Total time: 25 minutes

INGREDIENTS

For the vinaigrette:

5 slices	uncured reduced-sodium bacon
1	shallot, minced
¼ cup	apple cider vinegar
1 tbsp	brown sugar
1 tsp	Dijon mustard
1 tbsp	extra-virgin olive oil
¼ tsp	freshly ground black pepper

For the salad:

2 (4-oz)	containers crispy green-leaf lettuce (we prefer Little Leaf Farms)
1 (15.5-oz)	can white beans, drained and rinsed
1 cup	homemade or store-bought croutons

For the scallops:

1 lb	fresh sea scallops, tough side muscle removed, patted very dry
¼ tsp	freshly ground black pepper
⅛ tsp	kosher salt
1 tsp	avocado or canola oil
1 tbsp	unsalted butter

For serving:

1 tsp	fresh chives, sliced (optional)
1	lemon, cut into wedges

INSTRUCTIONS

For the vinaigrette: Add bacon to a skillet over medium heat and cook until crispy, turning every few minutes. Remove bacon and place on paper towels.

Add shallot to the bacon fat and cook 1–2 minutes until softened and beginning to brown, stirring constantly. Add apple cider vinegar, bring to a boil, then reduce heat to a simmer. Add brown sugar and mustard. Heat 1–2 more minutes until dressing is reduced slightly. Remove from heat. Whisk in extra-virgin olive oil and pepper. Pour hot dressing into a heat-safe bowl or jar. Set aside.

For the salad: Crumble the bacon slices. Add lettuce to four bowls. Top with white beans, croutons, and crumbled bacon.

For the scallops: Season the scallops on both sides with pepper and salt. Wipe out the skillet you used above with paper towels. Add oil and butter to the skillet over medium high heat. When pan is hot, add scallops (don't crowd them). Sear scallops for 2 minutes on one side, then flip and cook 1–2 more minutes until scallops are just barely opaque or to desired doneness. Remove from pan and place atop salads.

Whisk vinaigrette, then pour over salads. Sprinkle salads with chives. Serve with lemon wedges.

Nutrition Facts per Serving **Calories:** 385 / **Total fat:** 12g (15% DV) / **Saturated fat:** 4g (18% DV) / **Trans fat:** 0g / **Cholesterol:** 38mg (13% DV) / **Sodium:** 960mg (42% DV) / **Total carbohydrate:** 44.5g (16% DV) / **Dietary fiber:** 9g (32% DV) / **Total sugars:** 5.5g / **Added sugar:** 3.5g (7% DV) / **Protein:** 27g / **Vitamin D:** 0mcg (1% DV) / **Calcium:** 146mg (11% DV) / **Iron:** 5.5mg (31% DV) / **Potassium:** 1,025mg (22% DV)

Scallops with Bacon

Scallops with bacon–a.k.a. scallops topped with "real" bacon bits. These sea scallops are pan-seared in butter then topped with crispy bacon bits, chopped fresh parsley, and lemon zest. Perfect for a bite-sized appetizer.

Serves: 4
Course: Appetizer
Total time: 15 minutes

INGREDIENTS

1 tsp	salted butter
1 tsp	avocado or canola oil
1 lb	sea scallops, tough side muscle removed, patted dry
4 strips	bacon, cooked until crispy, crumbled
¼ cup	chopped fresh parsley
1	lemon, zested and cut into wedges

INSTRUCTIONS

Heat a nonstick skillet over medium high heat. Add butter and oil, swirl the pan to melt the butter. Once butter is hot and begins to foam, add the scallops. Do not crowd the scallops—you may need to work in batches.

Let scallops cook on the first side for about 2 minutes. Once the underside forms a nice golden crust, flip scallops and cook an additional 1–2 minutes, or until desired doneness. We like our scallops a bit undercooked in the center.

Plate the scallops; top with crumbled bacon, chopped parsley, and lemon zest. Serve immediately, with lemon wedges.

RECIPE NOTE: Make sure your bacon is crispy. No one likes soggy bacon, especially soggy bacon on top of scallops.

Nutrition Facts per Serving **Calories:** 130 / **Total fat:** 6g (8% DV) / **Saturated fat:** 2g (10% DV) / **Trans fat:** 0g / **Cholesterol:** 35mg (12% DV) / **Sodium:** 471mg (20% DV) / **Total carbohydrate:** 5g (2% DV) / **Dietary fiber:** 0.5g (2% DV) / **Total sugars:** 0.5g / **Added sugar:** 0g (0% DV) / **Protein:** 15g / **Vitamin D:** 0mcg (0% DV) / **Calcium:** 16mg (1% DV) / **Iron:** 1mg (4% DV) / **Potassium:** 264mg (6% DV)

Oysters, Mussels, and Clams

This chapter features a variety of recipes, both cooked and raw, using oysters, mussels, and clams, which are all filter-feeding bivalves. Bivalves have two shells that are hinged and contain a soft-bodied invertebrate, which is the part we eat. Oysters, mussels, and clams are highly sustainable, help clean our waterways by removing excess nitrogen from the water, and are packed with nutrition (protein, vitamin B12, iron, zinc, and more). They are also really fun to cook and display elegantly on a table—perfect for wowing guests—but also great for casual backyard everyday-type occasions. If you are intimidated by cooking shellfish, I encourage you to give one of these easy recipes a try. I promise, once you cook them once, you will realize how easy (and quick) they are to prepare. Another bonus of these three types of shellfish is that they are very affordable (they don't come with the heftier price tag of lobster, crab, or scallops)—yet another reason to add these bivalves to your table more often.

Choosing and Storing Oysters, Mussels, and Clams

- **The most important thing about purchasing live seafood is freshness.** Know and trust your fishmonger or retailer and where they are getting their shellfish. Ask questions about the shellfish, and feel comfortable that they are knowledgeable about answering those questions. Make sure the oysters, mussels, or clams are being stored properly at cold temperatures and that proper food-safety practices are being followed.
- **Some live shellfish have tags on the containers where they are sold** that contain information about the shellfish and processor and let you know they have followed national shellfish safety controls. You can look for/ask for these tags.
- **When you purchase the shellfish,** find out when they were harvested and how long you can store them. My advice is to use them as soon as possible. When we purchase oysters, mussels, or clams, I use them that day—possibly the next day, but typically you have a bit more wiggle room than that.
- **Keep the shellfish in the coldest part of the fridge,** which is typically the bottom shelf, in the back of the fridge. You can cover them with a slightly damp (not wet) cloth or newspaper.
- **If they came in a plastic bag,** remove them from that, as they need to breathe. If they came in a mesh bag, you can store them in that bag in a bowl with a damp (not wet) cloth over them. Or just store loosely in a bowl or on a baking sheet (for oysters, cup side down) covered in a damp towel. Drain any water that collects in the bowl. Do not store them in a sealed container and do not store them directly on or under ice, as fresh water can kill them.
- **Check each and every piece of shellfish for broken, cracked, or hollow shells,** discard those, as they are likely dead—remember you want your live shellfish to be alive. At home, I also smell each one and make sure they pass the "sniff" test—they should smell briny and clean like the ocean, not fishy, sour, or ammonia-like. Use your senses and make sure each piece smells, looks, and feels right.
- **Shells should be tightly closed.** If any shells are open, tap them gently on the counter. If the shellfish slowly closes, keep it. If it remains open, throw it away. When in doubt, throw it out. The exceptions are soft-shell clams (those shells won't be completely closed because the neck protrudes from the shell—in this case, touch the neck and if it moves, that should indicate the clam is alive) and razor clams, which have a naturally slightly opened shell.
- **When serving raw oysters or clams,** serve them shucked on top of plenty of ice.

Oysters 101

What kind of oysters should you look for?

Any kind you like! Nowadays, we all have access to fresh oysters regardless of where you live (near the sea or land-locked) because of refrigerated overnight shipping, so I encourage you to give oysters from all different locations a try. Island Creek Oysters has a great online shop (island creekoysters.com) offering FedEx Overnight service, so you know your oysters are arriving cold and fast.

   We live on Cape Cod, where we have access to endless varieties of oysters, each taking on its own merroir. Merroir (like terroir for wine) means that each oyster tastes like its surroundings—what it eats, the water it lives in, the temperature, the tides, the seaweed growing alongside it, and more. An oyster's flavor profile is a product of its environment.

How do you shuck oysters?

Oyster shucking can be intimidating, but after a little bit of practice, you can be on your way to becoming an oyster-shucking expert (or at least an amateur). Don't expect to get it on your first (or your tenth) try. But believe me, the skill will come.

- Prepare a tray with crushed ice and any oyster accompaniments.
- Discard any broken, cracked, or open oysters.
- Scrub your oysters with a firm brush—I use a vegetable brush—to remove grit, dirt, and debris from the oyster.
- You'll want to wear a protective glove on your non-knife-wielding hand to protect your hand from the shucking knife. Alternatively, use a kitchen towel for protection, but sometimes this doesn't offer adequate protection.
- Place your oyster on a flat working surface or place into your nondominant glove-protected hand. If placing the oyster on a flat surface, hold it still with your nondominant hand.
- Insert your oyster-shucking knife into the hinge of the oyster and gently rock your knife back and forth until you hear and feel a pop. This takes practice to get the angle and force just right.

- Wipe your knife clean of any gunk that was in the hinge.
- Keep the oyster steady, as you don't want to spill the liquor (oyster juice).
- Slide your knife right underneath the top shell and over top the oyster muscle, to remove the top shell; discard the top shell.

- Slide your knife underneath the oyster muscle to sever the muscle from the bottom shell. Keep the oyster meat on the bottom shell.
- Place the shucked oyster onto a tray with ice.
- Repeat for all of your oysters.
- If an oyster doesn't look right or smell right to you (it should smell fresh, like the sea), throw it out. Oysters should be plump, wet, and shiny inside (not dried out) with a creamy/tan color.

What should you serve with oysters?

We love oysters with lemon wedges and a basic mignonette. A mignonette sounds fancy, but it's not. Typical mignonettes combine vinegar, shallots, and black pepper. A good rule of thumb is you don't want the accompaniments to overwhelm the subtle flavor of the oysters. That being said, serve oysters with whatever and however *you* like. You make your own rules.

Aside from mignonettes, oysters are also often served with:

- Lemon wedges
- Cocktail sauce
- Horseradish
- Hot sauce

Young children and those who are pregnant, elderly adults, or those with weakened immune systems should not eat raw oysters but can safely eat cooked oysters, as long as they are cooked to a safe internal temperature of 145°F.

Jenny Ross and Andy Arch of Sea State in Bourne, Massachusetts, at their sea farm at the head of Buzzard's Bay

Sea State's Monk's Cove Oysters growing in their rack and bag system in Buzzard's Bay

Sea State's Monk's Cove Oysters at about two months old. They will be harvested in just over a year. These oysters have a hard shell and a deep cup from the wave action they receive in the bay, a punch of brine, and a mild vegetal sweetness on the finish.

Oysters on the Half Shell

Oysters with a champagne mignonette made with white wine vinegar, champagne, shallot, parsley, and black pepper.

Serves: 4
Course: Appetizer
Total time: 10 minutes

INGREDIENTS

12	oysters, shucked
2 tbsp	white wine vinegar
2 tbsp	dry champagne, prosecco, or cava sparkling wine
1 tbsp	minced shallot
1 tsp	chopped fresh parsley
¼ tsp	freshly ground black pepper

For serving:

1	lemon, cut into wedges

INSTRUCTIONS

Place shucked oysters over ice or rock salt on a chilled platter.

Combine vinegar, sparkling wine, shallot, parsley, and black pepper in a small bowl.

Serve oysters with mignonette and lemon wedges.

Nutrition Facts per Serving **Calories:** 56 / **Total fat:** 1g (1% DV) / **Saturated fat:** 0g (2% DV) / **Trans fat:** 0g / **Cholesterol:** 18mg (6% DV) / **Sodium:** 41mg (2% DV) / **Total carbohydrate:** 8.5g (3% DV) / **Dietary fiber:** 2.5g (9% DV) / **Total sugars:** 1g / **Added sugar:** 0g (0% DV) / **Protein:** 3.5g / **Vitamin D:** 0mcg (0% DV) / **Calcium:** 68mg (5% DV) / **Iron:** 3mg (17% DV) / **Potassium:** 213mg (5% DV)

Those with compromised immune systems, as well as those who are pregnant, infants, young children, and older adults, should not consume raw or undercooked fish and shellfish.

Oysters with Wild Blueberry Granita

Oysters on the half shell served with a frozen wild blueberry mignonette granita. The wild blueberries pair wonderfully with savory foods, like oysters. This recipe may sound and look fancy, but it's very simple–the granita is just a frozen mixture of wild blueberries, vinegar, shallot, and black pepper. Basically, a mignonette in a slushy consistency. This oyster platter is perfect for any celebratory occasion–or served in the summertime as a refreshing appetizer.

Serves: 4
Course: Appetizer
Total time: 10 minutes

INGREDIENTS

1 cup	frozen wild blueberries
½ cup	prosecco vinegar (or champagne or white wine vinegar)
1	shallot, trimmed
¼ tsp	freshly ground black pepper
1 dozen	oysters, scrubbed and shucked (make sure to sever the bottom of the oyster muscle so the oyster slides easily out of the shell)

For serving (optional):

Zest of 1 lemon

Flaky sea salt

INSTRUCTIONS

Add wild blueberries, vinegar, shallot, and black pepper to a small food processor. Pulse for about 30 seconds.

Place shucked oysters on a chilled serving platter lined with ice, Himalayan rock salt, or Celtic sea salt.

Top each oyster with about ¼–½ teaspoon of the wild blueberry granita. If desired, add a sprinkle of lemon zest and some finishing salt. Serve.

RECIPE NOTE: Freeze any leftover granita for future oyster platters. Thaw slightly, then scrape with a fork to break apart and fluff up prior to using.

Nutrition Facts per Serving **Calories:** 47 / **Total fat:** 1g (1% DV) / **Saturated fat:** 0g (1% DV) / **Trans fat:** 0g / **Cholesterol:** 18mg (6% DV) / **Sodium:** 41mg (2% DV) / **Total carbohydrate:** 6g (2% DV) / **Dietary fiber:** 1g (4% DV) / **Total sugars:** 3g / **Added sugar:** 0g (0% DV) / **Protein:** 2.5g / **Vitamin D:** 0mcg (0% DV) / **Calcium:** 35mg (3% DV) / **Iron:** 2.5mg (13% DV) / **Potassium:** 108mg (2% DV)

Those with compromised immune systems, as well as those who are pregnant, infants, young children, and older adults, should not consume raw or undercooked fish and shellfish.

Oyster Nutrition Highlights

Oysters are rich in protein and are an excellent source of iron, vitamin B3, vitamin B12, zinc, selenium, copper, and manganese.

Grilled Oysters with Garlic Butter

Shucked oysters topped with a garlicky herb butter and served with lemon wedges. This is a savory, briny, and insanely delicious appetizer. It's also a great way to serve oysters to oyster novices as well as those who are not ready to make the jump into the world of raw oysters.

Serves: 4
Course: Appetizer
Total time: 15 minutes

INGREDIENTS

1 stick	salted butter, softened
½ cup	basil leaves loosely packed, roughly chopped
¼ cup	parsley leaves loosely packed, roughly chopped
2 cloves	garlic, finely minced
1 tbsp	dry white wine
	Zest of 1 lemon, then cut into wedges
¼ tsp	freshly ground black pepper
12	oysters, scrubbed and shucked

INSTRUCTIONS

Preheat grill to high heat.

Combine butter, herbs, garlic, wine, lemon zest, and black pepper in a small bowl to make the garlic butter.

Add ½ teaspoon garlic butter to each shucked oyster. Place oysters on grill.

Reduce heat to medium high. Grill oysters for 6–8 minutes until bubbly and curled inward.

Remove carefully from grill using grill- or fire-safe gloves.

Serve with lemon wedges.

RECIPE NOTES:

• This recipe only uses a small amount of the garlicky herb butter. Save the rest for spreading on a baguette, corn, or serving atop any fish.

• You have many choices when it comes to grilling oysters. You can:

  ◦ Place oysters in an oyster-grilling dish (shown here).

  ◦ Place in a large grill-safe cast-iron skillet.

  ◦ Place directly on the grill, taking care not to spill the liquor.

  ◦ Crumble up a piece of tinfoil, stretch it back out, and nestle the oysters into the foil.

Nutrition Facts per Serving **Calories:** 85 / **Total fat:** 6.5g (8% DV) / **Saturated fat:** 4g (19% DV) / **Trans fat:** 0g / **Cholesterol:** 33mg (11% DV) / **Sodium:** 86mg (4% DV) / **Total carbohydrate:** 3.5g (1% DV) / **Dietary fiber:** 0.5g (2% DV) / **Total sugars:** 0.5g / **Added sugar:** 0g (0% DV) / **Protein:** 3g / **Vitamin D:** 0mcg (0% DV) / **Calcium:** 46mg (4% DV) / **Iron:** 2.5mg (14% DV) / **Potassium:** 130mg (3% DV)

Oysters Rockefeller

Oysters topped with a buttery shallot-and-spinach mixture then topped with crispy panko crumbs and shaved Parmesan cheese. This classic oyster dish seems fancy, but it's a very simple recipe. This is seafood comfort food right here! Even those who are hesitant about eating oysters will love these.

Serves: 4-6
Course: Appetizer
Total time: 30 minutes

INGREDIENTS

1 dozen	oysters, shucked, making sure to reserve the liquor (liquid inside the oyster)
2 tbsp	unsalted butter
1 small	shallot, minced
4 cups	baby spinach, chopped
¼ cup	seasoned panko breadcrumbs
¼ cup	shaved Parmesan cheese
2 tbsp	chopped parsley
	Freshly ground black pepper
1	lemon, cut into wedges

INSTRUCTIONS

Preheat oven to 425°F. Gather a small baking sheet and line with culinary rock salt. Or crumble up a piece of tinfoil, then stretch it back out, so the surface is rough and can hold the oysters.

Place the shucked oysters on the baking sheet either in the salt or into the foil. Be careful not to spill the oysters' liquor.

Heat the butter in a skillet over medium heat. Once melted and hot, add the shallot, stirring often, until translucent and softened. Add spinach and continue cooking for about 5 minutes until most of the liquid is absorbed, stirring frequently. Remove from heat.

Spoon the spinach mixture into the oysters, then top with breadcrumbs and shaved Parmesan.

Place into oven for 6–8 minutes until the oysters are bubbly and golden brown.

Remove from oven and top with parsley and freshly ground black pepper. Serve with lemon wedges.

RECIPE NOTES:

• If possible, choose oysters with a nice deep cup. These will hold the oyster liquor and spinach filling better than more shallow cups.

• Be careful when shucking your oysters to not spill the oyster liquor, as that liquid contains tons of briny flavor.

• When shucking your oysters, make sure to use your oyster knife to sever the muscle from the bottom shell. This will make eating these oysters much easier.

Nutrition Facts per Serving **Calories:** 139 / **Total fat:** 8.8g (11% DV) / **Saturated fat:** 5.0g (25% DV) / **Trans fat:** 0.3g / **Cholesterol:** 38mg (13% DV) / **Sodium:** 196mg (9% DV) / **Total carbohydrate:** 8.6g (3% DV) / **Dietary fiber:** 1.3g (5% DV) / **Total sugars:** 1.4g / **Added sugar:** 0.4g (1% DV) / **Protein:** 7.0g / **Vitamin D:** 0.1mcg (0% DV) / **Calcium:** 159mg (12% DV) / **Iron:** 3.4mg (19% DV) / **Potassium:** 284mg (6% DV)

Mussels 101

In New England, mussels from either Prince Edward Island (PEI) in Canada or Maine are readily available. On the Cape we also have access to some wild blue mussels in Chatham. I had a chance to go aboard the Fishing Vessel (F/V) *Mussla* to see some of these wild mussels, harvested just off the coast.

Mussels may seem intimidating to cook, but they are actually quick and easy. We eat them most often steamed, in a simple broth. Here's some of the basic information you need to know, along with simple tips for steaming mussels.

F/V *Mussla* dredging for mussels in Chatham, Massachusetts

How many pounds of mussels should you purchase per person?

- A good rule of thumb is to purchase about 1 pound of mussels per person for a main course or ½ pound per person for an appetizer.

How do you prep the mussels for steaming?

- Discard any mussels that are broken, cracked, hollow, or open. If open, gently tap them on the counter. If they close, keep them. If they stay open, toss them, as they're likely dead.
- Scrub the mussels under cold running water to remove any debris like grit or sand. You can use your hands or a scrub brush.
- If the mussels contain their beard (this is a black or green fibrous thread attached), tug gently to remove it before cooking.

Jenny aboard F/V *Mussla* with a handful of blue mussels

How do you steam mussels?

- After cleaning the mussels, set them aside.
- Sauté any flavoring ingredients in olive oil or butter (garlic, shallot, onions, etc.) over medium heat until fragrant in a large heavy-bottomed pot.
- Then add the mussels and liquid—you don't need much liquid. I typically only use ¼ to ½ cup of liquid for 1 pound of mussels. You want enough liquid to fully cover the bottom of your pot. Not to worry; there will still be plenty of liquid to mop up with crusty bread, as the mussels will release their juices once they open.
- Cover the pot. If you have a clear lid, that will work best because you can see if the mussels are beginning to open. Then, turn up the heat to high.
- Cook for about 2 minutes, then remove the lid and gently stir mussels. Remove any that have opened.

A handful of blue mussels

- Mussels are cooked through when their shells open up. Continue cooking for another 2–5 minutes until all the mussels have opened. Cooking time will vary depending on the size of the mussels, the cookware you're using, and the amount of mussels in the pot—the more mussels, the longer the cooking time.
- If any mussels don't open, discard them, as they are not safe to eat.
- Pour the mussels and broth into a serving dish—or bring the pot to the table and serve directly from the pot.

Pro Tip:

- Always serve mussels with crusty bread to sop up the broth.

Mussel with White Wine and Garlic

Mussels steamed with shallot, garlic, seaweed, and white wine (or rosé!), then topped with fresh parsley. This is an elegant, healthy, and stunningly simple dish that's perfect served as an appetizer or main dish. Serve with plenty of toasted and buttered bread for savoring every last drop of the broth.

Serves: 4 as an appetizer, 2 as a main course
Course: Appetizer or main course
Total time: 15 minutes

INGREDIENTS

2 lb	mussels, scrubbed and debearded
1 tbsp	unsalted butter
1 tbsp	extra-virgin olive oil
2	shallots, minced
2 cloves	garlic, minced
¼ cup	dry white wine or rosé
¼ cup	Ready-Cut Kelp, chopped (optional) (we use Atlantic Sea Farms)
¼ cup	chopped parsley

For serving:

Lemon wedges

Toasted baguette slices

INSTRUCTIONS

Put the mussels in a colander and rinse them in cold water. Inspect well. Discard any mussels with broken shells. If any mussels are open, gently tap them on the counter. If they close, they are fine to eat. If they remain open, discard. If you see any beard (this is the green piece—looks like seaweed), gently pull it off.

Add butter and extra-virgin olive oil to a large pot over medium heat. Add in minced shallot and minced garlic and cook just until they are softened, stirring frequently. This will take a few minutes.

Add the mussels into the pot, gently. Pour the wine and chopped kelp over the mussels and give them a gentle stir, coating the mussels. Place the lid on and increase the heat to high. After about 2 minutes, give the mussels a gentle stir—this will ensure they are cooking evenly. Remove any mussels that have opened and place in the serving bowl. Put the lid back on and continue cooking for few more minutes until most or all of the mussels have opened. Discard any mussels that haven't opened up to this point, as they're probably dead and not safe to eat.

Place mussels into serving bowls. Pour the broth over top of the mussels. Sprinkle each bowl with fresh parsley.

Serve with lemon wedges and toasted baguette slices for dipping in the broth.

Place a large bowl on the table for empty shells.

Nutrition Facts per Serving **Calories:** 373 / **Total fat:** 12.3g (16% DV) / **Saturated fat:** 3.4g (17% DV) / **Trans fat:** 0.2g / **Cholesterol:** 71mg (24% DV) / **Sodium:** 893mg (39% DV) / **Total carbohydrate:** 30.0g (11% DV) / **Dietary fiber:** 1.1g (4% DV) / **Total sugars:** 2.1g / **Added sugar:** 0.0g (0% DV) / **Protein:** 31.4g / **Vitamin D:** 0.0mcg (0% DV) / **Calcium:** 98mg (8% DV) / **Iron:** 10.9mg (61% DV) / **Potassium:** 819mg (17% DV)

Mussels in Beer

Mussels simply steamed with garlic, onion, and beer. This recipe couldn't be easier and is perfect as a beginner recipe for someone looking to make mussels for the first time. Serve as an appetizer or main course with lots of crusty bread for dipping into the broth.

Serves: 4 as an appetizer, 2 as a main course
Course: Appetizer or main course
Total time: 15 minutes

INGREDIENTS

2 lb	mussels, scrubbed and debearded
1 tbsp	unsalted butter
1 tbsp	extra-virgin olive oil
1	Vidalia onion, diced
2 cloves	garlic, minced
6 oz	lager or wheat ale of your choice (use one that you like to drink)
¼ cup	chopped parsley

For serving:

Lemon wedges

Hunks of baguette

INSTRUCTIONS

Put the mussels in a colander and rinse them in cold water. Inspect well. Discard any mussels with broken shells. If any mussels are open, gently tap them on the counter. If they close, they are fine to eat. If they remain open, discard. If you see any beard (this is the green piece—looks like seaweed), gently pull it off.

Add butter and extra-virgin olive oil to a large pot over medium heat. Add in onion and cook until translucent, about 5–8 minutes. Add in minced garlic and cook just until fragrant, stirring frequently, another 1–2 minutes.

Add the mussels into the pot gently. Pour the beer over the mussels and give them a gentle stir, coating the mussels. Place the lid on and increase the heat to high. After about 2 minutes, give the mussels a gentle stir—this will ensure they are cooking evenly. Remove any mussels that have opened and place in the serving bowl. Put the lid back on and continue cooking for a few more minutes until most or all of the mussels have opened. Discard any mussels that haven't opened up to this point, as they're probably dead and not safe to eat.

Place mussels into serving bowls. Pour the broth over top of the mussels. Sprinkle each bowl with fresh parsley.

Serve with lemon wedges and hunks of baguette.

Place a large bowl on the table for empty shells.

Nutrition Facts per Serving **Calories:** 277 / **Total fat:** 11.4g (15% DV) / **Saturated fat:** 3.2g (16% DV) / **Trans fat:** 0.2g / **Cholesterol:** 71mg (24% DV) / **Sodium:** 654mg (28% DV) / **Total carbohydrate:** 12.4g (4% DV) / **Dietary fiber:** 0.6g (2% DV) / **Total sugars:** 1.3g / **Added sugar:** 0.0g (0% DV) / **Protein:** 27.6g / **Vitamin D:** 0.0mcg (0% DV) / **Calcium:** 76mg (6% DV) / **Iron:** 9.3mg (52% DV) / **Potassium:** 803mg (17% DV)

Mussels Nutrition Highlights

Mussels are rich in protein and are an excellent source of iron, vitamin B1, vitamin B2, vitamin B3, vitamin B12, zinc, selenium, and manganese.

Serves: 4
Course: Main course
Total time: 1 hour

INGREDIENTS

2 tbsp	olive oil
1 medium	Vidalia onion, diced
3 stalks	celery, diced
2 cloves	garlic, finely minced
1 (28-oz) can	diced tomatoes
8 oz	clam juice
2 small	sweet potatoes, peeled, cut into 1-inch cubes
2	bay leaves
	Peel of 1 orange (peeled into thick strips)
1 tsp	hot sauce
1 tsp	saffron threads
1 tsp	fresh oregano
¼ cup	dry white wine
2 tsp	cornstarch
8 oz	cod (or other firm white fish), cut into 1-inch cubes
20	mussels, scrubbed
1 lb	shrimp (any size), peeled and deveined

For serving:

	Freshly ground black pepper
½ cup	fresh cilantro, chopped
	Crusty bread

Nonna's Seafood Stew

This easy yet elegant seafood stew comes from my mother-in-law, Coral, who has been making this recipe over the past 45 years, tweaking it ever so slightly each time. She originally learned how to make it from a good girlfriend when she lived in Brazil in the mid-1970s. We love the combination of mussels, shrimp, and cod in this recipe. It's hearty, warming, and perfect for chilly evenings. Serve with a large loaf of crusty bread.

INSTRUCTIONS

To a large Dutch oven or stockpot, add olive oil over medium heat. When hot, add onion, celery, and garlic and heat until softened and fragrant.

Add tomatoes, clam juice, sweet potatoes, bay leaves, orange peel, hot sauce, saffron, oregano, and wine. Simmer 20 minutes.

Add cornstarch to 1 tablespoon water, to dissolve. Mix well, then add to stew. Add fish and simmer gently 10 minutes more to avoid breaking up fish. Add mussels and shrimp. Cook 5 minutes more, or until shrimp are cooked through and opaque and mussels open. Discard any mussels that don't open.

Remove bay leaves and orange peel.

Sprinkle with freshly ground black pepper and cilantro.

Spoon into bowls. Serve with crusty bread, if desired.

RECIPE NOTE: If you cannot get fresh mussels, you could also use a frozen seafood medley, available at most grocers.

Nutrition Facts per Serving **Calories:** 356 / **Total fat:** 9.8g (13% DV) / **Saturated fat:** 1.5g (8% DV) / **Trans fat:** 0.0g / **Cholesterol:** 205mg (68% DV) / **Sodium:** 575mg (25% DV) / **Total carbohydrate:** 23.1g (8% DV) / **Dietary fiber:** 6.0g (21% DV) / **Total sugars:** 6.3g / **Added sugar:** 0.0g (0% DV) / **Protein:** 42.5g / **Vitamin D:** 0.5mcg (3% DV) / **Calcium:** 199mg (15% DV) / **Iron:** 5.8mg (32% DV) / **Potassium:** 1,314mg (28% DV)

Clams 101

There are countless types of edible clams, but the ones we eat most often here in New England are quahogs (hard-shell clams), soft-shell clams (steamers), and surf clams. The type of clams we cook with most at home are quahogs, which can vary by size and therefore by use: littlenecks are the smallest (at about 1½ inches wide), cherrystones are slightly larger (about 2½ inches wide), and chowders are the largest (3+ inches wide). Our favorites are little-necks, and we love to grill or steam them (we steam them in the same way we do mussels) until their shells open wide.

Adrian, Jenny's husband, clamming in Falmouth, MA

How many pounds of clams should you purchase per person?

- A good rule of thumb is to purchase about 1 pound of clams per person for a main course or ½ pound per person for an appetizer.

How do you prep clams for cooking?

- Most of the hard and soft-shelled clams you purchase at your fish market or grocery store will be cleaned of sand prior to being sold. Just ask your fishmonger or seafood counter associate if they are already purged of sand. If they are, just scrub them when you're ready to cook them and rinse them under cold water.
- If you are harvesting your own clams, especially soft-shell clams, you know that they likely contain sand and/or mud when gathered, so they will need to be cleaned. There are count-less online resources for purging clams of sand, so that will be your best resource, as it's not something we do regularly.

Littlenecks on the Grill with White Wine Sauce

Grilled littlenecks are served with an easy yet elegant buttery wine sauce. If you've never grilled clams, this is a really simple beginner recipe to try. We love serving these clams with crusty bread to soak up all the sauce.

Serves: 4
Course: Appetizer
Total time: 25 minutes

INGREDIENTS

2 tbsp	extra-virgin olive oil
1	shallot, minced
2 cloves	garlic, minced
½ cup	dry white wine
3 tbsp	unsalted butter, cut into pieces
2½ lb	littleneck clams, scrubbed
¼ cup	chopped parsley
	Juice of 1 lemon, cut in half lengthwise (use one half for squeezing over the clams, the other half to cut into wedges for serving)

For serving:

1	baguette, warmed

Clam Nutrition Highlights

Clams are packed with protein and are an excellent source of vitamin B3, vitamin B12, and selenium.

INSTRUCTIONS

Preheat grill to high heat. Clean and oil grates.

Add olive oil to a small saucepan over medium heat. When hot, add shallot and garlic. Cook for 1–2 minutes until fragrant, translucent, and softened, but doesn't develop color. Add wine and reduce to a simmer. Simmer for about 5 minutes until wine has reduced. Add butter, whisking to combine. Place on low heat and cover to keep warm.

Meanwhile, place clams on the grill and reduce heat to medium high. Cook for 5–8 minutes, or until clams open. Once they open, remove and place on a platter, taking care not to spill the juices. Discard any clams that have not opened.

Whisk the butter wine sauce and pour over clams. Sprinkle with parsley. Squeeze the half lemon over top of clams.

For serving: Serve with hunks of baguette for sopping up the sauce.

RECIPE NOTE: Discard any clams with broken shells or open shells that do not close when tapped gently, as the clams are likely dead. Use your eyes and nose–if any clam looks or smells off, get rid of it.

Nutrition Facts per Serving **Calories:** 307 / **Total fat:** 16.8g (22% DV) / **Saturated fat:** 6.6g (33% DV) / **Trans fat:** 0.4g / **Cholesterol:** 36mg (12% DV) / **Sodium:** 490mg (21% DV) / **Total carbohydrate:** 23.7g (9% DV) / **Dietary fiber:** 1.1g (4% DV) / **Total sugars:** 2.5g / **Added sugar:** 0.0g (0% DV) / **Protein:** 10.7g / **Vitamin D:** 0.0mcg (0% DV) / **Calcium:** 51mg (4% DV) / **Iron:** 2.6mg (14% DV) / **Potassium:** 130mg (3% DV)

Crab

This chapter features a variety of crab recipes, many of which are great for entertaining. In the United States, popular varieties of crab include blue, peekytoe, green, Dungeness, as well as Jonah, stone, king, snow crab, and more. We also import much of our crab. Crab is available in many different forms (live, cooked, fresh, frozen, canned, whole, sections, legs, etc.). And for many of us, the crab we see for purchase most often is pasteurized picked meat in plastic or tinned containers sold in the refrigerated section of the seafood department at our local grocer. The recipes in this chapter use that refrigerated crabmeat, but feel free to use fresh domestic or local fresh crabmeat if you can get your hands on it.

Choosing live crabs:

- If you are purchasing live crabs, make sure they are active and show leg movement.

Mini Crab Bites

Lump crabmeat, panko crumbs, tartar sauce, egg, and spices are mixed together, formed into bite-sized balls, then baked until they're crisp on the outside and tender on the inside. These simple and quick cakes are the perfect bites of crab goodness and would be a great appetizer for your seafood-lovin' guests. Oh, and kids love them too!

Makes: About 32 bites
Serves: 8
Course: Appetizer
Total time: 25 minutes

INGREDIENTS

1 lb	lump crabmeat, picked over for any shell fragments
1 cup	plain panko crumbs
½ cup	tartar sauce, plus more for dipping
1	egg, beaten
1¼ tsp	Old Bay Seasoning, plus more for sprinkling
½ tsp	garlic powder
¼ tsp	ground black pepper

For serving:

	Sea salt (optional)
1	lemon, cut into wedges
	Tartar sauce, for dipping

Crab Nutrition Highlights

Crab is rich in protein and is an excellent source of vitamin B3, vitamin B12, selenium, zinc, and copper.

INSTRUCTIONS

Preheat oven to 400°F. Line two baking sheets with aluminum foil. Spray each baking sheet with cooking spray.

Add crab, panko crumbs, tartar sauce, egg, Old Bay Seasoning, garlic powder, and black pepper to a large mixing bowl. Mix until combined.

Using a small ice cream scoop or a tablespoon, scoop the crab cake mixture into your hand, then roll into a ball, squeezing gently as you roll. Place each bite on the prepared baking sheet. Leave approximately an inch or so between bites. Continue making the bites until the mixture is gone. Sprinkle tops with additional Old Bay Seasoning.

Place into oven. Bake for 12–14 minutes, until bites are golden brown and set.

Remove from oven. Place bites onto a serving plate and sprinkle with sea salt. Serve with lemon wedges and additional tartar sauce for dipping.

Nutrition Facts per Serving **Calories:** 151 / **Total fat:** 5.4g (7% DV) / **Saturated fat:** 1.1g (5% DV) / **Trans fat:** 0.0g / **Cholesterol:** 81mg (27% DV) / **Sodium:** 700mg (30% DV) / **Total carbohydrate:** 11.9g (4% DV) / **Dietary fiber:** 0.7g (2% DV) / **Total sugars:** 2.2g / **Added sugar:** 2.0g (4% DV) / **Protein:** 12.9g / **Vitamin D:** 0.1mcg (0% DV) / **Calcium:** 81mg (6% DV) / **Iron:** 1.1mg (6% DV) / **Potassium:** 189mg (4% DV)

Crab-Stuffed Avocados with Kelp

Serves: 8
Course: Appetizer
Total time: 10 minutes

INGREDIENTS

12 oz   lump crabmeat, picked over for shell fragments

4 oz   Atlantic Sea Farms Ready-Cut Kelp, thawed, picked over for pebbles, and chopped

½   red onion, finely diced

1 tbsp   chopped fresh parsley

4   avocados, halved

For the dressing:

¼ cup   mayonnaise

2 tbsp   white wine vinegar

¼ tsp   kosher salt

¼ tsp   freshly ground black pepper

For serving:

Freshly ground black pepper

1   lemon, cut into wedges

Creamy, rich avocados stuffed with sweet lump crabmeat and umami-rich kelp (seaweed!) in a tangy dressing. These stuffed avocados are packed with all the umami-rich flavors of the sea, and they make the perfect appetizer, side dish, or even a quick lunch alongside some whole-grain crackers.

INSTRUCTIONS

Add lump crabmeat to a medium bowl. Using a fork, break up any large crab chunks. Add kelp, red onion, and parsley to the bowl. Toss well to combine.

Whisk together dressing ingredients and add to crab-and-kelp mixture. Mix to combine.

Place the avocado halves on a serving plate. Add crab-and-kelp mixture to the avocado halves. Top with black pepper. Serve with lemon wedges.

RECIPE NOTES:

• If preparing this as an appetizer ahead of time, squeeze lemon over the avocado halves so they don't brown prior to serving.

• This recipe can also be made as a crab, kelp, and avocado salad (versus stuffed into avocado halves). If you go the salad route, you can use 2 avocados instead of 4. Just prepare as directed, but add diced avocado to the crab-and-kelp mixture just before serving and toss gently.

Nutrition Facts per Serving

Calories: 207 / **Total fat:** 16.1g (21% DV) / **Saturated fat:** 2.4g (12% DV) / **Trans fat:** 0.0g / **Cholesterol:** 44mg (15% DV) / **Sodium:** 396mg (17% DV) / **Total carbohydrate:** 8.6g (3% DV) / **Dietary fiber:** 5.1g (18% DV) / **Total sugars:** 0.8g / **Added sugar:** 0.0g (0% DV) / **Protein:** 9.4g / **Vitamin D:** 0.0mcg (0% DV) / **Calcium:** 76mg (6% DV) / **Iron:** 1.2mg (6% DV) / **Potassium:** 493mg (10% DV)

Crab-Stuffed Portobello Mushrooms

Insanely delicious grilled portobellos stuffed with crabmeat. Basically, it's your favorite jumbo crab cake stuffed into a marinated and grilled portobello mushroom. These will be the heartiest and tastiest stuffed mushrooms you've had.

Serves: 4
Course: Main course
Total time: 45 minutes

INGREDIENTS

4 large	portobello mushrooms, cleaned and stem trimmed
½ cup	balsamic vinaigrette, or use citrus vinaigrette, homemade or store-bought
1 lb	lump crabmeat, picked over for shells
2	eggs, beaten
½ cup	seasoned panko crumbs
1 tbsp	grated Parmesan cheese
½ tbsp	Italian seasoning
⅛ tsp	kosher salt
¼ tsp	ground black pepper
¼ tsp	garlic powder

For serving:

¼ cup	shaved Parmesan cheese
¼ cup	chopped parsley
1	lemon, cut into wedges

INSTRUCTIONS

Add portobellos and vinaigrette to a resealable bag. Let marinate for at least 30 minutes, preferably longer.

Preheat grill to high heat. Clean and oil grates.

Combine crabmeat, eggs, panko crumbs, Parmesan, Italian seasoning, salt, pepper, and garlic powder.

Remove portobellos from marinade and place on grill, stem side down. Reduce heat to medium high and grill for 5 minutes. Flip portobellos and stuff with crab mixture (the topping will be heaping atop the mushrooms). Grill another 5–8 minutes until crab mixture is cooked through.

Remove portobellos from the grill and top with shaved Parmesan and chopped parsley. Serve with lemon wedges.

RECIPE NOTE: Marinating the mushrooms is optional, though it makes for a more delicious and flavorful end result.

Nutrition Facts per Serving **Calories:** 345 / **Total fat:** 16.0g (20% DV) / **Saturated fat:** 3.2g (16% DV) / **Trans fat:** 0.1g / **Cholesterol:** 221mg (74% DV) / **Sodium:** 1306mg (57% DV) / **Total carbohydrate:** 20.7g (8% DV) / **Dietary fiber:** 2.4g (9% DV) / **Total sugars:** 8.0g / **Added sugar:** 5.1g (10% DV) / **Protein:** 30.0g / **Vitamin D:** 0.9mcg (4% DV) / **Calcium:** 228mg (18% DV) / **Iron:** 2.5mg (14% DV) / **Potassium:** 732mg (16% DV)

Warm Crab Dip

Jumbo lump crabmeat, shredded cheddar, cream cheese, cottage cheese, Old Bay Seasoning, and panko crumbs are baked in a cast-iron skillet until hot and bubbly, then served with your favorite whole-grain crackers or pretzels. This lightened-up crab dip is the perfect appetizer for game day . . . or any day you're entertaining and need a comforting, crowd-pleasing warm dip.

Serves: 12
Course: Appetizer
Total time: 35 minutes

INGREDIENTS

8 oz	reduced-fat cream cheese
4 oz	reduced-fat cottage cheese
1 lb	lump crabmeat
¾ cup	shredded cheddar cheese, divided
2 tsp	Old Bay Seasoning, plus more for topping
½ tsp	garlic powder
¼ tsp	freshly ground black pepper
2 tbsp	panko crumbs
1 tbsp	chives, thinly sliced

For serving:

1	lemon, cut into wedges
	Crackers, baguette slices, and veggies

INSTRUCTIONS

Preheat oven to 350°F. Grease a medium cast-iron skillet with avocado or canola oil and place it inside the oven.

In a large mixing bowl, combine cream cheese, cottage cheese, crabmeat, ½ cup cheddar, Old Bay Seasoning, garlic powder, and black pepper. Gently mix with your hands to combine.

Remove skillet from oven. *Careful, skillet is hot!* Spoon crab mixture into skillet. Place into oven for 20 minutes.

Remove from oven and top with remaining ¼ cup cheddar and panko crumbs. Place back into the oven for 5–10 more minutes until cheese is melted and bubbly and panko crumbs are lightly toasted. Remove from oven.

Top dip with chives. Serve with lemon wedges and whole-grain crackers, baguette slices, or veggies.

Nutrition Facts per Serving **Calories:** 113 / **Total fat:** 6.1g (8% DV) / **Saturated fat:** 3.2g (16% DV) / **Trans fat:** 0.2g / **Cholesterol:** 55mg (18% DV) / **Sodium:** 473mg (21% DV) / **Total carbohydrate:** 3.3g (1% DV) / **Dietary fiber:** 0.2g (1% DV) / **Total sugars:** 1.2g / **Added sugar:** 0.1g (0% DV) / **Protein:** 11.1g / **Vitamin D:** 0.1mcg (0% DV) / **Calcium:** 127mg (10% DV) / **Iron:** 0.3mg (2% DV) / **Potassium:** 173mg (4% DV)

Crab Deviled Eggs

Eggs stuffed with lump crabmeat plus a touch of mayo, mustard, Old Bay Seasoning, and lemon juice. These deviled eggs are a seaworthy twist on the original deviled eggs and make a great addition to a brunch spread.

Serves: 6
Course: Breakfast or brunch
Total time: 40 minutes

INGREDIENTS

6	eggs
4 oz	lump crabmeat, picked over for shell fragments
3 tbsp	chopped chives, divided
2 tbsp	mayonnaise
1 tsp	stone ground mustard
1 tsp	Old Bay Seasoning
	Juice and zest of ½ lemon
¼ tsp	freshly ground black pepper

INSTRUCTIONS

Add eggs to a large pot in a single layer. Cover with 1 inch of water. Bring to a boil. Turn off heat and cover the eggs with a lid. Let sit for 10–12 minutes. Prepare an ice bath.

Drain water, remove eggs, and place in the ice bath to stop the cooking process. Let sit in the ice bath for 12–14 more minutes.

Peel eggs and slice in half with a sharp knife. Remove yolks with a spoon and place into mixing bowl. Smash yolks lightly with a fork.

Add crab, 2 tablespoons chives, mayonnaise, mustard, Old Bay Seasoning, lemon juice and zest, and pepper to the yolks. Mix well. Spoon mixture into egg whites. Top with remaining tablespoon chives.

Place any leftover filling in a small bowl and serve alongside deviled eggs.

Refrigerate until ready to serve.

Nutrition Facts per Serving **Calories:** 127 / **Total fat:** 8.9g (11% DV) / **Saturated fat:** 2.2g (11% DV) / **Trans fat:** 0.0g / **Cholesterol:** 207mg (69% DV) / **Sodium:** 324mg (14% DV) / **Total carbohydrate:** 1.2g (0% DV) / **Dietary fiber:** 0.2g (1% DV) / **Total sugars:** 0.7g / **Added sugar:** 0.0g (0% DV) / **Protein:** 9.8g / **Vitamin D:** 1.1mcg (5% DV) / **Calcium:** 46mg (4% DV) / **Iron:** 0.8mg (4% DV) / **Potassium:** 125mg (3% DV)

Shrimp

Shrimp is the no. 1 consumed seafood in the United States. Does that surprise you, or are you a shrimp enthusiast too? Shrimp is easy and quick to cook, unintimidating, readily available, and inexpensive, so it's not surprising it's a favorite to many. This chapter features a variety of shrimp recipes, from appetizers to tacos to pastas.

If you've ever wondered what the numbers on the shrimp packages mean (written as either U/15, 16/20, 21/25 or 16–20, 21–25, etc.), this is the "count" of shrimp and refers to the number of shrimp in 1 pound. So the larger the number, the more shrimp per pound and the smaller the shrimp. And the smaller the number, the fewer shrimp per pound and the larger the shrimp. For example, if you purchased 16-20 or 16/20 shrimp, that means there are 16 to 20 shrimp in 1 lb. This is very useful when shopping for shrimp and determining what size shrimp to purchase for your recipe.

Soy Ginger Shrimp Sliders

Grilled soy ginger–glazed shrimp on brioche buns with sriracha mayo and a gingery cabbage slaw. These Asian-inspired shrimp sliders are sweet and savory with just enough kick.

Serves: 4
Course: Main course
Total time: 25 minutes

INGREDIENTS

For the slaw:

¼ cup	reduced-fat mayonnaise
3 tbsp	seasoned rice vinegar
½ tsp	toasted sesame oil
1 (3-inch) piece	ginger root, grated, divided
½ medium	red or green cabbage, cored and thinly sliced
2	carrots, grated
1 bunch	scallions, white and green parts, thinly sliced; reserve a small amount of green parts for garnish

For the sriracha mayo:

¼ cup	reduced-fat mayonnaise
½ tsp	sriracha (adjust amount depending on heat preference)

For the shrimp glaze:

2 tbsp	honey
1 tbsp	reduced-sodium soy sauce
1 tbsp	mirin
1 tsp	sriracha
½ tsp	toasted sesame oil
	Reserved ginger (from slaw)
1 clove	garlic, minced

INSTRUCTIONS

For the slaw: Combine mayonnaise, rice vinegar, sesame oil, and half the ginger in a large mixing bowl. Whisk together. Add cabbage, carrot, and scallions. Mix well. Set aside.

For the sriracha mayo: Combine mayonnaise and sriracha in a small bowl. Mix well.

For the shrimp glaze: In a small bowl, combine honey, soy sauce, mirin, sriracha, sesame oil, remaining ginger, and garlic. Mix well. Reserve a small amount for drizzling after grilling the shrimp.

For the shrimp: Preheat grill to high heat. Clean and oil grates.

Pat shrimp very dry then thread onto skewers. Brush lightly with canola oil; sprinkle with salt and pepper.

Reduce grill heat to medium high. Add the shrimp and grill for 1 minute; flip then brush with glaze. Cook for 1 more minute, flip again, brush with glaze, then remove from heat once shrimp are cooked through and opaque.

To assemble: Spread each brioche bun with sriracha mayo. Top with grilled shrimp. Drizzle a bit of the reserved glaze over top of the shrimp. Top shrimp with slaw. Sprinkle with sesame seeds, if desired. Serve with remaining slaw.

For the shrimp:

1 lb	raw shrimp (21–25), peeled and deveined, tail removed, patted dry
½ tsp	canola oil
¼ tsp	kosher salt
⅛ tsp	ground black pepper

For assembly:

8	brioche slider buns, toasted
	Reserved scallions (from slaw)
	Black sesame seeds, optional

RECIPE NOTE: Feel free to use pre-shredded red cabbage as a time-saver.

Nutrition Facts per Serving **Calories:** 330 / **Total fat:** 10.6g (14% DV) / **Saturated fat:** 2.8g (14% DV) / **Trans fat:** 0.5g / **Cholesterol:** 92mg (31% DV) / **Sodium:** 512mg (22% DV) / **Total carbohydrate:** 46.4g (17% DV) / **Dietary fiber:** 5.2g (18% DV) / **Total sugars:** 20.3g / **Added sugar:** 13.3g (27% DV) / **Protein:** 13.3g / **Vitamin D:** 0.3mcg (1% DV) / **Calcium:** 116mg (9% DV) / **Iron:** 2.5mg (14% DV) / **Potassium:** 548mg (12% DV)

Shrimp 101

What should you look for when buying shrimp?

Domestic wild shrimp is harvested off the coasts of the United States, so if you can find domestic shrimp, buy it. Domestic seafood is sustainable seafood, as it's highly regulated and managed.

The majority of the shrimp available in the United States is imported from farms around the world, including Thailand, China, Vietnam, Central and South America, and more.

To make sure you're buying sustainably grown and harvested imported shrimp, look for third-party verifications on the package like Best Aquaculture Practices, Aquaculture Steward-ship Council, Fair Trade Certified, and others. You can also speak with your fishmonger or sea-food manager about where the shrimp comes from and what sustainability practices are used both at the retailer and the source of shrimp harvest.

Choose frozen shrimp that has nothing added (no preservatives)—you want the ingredient label to say: "shrimp." Some also have water and salt added, but avoid any other ingredients.

Bags of frozen shrimp are a great staple to keep in your freezer. We typically purchase raw, frozen, deveined shrimp with their shells and tails on. I find the shell-on shrimp have the most flavor. If you're in a hurry, you can purchase already-shelled shrimp—or frozen cooked shrimp (the latter is not our favorite because they can be rubbery, especially if you are heating them, but they're great in a pinch).

Oftentimes "fresh" shrimp at the fish counter is actually previously frozen, so be sure to ask your fishmonger if the shrimp was previously frozen. If it was, your better bet is to purchase fro-zen shrimp and thaw it yourself.

As far as shrimp size goes, choose whatever size the recipe calls for. You can usually substi-tute a different size than a recipe calls for and just adjust the cooking time accordingly.

How do you thaw frozen shrimp?

Thaw shrimp in the refrigerator overnight, or place it in a resealable bag in a large bowl with cold water. Change the water every 30 minutes. Or run cold water over it until thawed.

Serves: 4
Course: Appetizer
Total time: 20 minutes

INGREDIENTS

For the rolls:

16	rice paper spring roll wrappers
1 lb	cooked shrimp, peeled, deveined, and tail removed, or chopped lobster meat
1 cup	cooked brown rice
¼ head	red cabbage, thinly sliced
½	English cucumber sliced into matchsticks
2	carrots, shaved or cut into matchsticks
½ cup	mint leaves
¼ cup	Thai basil leaves (optional)
½ cup	roasted and salted peanuts crushed

For the spicy peanut sauce:

¼ cup	creamy peanut butter (unsalted, unsweetened)
2 tbsp	reduced-sodium soy sauce
1 tbsp	seasoned rice vinegar
1 tsp	sriracha (use more or less depending on your spice tolerance)
1 tsp	honey
1 tsp	toasted sesame oil
1 tsp	fresh grated ginger
½ tsp	fish sauce
¼ tsp	garlic powder

For serving:

1	lime, sliced into wedges

Shrimp (and Lobster) Summer Rolls

Rice paper wraps filled with shrimp or lobster, brown rice, red cabbage, cucumber, carrot, mint, Thai basil, and crushed peanuts, then served with spicy peanut sauce and lime wedges. This is a great interactive appetizer (or main dish) because everyone gets to make their own rolls and add as much or as little of each ingredient as they like.

INSTRUCTIONS

For the summer rolls: Place all ingredients into small bowls on the table or atop a large cutting board. Prepare a large pot or bowl of warm water and set on table.

Dip a rice paper wrap in the water (make sure all parts of the wrap have gotten wet) and lay on your plate—the wrap should soften and be pliable. If the water is too hot, the wrappers will be too sticky. Build your own spring roll and roll it like a mini burrito.

Serve with lime wedges and spicy peanut sauce (below).

For the spicy peanut sauce: Stir together all ingredients in a small microwave-safe bowl. Heat in the microwave in 10-second increments 2–3 times, stirring after each increment until smooth and combined.

RECIPE NOTES:

• Find rice paper spring roll wrappers in the international aisle of your local grocery store–or at Vietnamese or Chinese markets. They are also available online.

• Fresh summer rolls taste best as soon as you make them, but if you need to make them an hour or two prior to serving, place them spaced out on a baking sheet covered with a few damp paper towels then plastic wrap. This will help prevent them from drying out.

Nutrition Facts per Serving **Calories:** 643 / **Total fat:** 20.3g (26% DV) / **Saturated fat:** 3.7g (18% DV) / **Trans fat:** 0.0g / **Cholesterol:** 214mg (71% DV) / **Sodium:** 879mg (38% DV) / **Total carbohydrate:** 77.6g (28% DV) / **Dietary fiber:** 7.7g (28% DV) / **Total sugars:** 9.7g / **Added sugar:** 3.3g (7% DV) / **Protein:** 42.1g / **Vitamin D:** 0.0mcg (0% DV) / **Calcium:** 162mg (12% DV) / **Iron:** 2.8mg (15% DV) / **Potassium:** 949mg (20% DV)

Blackened-Shrimp Tacos

Jumbo shrimp tossed in blackening seasoning, then panfried in butter and stuffed into flour tortillas, along with sliced red cabbage, chunks of avocado, quick pickled onions, cilantro, and a cumin sour cream. Easy, quick, and bursting with freshness.

Serves: 4
Course: Main course
Total time: 20 minutes

INGREDIENTS

For the shrimp:

1 lb	raw shrimp (21–25), peeled and deveined, tail removed, patted dry
1 tsp	onion powder
1 tsp	garlic powder
1 tsp	cumin
1 tsp	paprika
½ tsp	kosher salt
½ tsp	ground black pepper
2 tbsp	unsalted butter
1 tsp	canola or avocado oil

For the sour cream:

½ cup	light sour cream
½ tsp	cumin
¼ tsp	garlic powder

For assembly:

12 street-sized	flour tortillas, warmed (either wrapped in a kitchen towel and heated for 30 seconds in the microwave or heated individually in a dry grill pan or skillet)
½ head	red cabbage, thinly sliced
1	avocado, cut into chunks
¼ cup	pickled red onion (recipe on page 208)
½ cup	cilantro, leaves and stems, roughly chopped

For serving:

1	lime, cut into wedges

INSTRUCTIONS

For the shrimp: Place shrimp in a large mixing bowl and pat very dry with a paper towel.

In a small bowl, mix together onion powder, garlic powder, cumin, paprika, salt, and pepper. Add seasoning mixture to the shrimp and toss to combine.

Heat butter and oil in a large cast-iron (or nonstick) skillet over medium high heat. Once the butter begins to bubble, add shrimp, making sure not to crowd the pan. If need be, cook shrimp in batches.

Flip shrimp after 1–2 minutes, once underside is browned. Cook another 1–2 minutes until shrimp is just opaque and cooked through. Don't overcook. Remove shrimp from heat.

For the sour cream: Combine the sour cream, cumin, and garlic powder. Mix well.

For assembly: Spread each warmed tortilla with sour cream mixture.

Top with red cabbage, blackened shrimp, avocado, pickled red onion, and cilantro.

Serve with lime wedges and more sour cream.

Nutrition Facts per Serving **Calories:** 531 / **Total fat:** 21.0g (27% DV) / **Saturated fat:** 8.0g (40% DV) / **Trans fat:** 0.3g / **Cholesterol:** 181mg (60% DV) / **Sodium:** 1,045mg (45% DV) / **Total carbohydrate:** 58.3g (21% DV) / **Dietary fiber:** 8.5g (30% DV) / **Total sugars:** 11.9g / **Added sugar:** 0.4g (1% DV) / **Protein:** 31.2g / **Vitamin D:** 0.1mcg (0% DV) / **Calcium:** 287mg (22% DV) / **Iron:** 5.3mg (29% DV) / **Potassium:** 904mg (19% DV)

Grilled Shrimp Lettuce Wraps

Colossal grilled shrimp, fresh corn, fresh herbs, and feta cheese served in Bibb lettuce leaves. These shrimp lettuce cups are summery, flavor-packed, and a crowd-pleaser.

Serves: 8
Course: Appetizer
Total time: 25 minutes

INGREDIENTS

For the corn salad:

4 ears	fresh corn, shucked
1 bunch	scallions, white and green parts, trimmed and thinly sliced
½ bunch	cilantro, roughly chopped
2–3 tbsp	extra-virgin olive oil
2 tbsp	seasoned rice vinegar
2	limes, juice of
¼ tsp	freshly ground black pepper
½ cup	feta cheese, crumbled
1 head	Bibb lettuce, separated into leaves

For the grilled shrimp:

1 lb	raw shrimp (12–14), peeled and deveined, patted dry
1 tbsp	canola or avocado oil
½ tsp	cumin
½ tsp	kosher salt
¼ tsp	garlic powder
¼ tsp	ground black pepper

For serving:

1	lime, cut into wedges

INSTRUCTIONS

Bring a large pot of water to a boil. Add corn and cook 3–5 minutes, or until tender. Remove corn from pot and let cool slightly.

Cut corn off the cobs with a sharp knife. Place kernels into a large bowl.

Add scallions, cilantro, olive oil, rice vinegar, lime juice, and freshly ground black pepper. Stir to combine. Gently stir in crumbled feta cheese. Spoon corn salad into Bibb lettuce leaves. Set aside.

Preheat grill to high heat. Clean and oil grates.

Drizzle shrimp with oil; sprinkle with cumin, salt, garlic powder, and pepper on both sides.

Reduce grill heat to medium high. Place shrimp onto grill. Grill shrimp for 1–2 minutes on each side or until opaque and cooked through. Remove from grill.

Top each lettuce cup with a grilled shrimp. Serve with lime wedges.

Nutrition Facts per Serving **Calories:** 159 / **Total fat:** 6.1g (8% DV) / **Saturated fat:** 1.8g (9% DV) / **Trans fat:** 0.1g / **Cholesterol:** 87mg (29% DV) / **Sodium:** 345mg (15% DV) / **Total carbohydrate:** 15.3g (6% DV) / **Dietary fiber:** 2.2g (8% DV) / **Total sugars:** 5.7g / **Added sugar:** 0.4g (1% DV) / **Protein:** 13.7g / **Vitamin D:** 0.0mcg (0% DV) / **Calcium:** 100mg (8% DV) / **Iron:** 1.2mg (7% DV) / **Potassium:** 374mg (8% DV)

Shrimp Scampi with Spinach

Linguine tossed with sautéed shrimp and baby spinach in a garlicky, buttery white wine sauce. This simple pasta meal is quick enough for a weeknight dinner but special enough for a weekend dinner. This dish is bright and fresh, yet comforting.

Serves: 4
Course: Main course
Total time: 25 minutes

INGREDIENTS

1 lb	linguine
2 tbsp	salted butter, divided
1 tbsp	extra-virgin olive oil
5 cloves	garlic, thinly sliced
¼ cup	dry white wine, such as Pinot Grigio
5 oz	fresh baby spinach
12 oz	raw shrimp (21–25), peeled and deveined, patted dry
¼ tsp	kosher salt
¼ tsp	ground black pepper
½ cup	fresh parsley, roughly chopped

For serving:

½ cup	shaved (or grated) Parmesan cheese
1	lemon, cut into wedges

INSTRUCTIONS

Bring a large pot of salted water to a boil. Add linguine and cook almost to al dente. Drain, reserving 1 cup of the pasta water. Place pasta back into pot.

Meanwhile, heat 1 tablespoon butter and 1 tablespoon olive oil in a medium skillet over medium heat. Once hot, add garlic and sauté 1–2 minutes, taking care not to burn the garlic. Add wine, bring to a boil, then reduce to a simmer. Simmer until wine has reduced a bit, then add spinach. Stir, then add to pasta.

In the same skillet you used for the spinach, add the remaining tablespoon of butter over medium high heat. Pat the shrimp dry again, then season with salt and pepper on both sides. Add to hot pan and cook about 1–2 minutes on each side, until opaque and just cooked through. Don't overcook!

Add shrimp and chopped parsley to the pasta and spinach and toss gently with tongs. Drizzle in a bit of pasta water, toss gently again (this should help smooth the sauce and provide silkiness to the dish). Add salt and pepper to taste.

Serve linguine with shaved Parmesan and lemon wedges for squeezing over top of bowls of scampi.

Nutrition Facts per Serving **Calories:** 719 / **Total fat:** 15.9g (20% DV) / **Saturated fat:** 6.7g (33% DV) / **Trans fat:** 0.3g / **Cholesterol:** 123mg (41% DV) / **Sodium:** 921mg (40% DV) / **Total carbohydrate:** 104.5g (38% DV) / **Dietary fiber:** 6.7g (24% DV) / **Total sugars:** 2.5g / **Added sugar:** 0.0g (0% DV) / **Protein:** 35.8g / **Vitamin D:** 0.1mcg (0% DV) / **Calcium:** 212mg (16% DV) / **Iron:** 5.7mg (32% DV) / **Potassium:** 522mg (11% DV)

Shrimp Nutrition Highlights

Shrimp is packed with protein and is an excellent source of vitamin B3, vitamin B12, zinc, selenium, and copper. It also contains a health-promoting antioxidant called astaxanthin.

Shrimp and Couscous Salad

Grilled shrimp served over top of pearled couscous tossed with baby arugula, white beans, parsley, red onion, extra-virgin olive oil, and apple cider vinegar. This fresh and tangy salad is perfect for enjoying with family and friends.

Serves: 4
Course: Main course
Total time: 25 minutes

INGREDIENTS

For the salad:

2 cups	cooked pearled couscous
2 cups	baby arugula, loosely packed
1 (15-oz) can	white beans, drained and rinsed
½	red onion, minced
¼ cup	flat-leaf parsley leaves, roughly chopped
¼ cup	extra-virgin olive oil
¼ cup	apple cider vinegar
¼ tsp	kosher salt
⅛ tsp	freshly ground black pepper

For the grilled shrimp:

8 oz	raw shrimp (21–25), peeled and deveined, patted dry
½ tsp	avocado or canola oil
¼ tsp	kosher salt
⅛ tsp	freshly ground black pepper

For serving:

1	lemon, cut into wedges

INSTRUCTIONS

Preheat grill to high heat. Clean and oil grates.

In a large bowl, combine couscous, arugula, beans, onion, parsley, olive oil, vinegar, salt, and pepper. Toss to combine. Add more salt, if needed. Set aside.

Brush shrimp with oil on both sides and season with salt and pepper. Add shrimp to the grill. Reduce heat to medium. Grill shrimp until they are just opaque, a few minutes on each side. Remove shrimp from heat.

Top couscous salad with grilled shrimp. Serve with lemon wedges.

Nutrition Facts per Serving **Calories:** 370 / **Total fat:** 14.7g (19% DV) / **Saturated fat:** 2.1g (10% DV) / **Trans fat:** 0.0g / **Cholesterol:** 78mg (26% DV) / **Sodium:** 572mg (25% DV) / **Total carbohydrate:** 39.4g (14% DV) / **Dietary fiber:** 6.3g (22% DV) / **Total sugars:** 1.9g / **Added sugar:** 0.0g (0% DV) / **Protein:** 20.5g / **Vitamin D:** 0.0mcg (0% DV) / **Calcium:** 129mg (10% DV) / **Iron:** 3.7mg (20% DV) / **Potassium:** 655mg (14% DV)

Shrimp Nachos

Tortilla chips loaded with shredded cheddar, black beans, shrimp, avocado, jalapeño, scallions, and cilantro, then drizzled with ranch dressing and served with salsa and lime wedges. Ready in less than 20 minutes, these nachos are the perfect game-day appetizer or weeknight meal!

Serves: 8-10
Course: Appetizer
Total time: 20 minutes

INGREDIENTS

For the shrimp:

12 oz	raw shrimp (21–25), peeled and deveined, patted very dry
1 tbsp + 1 tsp	extra-virgin olive oil, divided
½ tsp	cumin
½ tsp	chili powder
¼ tsp	garlic powder
¼ tsp	kosher salt

For the nachos:

6.5 oz	restaurant-style tortilla chips (half of a 13-oz bag)
8 oz	cheddar cheese, grated
½ cup	canned black beans, drained, rinsed, drained again
1	avocado, thinly sliced
1	jalapeño, halved, seeded, thinly sliced
1 bunch	scallions, white and green parts, thinly sliced
½ cup	cilantro, loosely packed, roughly chopped
	Freshly ground black pepper
2 tbsp	reduced-fat ranch dressing + more for serving

For serving:

Salsa

Lime wedges

INSTRUCTIONS

For the shrimp: Combine shrimp, 1 tablespoon olive oil, cumin, chili powder, garlic powder, and salt in a large bowl. Mix well so shrimp get covered in seasoning.

Add remaining teaspoon olive oil to a nonstick skillet over medium high heat. Once hot, add the shrimp. Avoid crowding the shrimp—cook them in batches if needed. Cook for 1–2 minutes on each side until shrimp are opaque throughout and cooked through. Remove from heat.

For the nachos: Preheat oven to 350°F. Prepare a baking sheet with parchment paper or aluminum foil.

Place chips evenly on baking sheet. Top evenly with cheese and beans.

Place in oven for 5–7 minutes, until cheese is melted and chips begin to brown on the edges.

Remove from oven.

Top with shrimp, avocado, jalapeño, scallions, cilantro, and black pepper.

Drizzle nachos with ranch dressing.

Serve with additional ranch dressing, salsa, and lime wedges.

RECIPE NOTES:

• Instead of avocado, you can substitute ¹/₂ cup prepared guacamole.

• As a time-saver, you can use cooked shrimp. Add them to the nachos prior to putting them in the oven so the shrimp can warm through.

Nutrition Facts per Serving **Calories:** 334 / **Total fat:** 19.4g (25% DV) / **Saturated fat:** 6.6g (33% DV) / **Trans fat:** 0.3g / **Cholesterol:** 87mg (29% DV) / **Sodium:** 571mg (25% DV) / **Total carbohydrate:** 24.7g (9% DV) / **Dietary fiber:** 4.6g (16% DV) / **Total sugars:** 1.8g / **Added sugar:** 0.2g (0% DV) / **Protein:** 17.4g / **Vitamin D:** 0.2mcg (1% DV) / **Calcium:** 277mg (21% DV) / **Iron:** 1.7mg (10% DV) / **Potassium:** 380mg (8% DV)

Grilled Shrimp with Chimichurri

Shrimp simply brushed with olive oil and sprinkled with garlic salt and black pepper, then grilled to perfection and finished with a bright and fresh chimichurri sauce. This is a quick, gorgeous, and flavor-packed dish that celebrates the fresh flavors of summer.

Serves: 4
Course: Main course
Total time: 20 minutes

INGREDIENTS

For the chimichurri:

- **½ cup** chimichurri (see recipe page 207)

For the shrimp:

- **12 oz** raw shrimp (31–40), peeled and deveined, patted very dry
- **½ tsp** avocado, canola, or olive oil
- **¼ tsp** garlic salt, or use kosher salt
- **⅛ tsp** freshly ground black pepper

For serving:

- **2 cups** cooked brown rice, warmed

INSTRUCTIONS

Preheat grill to high heat. Clean and oil grates.

Toss or brush shrimp with oil. Thread shrimp onto metal skewers (if you use wooden skewers, make sure to soak them in water for 30 minutes to prevent them from burning).

Sprinkle shrimp with garlic salt and pepper on both sides.

Add shrimp to the grill. Reduce heat to medium. Grill shrimp for 1–2 minutes on each side, just until opaque and cooked through.

Remove from grill.

For serving:

Place warmed cooked brown rice on a serving platter.

Top with grilled shrimp skewers.

Drizzle shrimp with chimichurri sauce. Serve additional chimichurri on the side.

Nutrition Facts per Serving **Calories:** 296 / **Total fat:** 12.6g (16% DV) / **Saturated fat:** 1.9g (9% DV) / **Trans fat:** 0.0g / **Cholesterol:** 117mg (39% DV) / **Sodium:** 258mg (11% DV) / **Total carbohydrate:** 27.9g (10% DV) / **Dietary fiber:** 2.2g (8% DV) / **Total sugars:** 0.4g / **Added sugar:** 0.0g (0% DV) / **Protein:** 18.1g / **Vitamin D:** 0.0mcg (0% DV) / **Calcium:** 67mg (5% DV) / **Iron:** 1.6mg (9% DV) / **Potassium:** 302mg (6% DV)

Buffalo Shrimp Sliders

Slider buns stuffed with panfried shrimp tossed in buffalo sauce, topped with blue cheese dressing, blue cheese crumbles, and thinly sliced celery. This is the ultimate game day appetizer for devouring while cheering on your favorite team.

Serves: 6
Course: Appetizer
Total time: 15 minutes

INGREDIENTS

1 tsp	canola or avocado oil
12 oz	raw shrimp (31–40), peeled and deveined, tail removed, patted very dry
1½ tbsp	buffalo sauce (mild, medium, or hot—your choice)
6	slider buns or dinner rolls
1 tbsp	salted butter, softened
1 head	celery, divided (thinly slice 3–4 stalks horizontally for the sliders and then cut the rest vertically into celery sticks for dipping in blue cheese)
¼ cup	reduced-fat blue cheese dressing, plus more for serving
2 oz	blue cheese crumbles
	Ground black pepper

INSTRUCTIONS

Heat oil in a large skillet over medium high heat until hot. Add shrimp, flipping after about 1 minute (once underside is seared and lightly browned). Cook another 1–2 minutes until shrimp is just opaque and cooked through. Don't overcook. Remove from heat and toss with buffalo sauce.

Toast buns and spread with butter.

Assemble sliders by placing 3 or 4 shrimp on each bottom slider bun, then topping with sliced celery, dressing, and blue cheese crumbles. Add the top slider bun.

Serve sliders with celery sticks and additional blue cheese for dipping.

RECIPE NOTE: This recipe makes 6 buffalo shrimp sliders. It will serve 6 people as an appetizer if other apps are being served. If you're making these sliders for a meal, it'll serve 3–4 people, as long as you're serving sides with it. Recipe can easily be doubled.

Nutrition Facts per Serving **Calories:** 209 / **Total fat:** 8.0g (10% DV) / **Saturated fat:** 3.7g (18% DV) / **Trans fat:** 0.2g / **Cholesterol:** 92mg (31% DV) / **Sodium:** 481mg (21% DV) / **Total carbohydrate:** 19.4g (7% DV) / **Dietary fiber:** 1.6g (6% DV) / **Total sugars:** 3.1g / **Added sugar:** 1.8g (4% DV) / **Protein:** 15.6g / **Vitamin D:** 0.1mcg (0% DV) / **Calcium:** 157mg (12% DV) / **Iron:** 1.4mg (8% DV) / **Potassium:** 333mg (7% DV)

Buffalo Shrimp Potato Skins

Potato skins stuffed with spicy buffalo shrimp, blue cheese, and diced celery, served with blue cheese dressing. This is a great appetizer for watching any sports game–or for serving as a party app!

Serves: 4
Course: Appetizer
Total time: 55 minutes

INGREDIENTS

4 medium	russet potatoes, scrubbed, poked a few times with a fork
1 tbsp	salted butter
1 tbsp	buffalo sauce (mild, medium, or hot—your choice), plus more for serving
12 oz	cooked shrimp (31–40), peeled and deveined, tail off
3 oz	blue cheese, crumbled
2 stalks	celery, diced
	Freshly ground black pepper

For serving:

	Additional buffalo sauce
¼ cup	reduced-fat blue cheese dressing
4 stalks	celery, sliced into sticks
4	carrots, sliced into sticks

INSTRUCTIONS

Preheat oven to 400°F. Place potatoes directly on rack and bake until fork-tender, about 30–40 minutes; time will vary depending on the size of your potatoes. Remove from oven.

Prepare a baking sheet with aluminum foil. Carefully (potatoes are hot!) cut potatoes in half lengthwise and scoop out flesh, leaving a thin flesh layer within each skin.

Place potato skins on baking sheet. Set potato flesh aside for another use— you won't need it in this recipe.

Place butter and buffalo sauce in a small microwave-safe bowl and microwave 15–30 seconds until butter is melted. Stir mixture together.

Brush buttery buffalo sauce onto each potato skin and place the skins back onto baking sheet. Place back in oven for 5 minutes.

Toss shrimp with remaining buttery buffalo mixture and set aside.

Remove potato skins from oven. Top each skin with 2 buffalo shrimp and blue cheese crumbles. Place back into oven for 2–3 minutes until shrimp are warmed through and cheese begins to melt. Remove from oven and top with diced celery and freshly ground pepper.

Serve potato skins with additional buffalo sauce, blue cheese dressing, and veggie sticks.

Nutrition Facts per Serving **Calories:** 403 / **Total fat:** 10.3g (13% DV) / **Saturated fat:** 6.1g (31% DV) / **Trans fat:** 0.3g / **Cholesterol:** 185mg (62% DV) / **Sodium:** 652mg (28% DV) / **Total carbohydrate:** 49.3g (18% DV) / **Dietary fiber:** 6.8g (24% DV) / **Total sugars:** 7.1g / **Added sugar:** 0.4g (1% DV) / **Protein:** 30.5g / **Vitamin D:** 0.1mcg (1% DV) / **Calcium:** 252mg (19% DV) / **Iron:** 2.7mg (15% DV) / **Potassium:** 1,586mg (34% DV)

Grilled Shrimp Wedge Salad

Crisp iceberg lettuce topped with grilled shrimp, charred red onion, and tomatoes. Sprinkled with crispy bacon and tangy blue cheese. This is your favorite wedge salad made *much* more exciting . . . and meal-worthy, especially alongside slices from a crusty loaf of multigrain bread.

Serves: 4
Course: Main course
Total time: 25 minutes

INGREDIENTS

1 lb	raw shrimp (31–40), peeled and deveined, patted very dry
½ cup	citrus or Italian vinaigrette, homemade or store-bought
1 pint	grape or cherry tomatoes
1	red onion, cut into 4 thick chunks
1 tsp	canola or avocado oil
1 head	iceberg lettuce, quartered
4 strips	bacon, cooked and crumbled
4 oz	blue cheese, crumbled
	Freshly ground black pepper, to taste

For serving:

	Balsamic glaze or balsamic vinegar
1	lemon, cut into wedges

INSTRUCTIONS

Preheat grill to high heat. Clean and oil grill grates.

Place shrimp and vinaigrette in a resealable plastic bag. Let shrimp marinate for 10–15 minutes.

Thread shrimp onto metal skewers (or wooden skewers that you've soaked in water for 30 minutes). Discard marinade.

Thread tomatoes onto additional skewers.

Brush tomatoes and red onion slices with oil.

Place shrimp, tomatoes, and red onion on the grill. Reduce heat to medium high.

Grill shrimp for 1–2 minutes on each side, or until shrimp just turns opaque and is cooked through (grilling time will vary depending on the size of the shrimp). Remove from grill.

Grill tomatoes and red onion until lightly charred on all sides, flipping/rotating a few times.

Assemble salads by placing a chunk of iceberg lettuce on each plate. Top with tomatoes, red onion, and shrimp. Sprinkle with crumbled bacon, blue cheese, and freshly ground black pepper. Drizzle with balsamic glaze. Serve with lemon wedges.

Nutrition Facts per Serving **Calories:** 327 / **Total fat:** 16.3g (21% DV) / **Saturated fat:** 7.0g (35% DV) / **Trans fat:** 0.2g / **Cholesterol:** 186mg (62% DV) / **Sodium:** 950mg (41% DV) / **Total carbohydrate:** 16.4g (6% DV) / **Dietary fiber:** 3.7g (13% DV) / **Total sugars:** 9.3g / **Added sugar:** 2.1g (4% DV) / **Protein:** 31.3g / **Vitamin D:** 0.2mcg (1% DV) / **Calcium:** 254mg (20% DV) / **Iron:** 1.6mg (9% DV) / **Potassium:** 832mg (18% DV)

Shrimp Scampi Spaghetti Squash Bowls

Roasted spaghetti squash tossed with extra-virgin olive oil, white wine, garlic, and spinach, then topped with sautéed shrimp and shaved Parmesan cheese and served in the spaghetti squash shell. This incredible spaghetti squash recipe is a fun spin on traditional shrimp scampi with linguine.

Serves: 4
Course: Main course
Total time: 45 minutes

INGREDIENTS

2 small	spaghetti squash, halved and seeded
2 tbsp	extra-virgin olive oil, divided
½ tsp	kosher salt, divided
¼ tsp	freshly ground black pepper, divided
3 tbsp	butter, divided
3 cloves	garlic, minced
¼ cup	dry white wine, such as Pinot Grigio
2 cups	loosely packed baby spinach
12 oz	raw shrimp (13–15), peeled and deveined, patted very dry
½ cup	shaved Parmesan cheese
1 tbsp	fresh parsley

For serving:

1	lemon, cut into wedges

INSTRUCTIONS

Preheat oven to 425°F. Prepare a baking sheet with aluminum foil.

Slice spaghetti squash in half. Remove seeds. Rub inside of spaghetti squash halves with 1 tablespoon extra-virgin olive oil. Sprinkle with ¼ teaspoon salt and ⅛ teaspoon pepper.

Roast for 30–35 minutes or until squash is tender and strands remove easily with a fork. Let cool slightly, then, using a fork, remove strands from the squash and place into a large mixing bowl. Set the spaghetti squash shells aside—you will stuff them later.

In a medium skillet, add 2 tablespoons butter and remaining 1 tablespoon extra-virgin olive oil over medium heat. When butter is melted, add minced garlic and lightly sauté 1–2 minutes. Add white wine and bring to a boil, then reduce to a simmer. Add baby spinach and remove from heat. Pour spinach mixture over top of spaghetti squash strands. Toss.

Season shrimp with remaining salt and pepper. In the same skillet, heat remaining 1 tablespoon butter over medium high heat. Once pan is hot and butter is melted, add shrimp. Cook 1–2 minutes until bottoms form a nice light-brown crust. Flip and cook until shrimp are no longer translucent, 1–2 minutes more. Don't overcook. Remove pan from heat.

Take the spaghetti squash shells and, using tongs, portion spaghetti squash mixture back into squash shells. Top with shrimp, shaved Parmesan, and parsley. Serve with lemon wedges.

Nutrition Facts per Serving **Calories:** 518 / **Total fat:** 21.5g (28% DV) / **Saturated fat:** 8.9g (45% DV) / **Trans fat:** 0.5g / **Cholesterol:** 151mg (50% DV) / **Sodium:** 832mg (36% DV) / **Total carbohydrate:** 63.6g (23% DV) / **Dietary fiber:** 13.5g (48% DV) / **Total sugars:** 23.6g / **Added sugar:** 0.0g (0% DV) / **Protein:** 25.3g / **Vitamin D:** 0.1mcg (1% DV) / **Calcium:** 369mg (28% DV) / **Iron:** 4.1mg (23% DV) / **Potassium:** 1,376mg (29% DV)

Swordfish, Tuna, and Striped Bass

This chapter highlights some of the larger, meatier fish of the sea—found in New England and beyond. Swordfish, tuna, and striped bass are great on the grill, and we also love tuna in a variety of raw and seared preparations—including one of our all-time favorite tuna dishes, tuna tartare avocado bowls (page 113). While most of the recipes in this chapter utilize fresh fish, I've also included some of my favorite canned-tuna recipes, as canned tuna is affordable, accessible, convenient, and delicious. I imagine it's likely a staple in your house like it is in ours.

How to choose and store:

- Trust your senses—use your sight, touch, and smell.
- Fresh fish should not smell overly fishy—it should smell clean and ocean fresh. If it has any scent of ammonia or smells a bit sour or fishy, don't buy it.
- Ask your fishmonger how long the fish has been in the display case and if it's been previously frozen.
- Purchase fish fillets and steaks that look firm and moist—the flesh should not be falling apart and there should be no strange discoloration or dry spots. If pressed, the flesh should spring back.
- Swordfish and tuna will have darker, full-flavored flesh toward the bloodline. The bloodline should be bright red (not brown), indicating freshness.
- Only purchase fish that is displayed on a thick bed of ice or refrigerated.
- When I purchase fresh fish and take it home from the market, I remove it from the paper it's wrapped in and place it in a sealed plastic bag. Then I place it on a small baking sheet and store it on the bottom shelf in the back of the fridge. This should be the coldest part of the refrigerator (make sure the fridge is set at a temperature of 40°F or less). Oftentimes I will lay one or two ice packs on top to keep it extra cold and to preserve freshness. Use the fish as soon as possible. We use fish on the same day of purchase or the next, but typically you are fine to use it within two days. If you aren't going to use it within that time frame, wrap tightly and freeze.
- When purchasing tuna for raw preparations, make sure you purchase sushi-grade tuna from a trusted, knowledgeable, and reputable source—and use it right away.

When is the fish cooked through?

- Fish is cooked through when the internal temperature reaches a safe 145°F in the thickest part of the flesh. Keep in mind that once you remove the fish from heat, its internal temperature will continue to rise, so it's safe to remove at 140°F.

- If you prefer your tuna seared, you'll want to remove it after briefly searing each side over high heat, leaving the center rare.
- A general rule of thumb is to cook fish for 10 minutes per inch of thickness, measured at the thickest part of the fillet—turning or flipping halfway through cooking time.
- Fish will flake easily with a fork in the thickest part of the flesh and will have lost its translucency.

Grilled Swordfish Piccata

Swordfish is simply grilled then topped with a buttery, tangy, and briny piccata pan sauce. This easy dinner is one of our favorite ways to serve this meaty, mild fish.

Serves: 4
Course: Main course
Total time: 20 minutes

INGREDIENTS

For the swordfish:

1½ lb	swordfish steaks
1 tsp	olive oil
⅛ tsp	kosher salt
⅛ tsp	freshly ground black pepper

For the pan sauce:

1 tbsp	olive oil
1	shallot, minced
2 cloves	garlic, sliced
½ cup	dry white wine, such as Pinot Grigio
2 tbsp	capers, drained
4 tbsp	unsalted butter, cut into 4 pieces
1	lemon, cut into thin rounds (use a few for the sauce, a few for serving)
2 tbsp	chopped fresh parsley

INSTRUCTIONS

Preheat grill to high heat. Clean and oil grates.

Brush swordfish with 1 teaspoon olive oil and sprinkle with salt and pepper.

Heat 1 tablespoon olive oil over medium heat in a skillet. Add shallot and garlic and heat until fragrant and translucent. Add wine, bring heat to medium high. Once boiling, reduce to a simmer. Simmer for about 5 minutes to reduce the sauce to half. Add capers and butter. Whisk sauce until smooth and combined. Add a few lemon slices to the pan. Keep warm over low heat.

Meanwhile, place swordfish on the grill and grill for 5 minutes on one side, flip, and grill until fish reaches an internal temperature of 140°F. Fish will continue rising in temperature, to a safe internal temperature of 145°F. Remove from heat and place on serving platter.

Whisk sauce well and pour over fish, reserving a bit of sauce for serving. Sprinkle with chopped parsley. Serve fish with lemon wedges.

Nutrition Facts per Serving **Calories:** 384 / **Total fat:** 25.8g (33% DV) / **Saturated fat:** 10.1g (51% DV) / **Trans fat:** 0.5g / **Cholesterol:** 126mg (42% DV) / **Sodium:** 298mg (13% DV) / **Total carbohydrate:** 2.7g (1% DV) / **Dietary fiber:** 0.5g (2% DV) / **Total sugars:** 0.7g / **Added sugar:** 0.0g (0% DV) / **Protein:** 29.2g / **Vitamin D:** 20.4mcg (102% DV) / **Calcium:** 24mg (2% DV) / **Iron:** 0.9mg (14% DV) / **Potassium:** 670mg (14% DV)

Swordfish Nutrition Highlights

Swordfish is rich in protein and is an excellent source of vitamin D, vitamin B3, vitamin B6, vitamin B12, phosphorous, and selenium.

Bluefin Tuna Toro Nachos

Serves: 4
Course: Appetizer
Total time: 20 minutes

INGREDIENTS

For the wontons:

20	wonton wrappers, cut in half on the diagonal
1 tbsp	avocado oil
¼ tsp	kosher salt

For the tuna:

1 tbsp	seasoned rice vinegar
1 tbsp	reduced-sodium soy sauce
	Juice of ½ lime
1 tsp	honey
1 tsp	sesame oil
1 tsp	freshly grated ginger
¼ tsp	sriracha
½ lb	sushi-grade bluefin tuna toro, cut into ¼-inch cubes

For assembly:

1 cup	shredded Napa cabbage
1 tsp	seasoned rice vinegar
½ tsp	toasted sesame oil
½ cup	seaweed salad (we use Atlantic Sea Farms)
1	avocado, cut into chunks
1 bunch	scallions (white and green parts), sliced
1 tsp	black sesame seeds
	Crushed teriyaki-flavored seaweed snacks (optional)

For serving:

2 tbsp	ginger slices
1 tbsp	wasabi mayo
1	lime, cut into wedges

Crisp wontons are topped with cabbage slaw, seaweed salad, avocado, scallions, and sesame seeds, then loaded up with sushi-grade fatty bluefin tuna that's been tossed in a soy-honey-ginger dressing. These nachos are over-the-top tasty and will be loved by all tuna enthusiasts.

INSTRUCTIONS

Preheat oven to 400°F. Line two baking sheets with parchment paper. Place wonton wrappers on parchment paper and brush on both sides with oil. Bake for 4 minutes, then rotate baking sheets (front to back/bottom to top rack). Bake another 2–4 minutes until crisp and lightly browned. Remove from oven. Sprinkle with salt.

Combine rice vinegar, soy sauce, lime juice, honey, sesame oil, ginger, and sriracha in a medium bowl. Whisk well. Add cubes of tuna and toss gently to combine.

Toss cabbage with rice vinegar and sesame oil. Place wontons onto a large serving platter in a single layer. Top with cabbage, tuna, seaweed salad, avocado, scallions, and black sesame seeds. Crush a few sheets of seaweed snacks over top. Serve nachos with ginger slices, wasabi mayo, and lime wedges.

RECIPE NOTE: You can substitute ahi tuna for the bluefin if you prefer.

Nutrition Facts per Serving **Calories:** 338 / **Total fat:** 15.0g (19% DV) / **Saturated fat:** 2.4g (12% DV) / **Trans fat:** 0.0g / **Cholesterol:** 25mg (8% DV) / **Sodium:** 467mg (20% DV) / **Total carbohydrate:** 32.8g (12% DV) / **Dietary fiber:** 5.1g (18% DV) / **Total sugars:** 3.4g / **Added sugar:** 1.7g (3% DV) / **Protein:** 19.2g / **Vitamin D:** 3.2mcg (16% DV) / **Calcium:** 61mg (5% DV) / **Iron:** 3.2mg (18% DV) / **Potassium:** 556mg (12% DV)

Those with compromised immune systems, as well as those who are pregnant, infants, young children, and older adults, should not consume raw or undercooked fish and shellfish.

Serves: 6
Course: Main course
Total time: 40 minutes

INGREDIENTS

For the slaw:

½	green cabbage, slivered
½ cup	reduced-fat mayonnaise
2 fingertip-size pieces	ginger root, peeled and finely minced, divided (reserve half for the marinade)
½ tsp	toasted sesame oil
¼ tsp	kosher salt
⅛ tsp	ground black pepper

For the tuna:

1 lb	sushi-grade ahi tuna
¼ cup	reduced-sodium soy sauce
¼ cup	seasoned rice vinegar
1 bunch	scallions, thinly sliced, white parts only (save the green parts for garnish)
2 tbsp	olive oil
1 tsp	toasted sesame oil
1 tsp	honey
	Reserved ginger from above
½ tsp	sriracha

For assembly:

12 small	flour tortillas, warmed
1	avocado, thinly sliced
½ cup	seaweed salad (we prefer Atlantic Sea Farms)
2 tbsp	wasabi mayo
	Black sesame seeds (optional)
	Reserved scallions, green parts

For serving:

	Additional wasabi mayo
1	lime, cut into wedges

Seared Tuna Tacos

Warm street-size flour tortillas topped with Asian slaw, seared soy ginger-marinated ahi tuna, seaweed salad, avocado, sliced scallions, and wasabi mayo. These Asian-inspired tacos are a tuna and seaweed salad lover's dream.

INSTRUCTIONS

Combine all slaw ingredients in a large bowl. Toss well. Chill until ready to serve.

Add tuna, soy sauce, rice vinegar, scallions, olive oil, toasted sesame oil, honey, ginger, and sriracha to a large resealable bag. Marinate for 15–20 minutes.

Preheat grill to high heat. Clean and oil grates.

Grill tuna for 1–2 minutes on each side, just to sear. Or cook until desired doneness. Remove from heat.

Slice tuna thinly against the grain.

Assemble tacos by adding slaw to each tortilla, then tuna, avocado, seaweed salad, wasabi mayo, black sesame seeds, and scallions.

Serve with additional wasabi mayo and lime wedges.

Nutrition Facts per Serving **Calories:** 601 / **Total fat:** 26.6g (34% DV) / **Saturated fat:** 6.0g (30% DV) / **Trans fat:** 0.1g / **Cholesterol:** 33mg (11% DV) / **Sodium:** 1,507mg (66% DV) / **Total carbohydrate:** 61.4g (22% DV) / **Dietary fiber:** 7.8g (28% DV) / **Total sugars:** 9.0g / **Added sugar:** 2.2g (4% DV) / **Protein:** 29.0g / **Vitamin D:** 4.3mcg (21% DV) / **Calcium:** 207mg (16% DV) / **Iron:** 5.5mg (31% DV) / **Potassium:** 699mg (15% DV)

Those with compromised immune systems, as well as those who are pregnant, infants, young children, and older adults, should not consume raw or undercooked fish and shellfish.

Tuna Nutrition Highlights

Tuna is rich in protein and is an excellent source of vitamin D, vitamin A, vitamin B3, vitamin B6, vitamin B12, selenium, phosphorous, and more.

Grilled Ahi Tuna with Chimichurri

Fresh ahi (also called yellowfin tuna) tuna steaks brushed with extra-virgin olive oil, sprinkled with salt and pepper, and seared briefly on the grill, then served with a bright, tangy, and fresh chimichurri sauce. These are the kind of easy, breezy meals that summer is all about.

Serves: 4
Course: Main course
Total time: 15 minutes

INGREDIENTS

For the tuna:

1½ lb	ahi (yellowfin) tuna steaks, patted dry
1 tsp	extra-virgin olive oil
¼ tsp	kosher salt
⅛ tsp	ground black pepper
½ cup	chimichurri (see recipe on page 207)

For serving:

1	lemon, cut into wedges

INSTRUCTIONS

Preheat grill to high heat. Clean and oil grates.

Brush tuna steaks (both sides) with extra-virgin olive oil and sprinkle with salt and pepper. Place tuna steaks on grill. Reduce heat to medium high. Cook for about 60 seconds, flip, and cook an additional 60 seconds, just to sear the tuna. If cooking the steaks through, continue cooking for a total of 8–10 minutes, flipping tuna halfway through cooking time, to an internal temperature of 140°F, or until desired doneness.

Remove from grill and place onto a serving plate. Spoon chimichurri over top.

Serve tuna with lemon wedges.

Nutrition Facts per Serving

Calories: 298 / **Total fat:** 12.8g (16% DV) / **Saturated fat:** 1.9g (10% DV) / **Trans fat:** 0.0g / **Cholesterol:** 65mg (22% DV) / **Sodium:** 345mg (15% DV) / **Total carbohydrate:** 3.2g (1% DV) / **Dietary fiber:** 1.0g (3% DV) / **Total sugars:** 0.6g / **Added sugar:** 0.0g (0% DV) / **Protein:** 40.7g / **Vitamin D:** 2.8mcg (14% DV) / **Calcium:** 30mg (2% DV) / **Iron:** 2.0mg (11% DV) / **Potassium:** 799mg (17% DV)

Those with compromised immune systems, as well as those who are pregnant, infants, young children, and older adults, should not consume raw or undercooked fish and shellfish.

Open-Faced Tuna Melt

Whole-grain bread topped with arugula, sliced summer tomato, tuna in olive oil, thick slices of cheddar, lots of freshly ground black pepper, basil, and balsamic glaze. A quick, easy, and fresh sandwich that's incredibly satisfying.

Serves: 2
Course: Sandwich
Total time: 5 minutes

INGREDIENTS

2 slices	hearty whole-grain bread
8 leaves	arugula
½ medium	tomato, sliced
1 (5-oz) can	tuna in olive oil, drained
4 thick slices	cheddar cheese
4 leaves	fresh basil
	Freshly ground black pepper
1 tsp	balsamic glaze

INSTRUCTIONS

Toast the bread slices. Preheat the broiler.

Place toasted bread on a piece of tinfoil. Top each slice with arugula, tomato, tuna, and cheddar.

Broil 1–2 minutes until the cheese is melted and bubbly. Remove from oven.

Top with fresh basil leaves, black pepper, and balsamic glaze.

Nutrition Facts per Serving **Calories:** 392 / **Total fat:** 20.4g (26% DV) / **Saturated fat:** 9.1g (46% DV) / **Trans fat:** 0.5g / **Cholesterol:** 53mg (18% DV) / **Sodium:** 473mg (21% DV) / **Total carbohydrate:** 18.8g (7% DV) / **Dietary fiber:** 2.7g (10% DV) / **Total sugars:** 3.1g / **Added sugar:** 1.6g (3% DV) / **Protein:** 32.5g / **Vitamin D:** 4.4mcg (22% DV) / **Calcium:** 383mg (29% DV) / **Iron:** 2.1mg (11% DV) / **Potassium:** 359mg (8% DV)

Jenny and her Mom, Mimi, on Nantucket

Serves: 4
Course: Sandwich or salad
Total time: 5 minutes

INGREDIENTS

1 (12-oz)	can solid white tuna in water, drained
½ cup	diced celery
½ cup	diced onion
½ cup	diced carrot
½ cup	diced dill pickle
½ cup	reduced-fat mayonnaise
2 tbsp	rice vinegar
½ tsp	freshly ground pepper
¼ tsp	seasoned salt

Mimi's Tuna Salad

This is my mom's tuna salad. Also known as the only tuna salad I will ever eat. Typically, I avoid mayo "salads," but this one I love because of the addition of all the veggies–celery, onion, carrot, and pickles. I also like the subtle sweetness that the rice vinegar gives. Mom used to pack this tuna salad on whole wheat for me for lunch in grade school, back 30+ years ago, and she's still making it weekly. This tuna salad is best eaten at the beach with Cape Cod Potato Chips stuffed inside.

INSTRUCTIONS

In a medium bowl combine tuna with celery, onion, carrot, pickle, mayonnaise, vinegar, pepper, and salt.

Serve in a pita, on a sandwich, or atop greens.

Nutrition Facts per Serving **Calories:** 184 / **Total fat:** 7.8g (10% DV) / **Saturated fat:** 1.6g (8% DV) / **Trans fat:** 0.0g / **Cholesterol:** 39mg (13% DV) / **Sodium:** 322mg (14% DV) / **Total carbohydrate:** 8.7g (3% DV) / **Dietary fiber:** 1.1g (4% DV) / **Total sugars:** 3.2g / **Added sugar:** 1.2g (2% DV) / **Protein:** 18.9g / **Vitamin D:** 1.5mcg (8% DV) / **Calcium:** 37mg (3% DV) / **Iron:** 0.9mg (5% DV) / **Potassium:** 321mg (7% DV)

Mediterranean Tuna Pizza

Toasted mini naan bread topped with feta cheese, baby kale or arugula, a Mediterranean tomato-parsley salad, and flaky white tuna. These simple and flavor-packed flatbread pizzas are perfect for lunch at home or even a quick dinner.

Serves: 4
Course: Main course
Total time: 15 minutes

INGREDIENTS

For the Mediterranean salad:

1 cup	grape tomatoes, halved
½ cup	parsley, leaves only (keep whole or chop)
½ medium	red onion, diced
¼ cup	capers, drained
¼ cup	extra-virgin olive oil
¼ cup	feta cheese crumbles
2 tbsp	red wine vinegar
⅛ tsp	kosher salt
⅛ tsp	ground black pepper

For the assembly:

8	mini naan bread rounds (sandwich size)
½ cup	crumbled feta cheese
2 cups	baby kale or arugula
2 (4.5-oz)	cans solid white albacore tuna in extra-virgin olive oil, drained
	Freshly ground black pepper

INSTRUCTIONS

Combine all salad ingredients in a medium-sized bowl. Mix well.

To each naan round, add feta. Place rounds into toaster oven and lightly toast. (You may want to place a piece of tinfoil under the rounds so the cheese doesn't fall onto the bottom of the toaster oven.)

Top rounds with arugula or baby kale. Spoon salad (with juices) atop toasted naan rounds. Top with chunks of tuna and freshly ground black pepper. Serve.

Nutrition Facts per Serving **Calories:** 496 / **Total fat:** 30.9g (40% DV) / **Saturated fat:** 10.3g (51% DV) / **Trans fat:** 0.6g / **Cholesterol:** 59mg (20% DV) / **Sodium:** 822mg (36% DV) / **Total carbohydrate:** 29.6g (11% DV) / **Dietary fiber:** 2.3g (8% DV) / **Total sugars:** 4.3g / **Added sugar:** 0.0g (0% DV) / **Protein:** 24.8g / **Vitamin D:** 2.1mcg (11% DV) / **Calcium:** 212mg (11% DV) / **Iron:** 3.0mg (17% DV) / **Potassium:** 486mg (10% DV)

Sesame-Crusted Ahi Tuna Power Bowls

Sesame seed-crusted ahi tuna, seared then served with brown rice, edamame, thinly sliced red cabbage, creamy avocado, shaved carrot, seaweed salad, ginger, and a rice vinegar vinaigrette. These Asian-inspired power bowls are a healthy, satisfying dinner (or lunch!) packed with flavor and tons of texture.

Serves: 4
Course: Main course
Total time: 20 minutes

INGREDIENTS

For the tuna:

1 lb	ahi tuna
2 tbsp	sesame seeds
2 tbsp	black sesame seeds
¼ tsp	garlic powder
⅛ tsp	kosher salt
1 tbsp	safflower oil or other neutral oil

For the bowls:

2 cups	cooked brown rice, warmed
1 cup	seaweed salad (we prefer Atlantic Sea Farms)
1 cup	cooked edamame
¼ medium	red cabbage, thinly sliced
1	avocado, thinly sliced
1 medium	carrot, peeled into ribbons
½ cup	salted peanuts, crushed
4	scallions, thinly sliced

For the dressing:

¼ cup	seasoned rice vinegar
½ tsp	sriracha
¼ tsp	toasted sesame oil

For serving:

	Pickled ginger
	Wasabi mayo
	Lime wedges

INSTRUCTIONS

Pat tuna very dry with a paper towel. Place sesame seeds, garlic powder, and salt on a large plate and mix with your hands. Place tuna on sesame seed mixture and press into the sesame seeds. Coat tuna on all sides.

Heat a nonstick skillet over medium high heat. Add oil and swirl. Once hot, add tuna. Sear tuna on both sides, 1–2 minutes per side, until sesame seeds turn golden. Remove from heat; set aside.

Add rice, seaweed salad, edamame, red cabbage, avocado, carrot, salted peanuts, and scallions equally to four bowls.

Thinly slice tuna, against the grain, and add to power bowls.

Whisk together dressing ingredients in a small bowl. Spoon dressing over bowls.

Serve bowls with pickled ginger, wasabi mayo, and lime wedges.

Nutrition Facts per Serving **Calories:** 670 / **Total fat:** 35.4g (45% DV) / **Saturated fat:** 5.6g (28% DV) / **Trans fat:** 0.1g / **Cholesterol:** 43mg (14% DV) / **Sodium:** 468mg (20% DV) / **Total carbohydrate:** 48.3g (18% DV) / **Dietary fiber:** 11.9g (42% DV) / **Total sugars:** 6.3g / **Added sugar:** 0.6g (1% DV) / **Protein:** 44.6g / **Vitamin D:** 6.4mcg (32% DV) / **Calcium:** 157mg (12% DV) / **Iron:** 5.4mg (30% DV) / **Potassium:** 1,279mg (27% DV)

Those with compromised immune systems, as well as those who are pregnant, infants, young children, and older adults, should not consume raw or undercooked fish and shellfish.

Tuna Tartare Avocado Bowls

Diced sushi-grade ahi tuna marinated briefly in soy sauce, rice vinegar, toasted sesame oil, honey, ginger, sriracha, and scallions, then stuffed into halved avocados, sprinkled with black sesame seeds, and served with pickled ginger and wasabi mayo. These tuna tartare avocado bowls are a tuna lover's dream. And they can be made in less than 20 minutes! Serve as an appetizer–or serve for dinner with brown rice plus roasted broccoli or a green salad with ginger dressing.

Serves: 4
Course: Appetizer
Total time: 20 minutes

INGREDIENTS

4	scallions, green parts only, sliced, divided
1 tbsp	reduced-sodium soy sauce
1 tbsp	seasoned rice vinegar
1 tsp	toasted sesame oil
1 tsp	honey
½ tsp	freshly grated ginger
¼ tsp	sriracha
2	avocados, halved, pitted
½ lb	sushi-grade ahi tuna, cut into ¼-inch cubes

For serving:

Black sesame seeds

Pickled ginger

INSTRUCTIONS

In a medium-sized bowl, whisk together the majority of the scallions, soy sauce, rice vinegar, toasted sesame oil, honey, ginger, and sriracha. Add the tuna. Stir gently to combine. Set aside.

Using a sharp knife, lightly score the avocados, as if you were going to dice them, but keep the flesh inside the avocados. Doing this will make the avocados easier to eat once you stuff them with the tuna. Spoon tuna mixture into the avocado halves.

Sprinkle tuna with reserved scallions and black sesame seeds. Serve with pickled ginger, and wasabi mayo.

RECIPE NOTE: You can place the tuna in the freezer for a few minutes to make it easier to slice.

Nutrition Facts per Serving **Calories:** 219 / **Total fat:** 14.4g (19% DV) / **Saturated fat:** 2.3g (12% DV) / **Trans fat:** 0.0g / **Cholesterol:** 22mg (7% DV) / **Sodium:** 182mg (8% DV) / **Total carbohydrate:** 8.8g (3% DV) / **Dietary fiber:** 5.1g (18% DV) / **Total sugars:** 2.2g / **Added sugar:** 1.5g (3% DV) / **Protein:** 15.2g / **Vitamin D:** 3.2mcg (16% DV) / **Calcium:** 26mg (2% DV) / **Iron:** 1.3mg (7% DV) / **Potassium:** 546mg (12% DV)

Those with compromised immune systems, as well as those who are pregnant, infants, young children, and older adults, should not consume raw or undercooked fish and shellfish.

Grilled Striped Bass with Cucumber and Jalapeño Salsa

Meaty, firm, and flaky striped bass is simply grilled then topped with a fresh, crisp, and just a tad-bit spicy cucumber and jalapeño salsa. Striped bass is an incredibly delicious eating fish–it's slightly sweet, buttery, and mild.

Serves: 4
Course: Main course
Total time: 20 minutes

INGREDIENTS

For the striped bass:

1½ lb	striped bass, skin on, cut into 4 equal portions
1 tsp	extra-virgin olive oil
¼ tsp	kosher salt
¼ tsp	ground cumin
⅛ tsp	ground black pepper

For the salsa:

1 medium	cucumber, seeded, diced
1 medium	tomato, diced
1	jalapeño, seeded, finely diced
¼ medium	red onion, diced
½ cup	cilantro, chopped
1 clove	garlic, minced
	Zest and juice of 1 lime
1 tbsp	extra-virgin olive oil
¼ tsp	kosher salt
¼ tsp	cumin
⅛ tsp	freshly ground black pepper

For serving:

¼ cup	crumbled feta cheese (optional)
1	lime, cut into wedges

INSTRUCTIONS

Preheat grill to high heat. Clean and oil grates.

Pat striped bass fillets very dry. Brush on both sides with extra-virgin olive oil and sprinkle the flesh side with salt, cumin, and black pepper.

In a large bowl, combine cucumber, tomato, jalapeño, red onion, cilantro, garlic, lime juice and zest, extra-virgin olive oil, salt, cumin, and black pepper. Add more salt to taste, if needed.

Place striped bass onto the grill, skin side up. Flip after 3–4 minutes—fish should release easily from the grill when it's ready to flip. Cook another 3–4 minutes, until fish is opaque, firm, and flakes easily with a fork. Remove from grill.

Plate fish on a serving platter. Spoon salsa over top of fish. Sprinkle with feta cheese. Serve with lime wedges.

RECIPE NOTES:

• If you like more heat, don't seed the jalapeño, just finely dice it. We tend to like less heat–I find this salsa to have the perfect amount of heat without being too spicy. Remember to use gloves when handling the jalapeño–and, most importantly, don't touch your eyes after handling. Wash those hands well!

• If you don't like feta, you can leave it out. It does add a nice creaminess and saltiness to the salsa and takes away some of the heat from the jalapeño.

Nutrition Facts per Serving **Calories:** 235 / **Total fat:** 8.5g (11% DV) / **Saturated fat:** 1.5g (8% DV) / **Trans fat:** 0g / **Cholesterol:** 137mg (46% DV) / **Sodium:** 414mg (18% DV) / **Total carbohydrate:** 8g (3% DV) / **Dietary fiber:** 2g (8% DV) / **Total sugars:** 2.5g / **Added sugar:** 0g (0% DV) / **Protein:** 31g / **Vitamin D:** 0mcg (0% DV) / **Calcium:** 56mg (4% DV) / **Iron:** 2mg (12% DV) / **Potassium:** 660mg (14% DV)

Striped Bass Nutrition Highlights

Striped bass is rich in protein and is an excellent source of vitamin B12, vitamin B3, and selenium.

Skate, Bluefish, Black Sea Bass, Monkfish, and Squid

This chapter highlights some of the most delicious and most underutilized (and underappreciated) wild local species found in New England and beyond. Some of these species you will find on restaurant menus, but they are much less often purchased and cooked at home. They are abundant in our local waters, yet the local demand remains low—so much of it is exported or sent to other areas of the country. I would encourage you to try some of this local seafood—you will likely find a new favorite among them. Many of these species are seasonal, but you can also find them year-round flash-frozen.

How to choose and store:

- Trust your senses—use your sight, touch, and smell.
- Fresh fish should not smell overly fishy—it should smell clean and ocean fresh. If it has any scent of ammonia or smells a bit sour or fishy, don't buy it.
- Ask your fishmonger how long the fish has been in the display case and if it's been previously frozen.
- Purchase fish that look firm and moist—the flesh should not be falling apart and there should be no discoloration or dry spots. If pressed, the flesh should spring back.
- Only purchase fish that is refrigerated or displayed in a case on a thick bed of ice.
- When I purchase fresh fish and take it home from the market, I remove it from the paper it's wrapped in and place it in a sealed plastic bag. Then I place it on a small baking sheet and store it on the bottom shelf in the back of the fridge. This should be the coldest part of the refrigerator (make sure the fridge is set at a temperature of 40°F or less). Oftentimes I will lay one or two ice packs on top to keep it extra cold and to preserve freshness. Use the fish as soon as possible. We use fish on the same day of purchase or the next, but typically you are fine to use it within two days. If you aren't going to use it within that time frame, wrap tightly and freeze.

When is fish cooked through?

- Fish is cooked through when the internal temperature reaches a safe 145°F in the thickest part of the flesh. Keep in mind that once you remove the fish from heat, its internal temperature will continue to rise, so it's safe to remove at 140°F.
- A general rule of thumb is to cook fish for 10 minutes per inch of thickness, measured at the thickest part of the fillet—turning or flipping halfway through cooking time.
- Fish will flake easily with a fork in the thickest part of the flesh and will have lost its translucency.

Skate Wings with Garlic

Skate wings simply sautéed with smashed garlic and lemon. We love this simple preparation of skate because it allows the delicate texture and mild flavor to shine through.

Skates are related to stingrays and sharks. They are bottom-dwelling fish with fillets (wings) that look like an open fan. The muscle tissue of the fillets has striated bands, giving it an interesting texture with an almost scallop-like flavor. Because skate wings are thin, they cook very quickly.

Serves: 4
Course: Main course
Total time: 15 minutes

INGREDIENTS

1½ lb	skate wing fillets
¼ tsp	kosher salt
¼ tsp	freshly ground black pepper
1 tbsp	safflower or canola oil
4 whole cloves	garlic, smashed
1	lemon, cut into rings, divided
2 tbsp	unsalted butter
2 tbsp	fresh chopped parsley

INSTRUCTIONS

Pat skate very dry with a paper towel. Season with salt and pepper.

Add oil to a large skillet over medium high heat. Once hot and glistening, add skate wings to the skillet (use two pans if needed) and smashed garlic. Sauté for 3–4 minutes until a nice golden crust forms, add 2–3 lemon slices and butter, then flip and cook another 1–2 minutes until fish is opaque and cooked through.

Plate and top with chopped fresh parsley. Serve with remaining lemon slices.

Nutrition Facts per Serving **Calories:** 198 / **Total fat:** 9.9g (13% DV) / **Saturated fat:** 4.0g (13% DV) / **Trans fat:** 0.2g / **Cholesterol:** 24mg (8% DV) / **Sodium:** 355mg (15% DV) / **Total carbohydrate:** 2.0g (1% DV) / **Dietary fiber:** 0.4g (1% DV) / **Total sugars:** 0.3g / **Added sugar:** 0.0g (0% DV) / **Protein:** 26.5g / **Vitamin D:** 0.1mcg (1% DV) / **Calcium:** 82mg (6% DV) / **Iron:** 1.1mg (6% DV) / **Potassium:** 479mg (10% DV)

Skate Nutrition Highlights

Skate is rich in protein and is an excellent source of vitamin B3, vitamin B12, vitamin B6, and selenium.

Easy Grilled Bluefish with Lemon and Dill

This simple bluefish recipe allows the full flavor of the fish to shine. The lemon and dill add freshness and brightness and complement the bluefish's rich flavors. If you've never tried fresh bluefish, it is a fatty fish (rich in heart-healthy omega-3 fatty acids) and has a strong flavor, not too dissimilar to salmon. *Note:* The raw flesh of fresh bluefish is naturally brown or a light grayish blue–this is not an indicator of spoiling.

Serves: 4
Course: Main course
Total time: 30 minutes

INGREDIENTS

1½ lb	bluefish fillet, patted dry, cut into 4 pieces
¼ cup	extra-virgin olive oil
	Juice of 1 lemon
1 tbsp	whole-grain mustard
2 cloves	garlic, minced
¼ tsp	kosher salt

For serving:

	Freshly ground black pepper
2 tbsp	chopped fresh dill
	Lemon wedges

INSTRUCTIONS

Add the bluefish to a shallow glass container or resealable bag. Pour in olive oil, lemon juice, mustard, garlic, and salt. Let the fish sit at room temperature in the marinade for 15–20 minutes.

Meanwhile, preheat the grill to high heat. Clean and oil the grates very well—this will help prevent the fish from sticking.

Reduce grill heat to medium high and place fish skin side up on the grill. Cover and grill for 3–4 minutes. Flip and grill another 2–3 minutes, until fish is opaque and flakes easily with a fork in the thickest part of the flesh. Remove from heat.

Sprinkle bluefish with black pepper and dill. Serve with lemon wedges.

Nutrition Facts per Serving **Calories:** 343 / **Total fat:** 21.3g (27% DV) / **Saturated fat:** 3.5g (17% DV) / **Trans fat:** 0.0g / **Cholesterol:** 101mg (34% DV) / **Sodium:** 249mg (11% DV) / **Total carbohydrate:** 1.8g (1% DV) / **Dietary fiber:** 0.3g (1% DV) / **Total sugars:** 0.4g / **Added sugar:** 0.0g (0% DV) / **Protein:** 34.6g / **Vitamin D:** 23.2mcg (116% DV) / **Calcium:** 21mg (2% DV) / **Iron:** 1.1mg (6% DV) / **Potassium:** 665mg (14% DV)

Bluefish Nutrition Highlights

Bluefish is packed with protein and is an excellent source of vitamin D, vitamin B12, vitamin B3, vitamin B6, and selenium.

Bluefish Taco Bites

Grilled bluefish topped with slaw, guacamole, pickled onions, jalapeño, and sour cream stuffed into scoop style tortilla chips. These light fish taco bites are flavorful, fun, and crowd-pleasing.

Serves: 6–8
Course: Appetizer
Total time: 25 minutes

INGREDIENTS

For the bluefish:

½ lb	bluefish fillet, skin on, patted dry
1 tsp	canola or grapeseed oil or other high-heat, neutral-cooking oil
¼ tsp	freshly ground black pepper
⅛ tsp	kosher salt
1	lime, cut into wedges (use two wedges for the fish, the rest for serving)

For the slaw:

3 cups	shredded cabbage or coleslaw mix (without dressing)
2 tbsp	reduced-fat mayonnaise
2 tbsp	white wine vinegar
	Kosher salt, to taste
	Freshly ground black pepper, to taste

Assembly:

50	whole-grain tortilla "scoop" chips (approximately half of a 10-oz bag)
½ cup	guacamole, prepared or homemade (see page 183 for homemade guacamole)
¼ cup	quick pickled onion (see page 208)
¼ cup	reduced-fat sour cream
1	jalapeño, very thinly sliced
¼ cup	cilantro leaves

INSTRUCTIONS

Preheat grill to high heat.

Place fish on a piece of aluminum foil. Brush fish with oil and sprinkle with black pepper and salt. Squeeze two lime wedges over top of fish.

Reduce the grill heat to medium high. Place the foil (with fish) on the grill. Cover and grill for 6–8 minutes, until fish flakes easily with a fork when inserted in the thickest part of the fillet. Cooking time will depend on the thickness of the fillet. Remove fish from heat. Flake fish.

Combine cabbage, mayonnaise, and vinegar in a medium bowl. Season with salt and pepper to taste.

To assemble, place two scoop chips on top of each other.

Add a small amount of slaw to each chip. Top with flaked fish, guacamole, and pickled red onion. Drizzle with sour cream, then top with a jalapeño slice and cilantro leaves. Serve with remaining lime wedges.

RECIPE NOTES:

• Do not prepare these bites ahead of time, as they will get soggy. Prepare right before serving, and don't allow them to sit.

• Use either whole-grain or regular chips, depending on preference.

Nutrition Facts per Serving **Calories:** 157 / **Total fat:** 5.7g (7% DV) / **Saturated fat:** 1.3g (6% DV) / **Trans fat:** 0.0g / **Cholesterol:** 21mg (7% DV) / **Sodium:** 112mg (5% DV) / **Total carbohydrate:** 19.1g (7% DV) / **Dietary fiber:** 2.9g (10% DV) / **Total sugars:** 1.9g / **Added sugar:** 0.1g (0% DV) / **Protein:** 8.4g / **Vitamin D:** 3.9mcg (19% DV) / **Calcium:** 53mg (4% DV) / **Iron:** 0.9mg (5% DV) / **Potassium:** 325mg (7% DV)

Black Sea Bass with Garden Salsa

An easy summer recipe for cumin- and garlic-spiced black sea bass with a colorful tomato salsa. Black sea bass is a mild, lean, white fish with a moderately firm texture and a delicate flavor. It's a very good eating fish.

Serves: 4
Course: Main course
Total time: 20 minutes

INGREDIENTS

1½ lb	black sea bass fillets (check fillets carefully for pin bones), skin on, descaled
1 tsp	extra-virgin olive oil
½ tsp	ground cumin
½ tsp	garlic powder
½ tsp	ground black pepper
¼ tsp	kosher salt

For the salsa:

2 medium	tomatoes, diced (or about 2 cups cherry tomatoes, halved)
1	jalapeño, seeded and finely diced (if you prefer more heat, keep the seeds in)
¼ medium	red onion, diced
½ cup	loosely packed cilantro, chopped
1 clove	garlic, finely minced
	Juice of 1 lime
1 tbsp	extra-virgin olive oil
¼ tsp	kosher salt
¼ tsp	ground cumin
¼ tsp	ground black pepper

For serving:

	Sea salt, to taste (optional)
1	lime, cut into wedges

INSTRUCTIONS

Preheat grill to high heat. Clean and oil grates well (this will help prevent the fish from sticking).

Pat fish dry with a paper towel. Brush with olive oil and sprinkle with cumin, garlic, black pepper, and salt on both sides.

In a large bowl, combine tomatoes, jalapeño, red onion, cilantro, garlic, lime juice, extra-virgin olive oil, salt, cumin, and pepper. Stir well. Add more salt to taste, if needed. Set aside.

Reduce grill heat to medium high. Place fish on the grill, skin side up, flipping after 2–3 minutes. Grill until fish is opaque and flakes easily with a fork. These fillets tend to be thin, so they will cook in just a few minutes. Remove from grill.

Spoon salsa over fish. Sprinkle with sea salt.

Serve with lime wedges and additional salsa.

> ## Black Sea Bass Nutrition Highlights
>
> Black sea bass is rich in protein and is an excellent source of vitamin D, vitamin B1, vitamin B3, vitamin B12, phosphorous, and selenium.

RECIPE NOTES:

• Black sea bass fillets tend to have quite a few pin bones. Prior to grilling, check fillets carefully and pull out any pin bones with tweezers or your fingers.

• The skin of black sea bass tends to curl up with heat, so you can score the skin prior to grilling to prevent the flesh and skin from curling up. This is optional and won't affect the flavor of the fish.

• You can also sprinkle with feta cheese, for a salty, briny twist.

Nutrition Facts per Serving **Calories:** 232 / **Total fat:** 8g (11% DV) / **Saturated fat:** 1.5g (8% DV) / **Trans fat:** 0g / **Cholesterol:** 70mg (23% DV) / **Sodium:** 414mg (18% DV) / **Total carbohydrate:** 7g (3% DV) / **Dietary fiber:** 1.5g (6% DV) / **Total sugars:** 2.5g / **Added sugar:** 0g (0% DV) / **Protein:** 32.5g / **Vitamin D:** 9.5mcg (48% DV) / **Calcium:** 42mg (3% DV) / **Iron:** 1mg (7% DV) / **Potassium:** 660mg (14% DV)

Panfried Monkfish

Monkfish fillets sautéed in olive oil and butter with smashed whole garlic cloves and lemon slices. This is a simple, foolproof fish dinner that comes together in minutes.

Serves: 4
Course: Main course
Total time: 15 minutes

INGREDIENTS

2 tbsp	extra-virgin olive oil
1½ lb	monkfish fillets, membrane removed
¼ tsp	kosher salt
¼ tsp	freshly ground black pepper
4 cloves	garlic, smashed
1	lemon, sliced into rings
2 tbsp	salted butter
¼ cup	dry white wine
¼ cup	loosely packed parsley, chopped

INSTRUCTIONS

Add olive oil to a large skillet over medium heat. Pat monkfish very dry and season fillets on both sides with salt and pepper.

When pan is hot, add monkfish to the skillet along with garlic cloves and lemon slices. Flip fish after 3–4 minutes. Add butter and white wine to the skillet when you flip the fish.

Spoon the melted butter and wine over top of the fish as it finishes cooking, another 3–4 minutes, depending on the thickness of the fillets. Monkfish is cooked through when it's opaque throughout, flakes easily, and becomes slightly firm.

Remove from heat and top with chopped parsley, salt, and pepper to taste. When plating the monkfish, include the panfried lemon rings and garlic cloves, as well as the pan juices.

Serve with lemon wedges.

Monkfish 101

What is monkfish?

- Monkfish is a firm, meaty, mild-flavored, and slightly sweet-tasting fish. Monkfish actually has a flavor and texture very similar to lobster—in fact, it is often called the poor man's lobster. It's like lobster without the price tag . . . and without the shell! It is so delicious. The fillets vary from white to pinkish to grayish. The fillets should smell fresh like the sea, not fishy.
- Because monkfish is firm and meaty, it doesn't fall apart easily, making it a great choice for most any type of cooking method, including grilling, roasting, in soups and chowders, pan-frying, and more.
- One important thing to note about monkfish is that oftentimes when you purchase it, it will still have a gray membrane surrounding the fillet. This thin membrane needs to be removed (most of it anyway). You'll do that using a paring knife, carefully. It's not necessary to remove all of the membrane—just do the best you can, because it will seize up when you cook the monkfish, making it a bit unpleasant to eat. If you have a great fish market, ask them to remove the membrane for you. If that's not an option, don't be intimidated by removing the membrane—it takes a few minutes (and a bit of practice), but it's worth it because monkfish really is one of the most delicious fish out there!

Monkfish Nutrition Highlights

Monkfish is rich in protein and is an excellent source of vitamin B12, vitamin B3, and selenium.

Nutrition Facts per Serving **Calories:** 267 / **Total fat:** 15g (20% DV) / **Saturated fat:** 5g (26% DV) / **Trans fat:** 0g / **Cholesterol:** 59mg (20% DV) / **Sodium:** 227mg (10% DV) / **Total carbohydrate:** 3g (1% DV) / **Dietary fiber:** 0.5g (2% DV) / **Total sugars:** 0.5g / **Added sugar:** 0g (0% DV) / **Protein:** 26g / **Vitamin D:** 2.5mcg (14% DV) / **Calcium:** 32mg (2% DV) / **Iron:** 1mg (6% DV) / **Potassium:** 774mg (16% DV)

Crispy Panfried Calamari

Calamari is quickly panfried in olive oil and butter and topped with garlicky and buttery crispy panko crumbs. This is a better-for-you alternative to deep-fried calamari–but it's just as tasty!

Serves: 4-6
Course: Appetizer
Total time: 10 minutes

INGREDIENTS

1 lb	squid, bodies and tentacles
1 tbsp + 1 tsp	olive oil, divided
1 tbsp + 1 tsp	unsalted butter
2 cloves	garlic, minced
¼ cup	seasoned panko crumbs
1 tbsp	chopped fresh parsley

For serving:

	Lemon wedges

INSTRUCTIONS

Pat the squid very dry. Slice the squid bodies into approximately ⅛-inch rings.

Heat 1 tablespoon olive oil and 1 teaspoon butter in a large skillet over medium high heat. Once hot, add the garlic and sauté until fragrant, about a minute. Add the seasoned panko crumbs, stirring frequently, until toasted, about 3–5 minutes. Stay close so breadcrumbs don't burn. Remove breadcrumbs from heat and pour into a bowl. Set aside.

Place the skillet back over medium high heat and add remaining teaspoon olive oil. Once hot, add the squid. Sauté for 1–2 minutes, flip, add remaining 1 tablespoon butter, and sauté another 1–2 minutes until cooked through. Squid is cooked through when it turns opaque and milky white. Do not overcook—overcooked squid becomes tough and rubbery.

Place squid on a serving platter. Sprinkle with breadcrumbs and parsley.

Serve with lemon wedges.

Nutrition Facts per Serving **Calories:** 131 / **Total fat:** 6.7g (9% DV) / **Saturated fat:** 2.3g (12% DV) / **Trans fat:** 0.1g / **Cholesterol:** 164mg (55% DV) / **Sodium:** 60mg (3% DV) / **Total carbohydrate:** 5.7g (2% DV) / **Dietary fiber:** 0.2g (1% DV) / **Total sugars:** 0.3g / **Added sugar:** 0.3g (1% DV) / **Protein:** 11.2g / **Vitamin D:** 0.0mcg (0% DV) / **Calcium:** 34mg (3% DV) / **Iron:** 0.7mg (4% DV) / **Potassium:** 150mg (3% DV)

Squid 101

Squid is closely related to the octopus. The edible parts of the squid include the tentacles, tube, and wings. Squid's black ink is often used for pasta or other dishes. You'll want to purchase cleaned squid, as the cleaning process is quite time-consuming and messy—we did that once and won't do it again! Fresh squid should be shiny and white with no fishy or off-putting smell. Frozen squid is also readily available. Squid has a mild, slightly sweet flavor and a firm, chewy texture. It is best either cooked over high heat for a very short time until just opaque—or cooked for a longer period of time over lower heat. Overcooked squid becomes very tough, but you can tenderize it again by continuing to cook it until it softens back up.

Grilled Squid Arugula Salad

Grilled squid served over top of baby arugula, white beans, croutons, fresh parsley, and shaved Parmesan with a lemony vinaigrette. This salad is bright and fresh.

Serves: 4
Course: Appetizer or salad
Total time: 15 minutes

INGREDIENTS

For the vinaigrette:

¼ cup	extra-virgin olive oil
	Juice of 1 lemon
1 tsp	honey
1 clove	garlic, minced
⅛ tsp	kosher salt
⅛ tsp	freshly ground black pepper

For the salad:

1 lb	squid, bodies and tentacles
1 tsp	canola oil
⅛ tsp	kosher salt
⅛ tsp	freshly ground black pepper
5 oz	baby arugula
1 (15-oz) can	white beans, drained and rinsed
1 cup	store-bought or homemade croutons
¼ cup	chopped parsley
¼ cup	shaved Parmesan cheese

INSTRUCTIONS

Preheat grill to high heat. Clean and oil grates.

Make the vinaigrette by combining olive oil, lemon juice, honey, garlic, salt, and pepper. Whisk well.

Brush squid with canola oil and sprinkle with salt and pepper.

Place squid on the grill, grilling for 1–2 minutes per side until fully opaque. Time will vary, depending on the size of your squid. Don't overcook.

Place arugula on a large serving platter. Top with white beans, squid, croutons, parsley, and shaved Parmesan. Drizzle with vinaigrette. Serve.

Nutrition Facts per Serving **Calories:** 400 / **Total fat:** 18.8g (24% DV) / **Saturated fat:** 3.7g (19% DV) / **Trans fat:** 0.1g / **Cholesterol:** 241mg (80% DV) / **Sodium:** 337mg (15% DV) / **Total carbohydrate:** 31.1g (11% DV) / **Dietary fiber:** 5.7g (20% DV) / **Total sugars:** 3.2g / **Added sugar:** 1.5g (3% DV) / **Protein:** 27.4g / **Vitamin D:** 0.0mcg (0% DV) / **Calcium:** 252mg (19% DV) / **Iron:** 4.6mg (25% DV) / **Potassium:** 789mg (17% DV)

Squid Nutrition Highlights

Squid is rich in protein and is an excellent source of copper, selenium, vitamin B12, vitamin B3, and vitamin B2.

White Fish

This chapter is full of tasty white-fish recipes, from tacos to fish bites. And by white fish, we're talking cod, haddock, pollock, halibut, mahimahi, and more. There are so many flaky white fish out there, and the great thing about them is that they are mild, incredibly versatile, and, for the most part, can be interchanged depending on what you are able to get at your local fish market or grocer. If a recipe calls for haddock and you have pollock, use the pollock. If you head to the fish market in search of halibut and it just doesn't look great, make a switch to another white fish. Be flexible and open to swapping out one fish for another, depending on what's available and what is freshest that day. Just remember to adjust cooking time depending on the thickness of the fillets.

White Fish 101

How to choose and store white fish:

- Trust your senses—use your sight, touch, and smell.
- Fresh fish should not smell overly fishy—it should smell clean and ocean fresh. If it has any scent of ammonia or smells a bit sour or fishy, don't buy it.
- Ask your fishmonger how long the fish has been in the display case and if it's been previously frozen. Only purchase fish that is refrigerated or displayed in a case on a thick bed of ice.
- Purchase fish fillets that look firm—the flesh should not be falling apart and there should be no discoloration or dry spots. If pressed, the flesh should spring back. Whole fish should have red gills and firm flesh.
- When we purchase fresh fish, we remove it from the paper it's wrapped in and place it in a sealed plastic bag. Then we place it on a small baking sheet and store it on the bottom shelf in the back of the fridge. This should be the coldest part of the refrigerator (make sure the fridge is set at a temperature of 40°F or less). Oftentimes I will lay one or two ice packs on top to keep it extra cold—this will keep it fresh. Use the fish as soon as possible. We use fish on the same day of purchase or the next, but typically you are fine to use it within two days. If you aren't going to use it within that time frame, wrap tightly and freeze.

When is white fish cooked through?

- White fish is cooked through when the internal temperature reaches a safe 145°F in the thickest part of the flesh. Keep in mind that once you remove the fish from heat, its internal temperature will continue to rise, so we take the fish off the heat a few degrees before that. You don't want to overcook white fish, but you also don't want to undercook it.
- White fish will flake easily with a fork in the thickest part of the flesh and will have turned from translucent to opaque.
- A general rule of thumb is to cook fish for 10 minutes per inch of thickness, measured at the thickest part of the fillet—turning or flipping halfway through cooking time.

Can you grill white fish?

- Yes! Some of the thicker, meatier cuts of white fish will hold up well on the grill on their own—e.g., halibut, mahimahi—but for thinner fillets like cod, pollock, haddock, black sea bass, etc., I like to place them first onto foil and then onto the grill so you don't lose any of the fish between the grill grates. If you do this, you don't need to flip the fish halfway through cooking time. Just keep it on the grill until the fish is cooked through.

Halibut with Roasted Tomatoes and Basil

Serves: 4
Course: Main course
Total time: 1 hour, 10 minutes

INGREDIENTS

3 cups	cherry tomatoes
4 cloves	garlic
¼ cup	extra-virgin olive oil
1 tbsp	balsamic vinegar
¼ tsp	kosher salt
¼ tsp	freshly ground black pepper

For the halibut:

1½ lb	halibut fillet, skin on, cut into 4 pieces
¼ tsp	kosher salt
¼ tsp	freshly ground black pepper
1 tbsp	safflower or canola oil
1 tbsp	unsalted butter

For serving:

¼ cup	basil, torn or slivered
	Lemon wedges (optional)

Halibut Nutrition Highlights

Halibut is rich in protein and is an excellent source of vitamin D, vitamin B6, vitamin B3, vitamin B12, phosphorous, and selenium.

Cherry tomatoes with garlic, olive oil, and balsamic vinegar are roasted until jammy, then served on top of simply sautéed halibut, all topped with fresh basil. This meal is perfect for late summer dinners when you have an abundance of garden tomatoes. Halibut fillets can be on the thicker side, so they will take longer to cook than a thinner white fish like cod or haddock.

INSTRUCTIONS

Preheat oven to 375°F. Add tomatoes, garlic, olive oil, balsamic vinegar, salt, and black pepper to a baking dish. Stir to combine. Roast for 45 minutes to an hour. Remove from oven.

Pat halibut very dry with a paper towel. Season with salt and pepper. Add oil to a large skillet over medium high heat. Once hot and glistening, add the halibut, skin side up. Cook for 4–5 minutes, until golden brown on the underside. Flip, add butter, and cook an additional 3–5 minutes, depending on thickness of the fillet. Spoon melted butter over top of the fish as it finishes cooking. When cooked through, fish should flake easily with a fork and should be just opaque throughout. Remove from heat.

Plate fish, then spoon tomato and garlic mixture over top and sprinkle with fresh basil. Serve with lemon wedges.

Nutrition Facts per Serving **Calories:** 355 / **Total fat:** 22.2g (28% DV) / **Saturated fat:** 4.4g (22% DV) / **Trans fat:** 0.2g / **Cholesterol:** 87mg (29% DV) / **Sodium:** 410mg (18% DV) / **Total carbohydrate:** 7.0g (3% DV) / **Dietary fiber:** 1.7g (6% DV) / **Total sugars:** 4.2g / **Added sugar:** 0.0g (0% DV) / **Protein:** 31.4g / **Vitamin D:** 7.7mcg (38% DV) / **Calcium:** 38mg (3% DV) / **Iron:** 0.9mg (5% DV) / **Potassium:** 1,046mg (22% DV)

Grilled Cod Tacos with Charred Red Cabbage

Warmed corn tortillas topped with smashed avocado, grilled seasoned cod, charred red cabbage, crumbled queso fresco, and grilled scallions. Serve with lots of fresh lime wedges. You'll love this fresh, healthy, flavor-packed twist on fish tacos.

Serves: 4
Course: Main course
Total time: 40 minutes

INGREDIENTS

1 lb	cod, haddock, or other white-fish fillets
1 small head	red cabbage cut into 1-inch slices, core kept intact
1 bunch	scallions, root end trimmed
1½ tbsp	extra-virgin olive oil
1 tsp	Old Bay Seasoning
¼ tsp	kosher salt
¼ tsp	ground black pepper

For serving:

2	limes, one sliced in half, the other cut into wedges
8–10 small	corn tortillas, warmed
2	avocados, smashed, or prepared guacamole
5 oz	queso fresco cheese, crumbled

INSTRUCTIONS

Preheat grill to high heat. Clean and oil grates.

Place cod on aluminum foil and red cabbage and scallions on a plate to prepare for grilling. Drizzle cod, red cabbage, and scallions with extra-virgin olive oil. Sprinkle Old Bay Seasoning over top of cod. Sprinkle salt and pepper over top of red cabbage and scallions.

Reduce grill heat to medium high. Place cod (keep on aluminum foil—this will prevent any fish from falling through the grill grates) onto one side of the grill. Place red cabbage slices onto the other side of the grill. Place scallions onto the top rack of the grill away from direct heat.

Grill fish and veggies until cabbage is lightly charred and fish is cooked through and flakes easily with a fork. Flip cabbage halfway through cooking time. Remove fish and veggies from grill. Squeeze the halved lime over top of the fish and flake the fish. When cooled slightly, roughly chop red cabbage and scallions.

Assemble tortillas by spreading each with smashed avocado, red cabbage, flaked cod, scallions, and queso fresco. Serve with lime wedges.

RECIPE NOTE: To heat tortillas, place a cast-iron skillet over medium heat. Add tortillas and heat 30-60 seconds, flip, then heat an additional 30-60 seconds or until tortilla puffs a bit and develops a bit of color and light char. Repeat with all tortillas and keep warm in a clean dish towel. Alternatively, you can carefully heat tortillas one at a time directly over a gas flame, flipping tortillas with tongs and keeping a very close watch so they don't catch fire. You can also place a stack inside a clean dish towel and heat for 30 seconds in the microwave.

Nutrition Facts per Serving **Calories:** 462 / **Total fat:** 25.5g (33% DV) / **Saturated fat:** 7g (35% DV) / **Trans fat:** 0g / **Cholesterol:** 73mg (24% DV) / **Sodium:** 664mg (29% DV) / **Total carbohydrate:** 31.5g (11% DV) / **Dietary fiber:** 10g (36% DV) / **Total sugars:** 8g / **Added sugar:** 0g (0% DV) / **Protein:** 31.5g / **Vitamin D:** 2mcg (10% DV) / **Calcium:** 323mg (25% DV) / **Iron:** 2.5mg (15% DV) / **Potassium:** 1051mg (22% DV)

Cod Nutrition Highlights

Cod is rich in protein and provides an excellent source of vitamin B12, selenium, and vitamin B3.

Panko Baked Cod

Cod loin fillets topped with a mixture of Italian-seasoned panko crumbs, grated Parmesan, chopped parsley, lemon zest, sun-dried tomatoes, and extra-virgin olive oil, then baked until the topping is crisp and golden and the fish is flaky and succulent. You will love the crunchy texture and Mediterranean flavor of this cod. It will easily become a favorite fish dinner in your home, as it has in ours! This recipe is also great with haddock–or any white fish. Just adjust cooking time depending on thickness of your loin or fillet.

Serves: 4
Course: Main course
Total time: 20 minutes

INGREDIENTS

1¼ lb	cod loin, patted dry, cut into 4 equal portions
¼ cup	Italian-seasoned panko crumbs
2 tbsp	fresh parsley, chopped
1½ tbsp	sun-dried tomatoes in herbs and oil, drained and chopped
1 tbsp	grated Parmesan cheese
1 tbsp	extra-virgin olive oil, plus more for drizzling
	Zest of 1 lemon, then cut into wedges
¼ tsp	kosher salt
⅛ tsp	ground black pepper

For serving:

Lemon wedges

INSTRUCTIONS

Preheat oven to 425°F. Line a baking sheet with aluminum foil. Place cod loin on baking sheet.

In a small bowl, combine panko crumbs, parsley, sun-dried tomatoes, Parmesan, olive oil, lemon zest, salt, and pepper.

Mound panko mixture on top of each piece of cod. Drizzle cod loin with additional olive oil, if desired. (I like to do this for added richness, moisture, and flavor.)

Bake cod for 12–15 minutes, until cooked through and it flakes easily with a fork. Remove from oven.

Serve with lemon wedges, your favorite roasted veggies (broccoli or cauliflower would be great), and a loaf of whole-grain bread.

RECIPE NOTE: Cod loin is thicker (fatter) and shorter than a cod fillet. The cod loin is considered a premium cut, but the flavor is exactly the same as the rest of the fillet, so choose what you have access to. Note that cooking time will vary depending on the thickness of the loin or cod fillet that you're using.

Nutrition Facts per Serving **Calories:** 178 / **Total fat:** 5.5g (7% DV) / **Saturated fat:** 1g (5% DV) / **Trans fat:** 0g / **Cholesterol:** 62mg (21% DV) / **Sodium:** 296mg (13% DV) / **Total carbohydrate:** 5g (2% DV) / **Dietary fiber:** 1g (3% DV) / **Total sugars:** 1g / **Added sugar:** 0g (0% DV) / **Protein:** 26.5g / **Vitamin D:** 1mcg (6% DV) / **Calcium:** 44mg (3% DV) / **Iron:** 1mg (6% DV) / **Potassium:** 352mg (7% DV)

Panfried Fish Tacos

Cumin-spiced cod, panfried, then added to tortillas with guacamole, baby greens, *cotija* cheese, cilantro, and scallions. So much flavor. Just add a margarita! We've used cod here, but you can use any white fish.

Serves: 4
Course: Main course
Total time: 15 minutes

INGREDIENTS

For the panfried cod:

1 lb	cod or haddock fillet
½ tsp	ground cumin
¼ tsp	garlic powder
¼ tsp	kosher salt
1 tsp	avocado or canola oil, or any neutral oil

For the tacos:

8	corn or flour tortillas, warmed
½ cup	guacamole or 1 avocado, thinly sliced
2 cups	baby spring mix
½ cup	chopped cilantro
1 bunch	scallions, white and green parts, thinly sliced
2 oz	*cotija* cheese, crumbled

For serving

1	lime, cut into wedges

INSTRUCTIONS

Dry fish well with paper towel. Season on both sides with cumin, garlic powder, and salt.

Heat oil in a medium skillet over medium high heat. When pan is hot, add fish.

Cook 3–4 minutes on one side, flip, then cook another few minutes until fish is opaque and flakes easily with a fork. Remove from heat and flake.

Assemble tacos by spreading guacamole or avocado on the tortillas, then topping with baby greens, fish, cilantro, scallions, and cheese.

Serve with lime wedges.

Nutrition Facts per Serving **Calories:** 307 / **Total fat:** 14g (18% DV) / **Saturated fat:** 4.5g (22% DV) / **Trans fat:** 0g / **Cholesterol:** 63mg (21% DV) / **Sodium:** 628mg (27% DV) / **Total carbohydrate:** 19g (7% DV) / **Dietary fiber:** 4.5g (16% DV) / **Total sugars:** 2g / **Added sugar:** 0g (0% DV) / **Protein:** 27g / **Vitamin D:** 1mcg (6% DV) / **Calcium:** 181mg (14% DV) / **Iron:** 2mg (12% DV) / **Potassium:** 557mg (12% DV)

Blackened Mahimahi

Mahimahi fillets coated in blackening seasoning then panfried in butter until crispy on the outside and tender and flaky on the inside. These meaty blackened fillets are topped with a simple creamy and cooling guacamole.

Serves: 4
Course: Main course
Total time: 15 minutes

INGREDIENTS

For the guacamole:

2	avocados, pitted, cut into chunks
¼	red onion, diced
¼ cup	cilantro leaves, roughly chopped
	Juice of 1 lime
¼ tsp	kosher salt
¼ tsp	freshly ground black pepper

For the mahimahi:

1½ lb	mahimahi fillet (if frozen, thawed), skinless, cut into 4 fillets
1 tsp	onion powder
1 tsp	paprika
1 tsp	garlic powder
1 tsp	dried oregano
1 tsp	dried thyme
½ tsp	kosher salt
¼ tsp	ground black pepper
1 tbsp	canola or avocado oil
1–2 tbsp	salted butter

For serving:

1	lime, cut into wedges

INSTRUCTIONS

Combine avocado chunks, red onion, cilantro, lime juice, salt, and pepper. Adjust seasoning to your liking. Set aside.

Using a paper towel or kitchen towel, pat the mahimahi fillets very dry on both sides. This will help the fish develop a nice crust.

To make the blackening seasoning, combine onion powder, paprika, garlic powder, oregano, thyme, salt, and pepper together in a small bowl. Mix well.

Sprinkle the blackening seasoning liberally on all sides of the fillets. Using your hands, press the seasoning into the fish.

Add oil and butter to a large cast-iron skillet over medium high heat. (Be sure to turn the exhaust fan on and open kitchen windows, as blackening can create quite a bit of smoke.) When pan is hot, carefully add the fish. Cook fillets for 3–4 minutes, until a nice dark crust appears on one side. Flip mahimahi and cook another 3–4 minutes, until cooked through. Cooking time will vary depending on the thickness of the fillets. Mahimahi is cooked through when the internal temperature reaches 145°F in the center of the thickest part of the fillet, as measured with a meat thermometer—pull it off the heat a few degrees before this, as fish will continue cooking once removed from heat. Fish will have turned from translucent flesh to white and opaque throughout and will flake easily with a fork.

Remove from skillet. Serve mahimahi with a dollop of chunky guacamole and lime wedges.

Nutrition Facts per Serving **Calories:** 333 / **Total fat:** 18g (23% DV) / **Saturated fat:** 4g (19% DV) / **Trans fat:** 0g / **Cholesterol:** 132mg (44% DV) / **Sodium:** 619mg (27% DV) / **Total carbohydrate:** 11g (4% DV) / **Dietary fiber:** 6g (21% DV) / **Total sugars:** 1g / **Added sugar:** 0g (0% DV) / **Protein:** 33.5g / **Vitamin D:** 4mcg (21% DV) / **Calcium:** 59mg (5% DV) / **Iron:** 3mg (17% DV) / **Potassium:** 1,135mg (24% DV)

Mahimahi Nutrition Highlights

Mahimahi is rich in protein and is an excellent source of vitamin B12, selenium, and vitamin B3.

Baked Fish Bites

Serves: 4
Course: Main course or appetizer
Total time: 30 minutes

Nuggets of fresh cod breaded in Italian-seasoned panko crumbs then baked until crispy and golden brown. A kid favorite and far tastier than chicken fingers! Also a healthier alternative to fish sticks. And these fish bites make a great appetizer for adults, paired with your favorite local beer.

INGREDIENTS

1 lb	cod loin or other white fish, cut into about 1-inch pieces
¼ cup	whole-wheat flour
½ tsp	garlic powder
¼ tsp	kosher salt
¼ tsp	ground black pepper
2	eggs, beaten
1½ cups	Italian-seasoned panko crumbs
1 tsp	Italian seasoning
1 tsp	avocado oil

For serving:

Flaky sea salt

Tartar sauce

Lemon wedges

INSTRUCTIONS

Preheat oven to 425°F. Spray a large cooking sheet well with avocado or vegetable oil spray.

Pat fish very dry with a paper towel.

Combine whole-wheat flour, garlic powder, salt, and black pepper in a medium-sized shallow bowl. Place beaten eggs in another bowl. Combine panko and Italian seasoning in another medium-sized shallow bowl.

Dredge each piece of fish in the flour first (shaking off excess), then into the beaten egg, then into the panko mixture (coating both sides of the fish), then place onto the baking sheet.

Spray fish bites evenly with oil spray, then drizzle a thin stream of avocado oil over top of the bites (this will help them crisp up).

Bake for 12–15 minutes until fish flakes easily with a fork and is cooked through—timing will vary depending on the size of the fish bites.

Remove from oven and sprinkle with flaky sea salt.

Serve bites with tartar sauce and lemon wedges.

Nutrition Facts per Serving **Calories:** 255 / **Total fat:** 5.5g (7% DV) / **Saturated fat:** 1g (7% DV) / **Trans fat:** 0g / **Cholesterol:** 131mg (44% DV) / **Sodium:** 406mg (18% DV) / **Total carbohydrate:** 23g (8% DV) / **Dietary fiber:** 2.2g (8% DV) / **Total sugars:** 2g / **Added sugar:** 1.5g (3% DV) / **Protein:** 27g / **Vitamin D:** 1.5mcg (7% DV) / **Calcium:** 74mg (6% DV) / **Iron:** 2mg (13% DV) / **Potassium:** 334mg (7% DV)

Salmon

This chapter is full of tasty salmon recipes (America's no. 2 favorite seafood—behind shrimp but ahead of canned tuna). Whether you prefer sustainably grown and harvested farmed or wild salmon, salmon across the board is one of the healthiest foods you can eat, mainly because of the heart and brain-health-promoting omega-3 fatty acids found in the fish. Flavor profiles differ across all the salmon varieties, with farmed salmon generally having a milder flavor and wild salmon having a fuller flavor. Salmon are anadromous fish, meaning they are born in rivers and streams (fresh water), then they migrate to the ocean (salt water) to grow and stay for their adult life before returning to the fresh water to reproduce, then die. In the United States we have six main types of salmon: farmed Atlantic salmon (commercial and recreational fishing for wild Atlantic salmon is prohibited in the United States because of overfishing, so all Atlantic salmon available in the United States is farmed) and wild Pacific chinook (king salmon), chum (keta salmon), coho, pink, and sockeye salmon. Much, but not all, of our farmed salmon in the United States is imported, coming from different farms around the world.

For the recipes in this chapter, feel free to use whatever type of salmon you prefer; just adjust the cooking time depending on the thickness of your fillets. And an important note: Wild salmon is leaner and will cook more quickly than farmed salmon, so check on it a few minutes earlier than you would farmed salmon. You could also use arctic char or steelhead trout, which have a similar flavor, richness, color, and texture.

Salmon 101

Salmon and other fatty fish are brain food:

Fatty and oily fish like salmon (farmed and wild), trout, mackerel, herring, and tuna are loaded with omega-3 fatty acids, which are beneficial for brain, eye, and heart health. On page 243 you'll find a chart that outlines the different species of seafood and the corresponding amount of omega-3 fats. This chart can serve as a great resource when seeking out omega-3-rich seafood.

How to choose and store salmon:

- Trust your senses—use your sight, touch, and smell.
- Fresh fish should not smell overly fishy—it should smell clean and ocean fresh. If it has any scent of ammonia or smells a bit sour or fishy, don't buy it.
- Ask your fishmonger how long the fish has been in the display case and if it's been previously frozen, to give you an idea of freshness.
- Purchase fish fillets that look firm and moist—the flesh should not be falling apart and there should be no discoloration or dry spots. If pressed, the flesh should spring back. Whole fish should have red gills and firm flesh.
- Only purchase fish that is refrigerated or displayed in a case on a thick bed of ice.
- When I purchase fresh fish and take it home from the market, I remove it from the paper it's wrapped in and place it in a sealed plastic bag. Then I place it on a small baking sheet and store it on the bottom shelf in the back of the fridge. This should be the coldest part of the refrigerator (make sure the fridge is set at a temperature of 40°F or less). Oftentimes I will lay one or two ice packs on top to keep it extra cold and to preserve freshness. Use the fish as soon as possible. We use fish on the same day of purchase or the next, but typically you are fine to use it within two days. If you aren't going to use it within that time frame, wrap tightly and freeze.

- When purchasing salmon for raw preparations, make sure you purchase sushi-grade salmon from a trusted, knowledgeable, and reputable source—and use it right away.

When is salmon cooked through?

- Salmon is cooked through when the internal temperature reaches a safe 145°F in the thickest part of the flesh. Keep in mind that once you remove the fish from heat, its internal temperature will continue to rise, so it's safe to remove at 140°F. If you prefer your salmon slightly undercooked, you'll want to remove it prior to 140°F. We typically remove our salmon between 125°F and 135°F because we prefer it slightly undercooked.
- A general rule of thumb is to cook fish for 10 minutes per inch of thickness, measured at the thickest part of the fillet—turning or flipping halfway through cooking time.
- Since salmon (especially farmed salmon) is a fatty fish, you have a bit more wiggle room before salmon overcooks.
- Salmon will flake easily with a fork in the thickest part of the flesh and will have lost its translucency.

Don't skip the canned salmon!

- Canned salmon is a staple in our pantry and shouldn't be forgotten. We love using canned salmon to make quick salmon burgers or patties. It's also great in salmon salad (like tuna salad, except with salmon).

Check for pin bones.

- With salmon, it's a good idea to check for pin bones (thin needlelike bones), typically found in the middle of the fillet, and pull any out with tweezers or needle-nosed pliers. Most fish markets and fish counters will have removed most of them, but it's not uncommon to still find a few in your fillet.

Grilled Salmon with Summer Corn Salad

Grilled salmon rubbed with cumin and brown sugar and served atop a summer corn salad that combines fresh corn, garden tomatoes, red onion, mozzarella, basil, extra-virgin olive oil, and white wine vinegar. This is the ultimate summer meal–guaranteed to please anyone at your table.

In the cool weather months, we make this salmon in the oven instead of on the grill, and without the corn salad.. Cook at 425°F until desired doneness, estimating about 10 minutes per inch of thickness. We typically broil for the last 1-2 minutes to get a nice crust on the fish.

Serves: 6
Course: Main course
Total time: 45 minutes

INGREDIENTS

For the salmon:

2 lb	salmon fillet, center cut, skin on, cut into 4 portions
1 tbsp	cumin
1 tbsp	light brown sugar
1 tsp	garlic powder
½ tsp	kosher salt

For the corn salad:

5 ears	fresh corn, shucked
1 pint	cherry tomatoes, halved
8 oz	pearl mozzarella balls (or cubed mozzarella)
½	red onion, diced
¼ cup + 2 tbsp	extra-virgin olive oil
¼ cup	white wine vinegar
¼ tsp	kosher salt
⅛ tsp	freshly ground black pepper
½ cup	basil, slivered or torn

For serving:

1	lime, cut into wedges

INSTRUCTIONS

Prepare a large piece of aluminum foil. Place salmon portions onto the foil, skin side down. Pat salmon dry with a paper towel. Combine cumin, light brown sugar, garlic powder, and salt in a small bowl. Coat salmon on top and sides with spice rub. Set aside, at room temperature, for 30 minutes while you make the corn salad.

Heat a large pot filled halfway with water over high heat until boiling. Add corn, cover, bring back to a boil, then lightly boil for 3–5 minutes. Remove corn from pot with tongs. Once corn is cool enough to handle, slice the corn off the cobs into a large serving bowl.

Add tomatoes, mozzarella, red onion, extra-virgin olive oil, white wine vinegar, salt, and pepper to the bowl with the corn. Toss to combine. Add in basil and toss again gently. Season with more salt and pepper, if needed.

Preheat grill to high heat. Clean grates. Place salmon (keeping it on the foil) onto grill and reduce heat to medium high. Grill until salmon flakes easily with a fork and until it's just barely opaque in the thickest part of the fillet. You do not need to flip the salmon. Remove salmon from the grill. Using tongs, place fillets over top of corn salad.

Serve with lime wedges, your favorite loaf of bread, and softened butter.

RECIPE NOTE: This corn salad goes well with any seafood, so feel free to top it with something other than salmon–like scallops, black sea bass, striped bass fillets, or other fish.

Nutrition Facts per Serving **Calories:** 592 / **Total fat:** 34g (43% DV) / **Saturated fat:** 9g (45% DV) / **Trans fat:** 0g / **Cholesterol:** 110mg (37% DV) / **Sodium:** 378mg (16% DV) / **Total carbohydrate:** 28g (10% DV) / **Dietary fiber:** 3.5g (13% DV) / **Total sugars:** 9g / **Added sugar:** 2g (4% DV) / **Protein:** 46g / **Vitamin D:** 34mcg (169% DV) / **Calcium:** 312mg (24% DV) / **Iron:** 2mg (12% DV) / **Potassium:** 1,115mg (24% DV)

Air Fryer Teriyaki Salmon

Salmon fillets marinated in a quick teriyaki sauce, then air-fried to perfection until crisp on the outside and perfectly flaky and tender on the inside. This easy recipe cooks in less than 10 minutes, making it a great family-friendly weeknight dinner option.

Serves: 4
Course: Main course
Total time: 45 minutes

INGREDIENTS

½ cup	reduced-sodium soy sauce
¼ cup	mirin
2 tbsp	dark brown sugar
½ tsp	toasted sesame oil
2 cloves	garlic, minced
1 inch	finger ginger, minced (about 1 tbsp)
1½ lb	salmon fillet, skin on, cut into 4 equal-sized pieces

For serving:

Black sesame seeds

Lime wedges

INSTRUCTIONS

Make the teriyaki sauce by whisking together soy sauce, mirin, brown sugar, sesame oil, garlic, and ginger in a small saucepan over medium heat. Bring to a boil, then reduce to a simmer. Simmer for 5 minutes, then remove from heat. Cool.

Add ¾ of the sauce to a ziplock bag or glass container. Add the salmon. Set aside for 20–30 minutes at room temperature.

Pour the remaining ¼ of the sauce into a small serving bowl. You will use this later to serve with the salmon as a dipping sauce.

Preheat your air fryer to 390°F. Wipe or spray your air fryer basket with avocado oil or other high-heat cooking oil.

Remove salmon from teriyaki marinade (discard remaining marinade that was with the fish), shaking off excess, and place salmon in the air fryer, spacing the fillets so they don't touch each other. Cook salmon for 5–6 minutes, or until desired doneness—time will vary depending on the thickness of your salmon fillets and the variation in air fryers. Salmon is cooked through at an internal temperature of 145°F, but keep in mind the fish will continue cooking once you remove it from the air fryer, so pull it out at about 140°F (or less if you prefer it slightly undercooked).

Plate salmon. Sprinkle with black sesame seeds and serve with lime wedges. Serve with reserved sauce.

RECIPE NOTES:

• Every air fryer cooks a bit differently, so cooking time may need to be adjusted based on your air fryer, as well as the thickness of your salmon fillets.

• Mirin is a sweet Japanese rice wine, available in most grocery stores near the Asian condiments.

• If you're using store-bought teriyaki sauce, use 3/4-1 cup.

• Do not use marinade used on the raw fish for serving on the finished dish.

Nutrition Facts per Serving **Calories:** 315 / **Total fat:** 13g (16% DV) / **Saturated fat:** 3g (15% DV) / **Trans fat:** 0g / **Cholesterol:** 96mg (32% DV) / **Sodium:** 464mg (20% DV) / **Total carbohydrate:** 6.5g (2% DV) / **Dietary fiber:** 0.5g (2% DV) / **Total sugars:** 3g / **Added sugar:** 2g (4% DV) / **Protein:** 38.5g / **Vitamin D:** 38mcg (189% DV) / **Calcium:** 31g (2% DV) / **Iron:** 1.1mg (6% DV) / **Potassium:** 787mg (17% DV)

Teriyaki Salmon Bowl

Teriyaki salmon served over top of brown rice with cucumber, edamame, avocado, seaweed salad, scallions, and pickled ginger. This healthy salmon rice bowl is savory, sweet, and satisfying—and makes the perfect "meal in a bowl" for lunch or dinner.

Serves: 4
Course: Main course
Total time: 10 minutes

INGREDIENTS

1 recipe	air fryer teriyaki salmon (see page 152)
3 cups	cooked warm brown or white rice
1	English cucumber, thinly sliced
2 cups	shelled cooked edamame
1	avocado, thinly sliced
1 cup	seaweed salad (we use Atlantic Sea Farms)
4	scallions, green parts only, sliced
2 tbsp	pickled ginger

For serving:

	Black sesame seeds
1	lime, cut into wedges

INSTRUCTIONS

Make air fryer teriyaki salmon recipe (page 152). Assemble bowls by dividing rice among 4 bowls. Add salmon, cucumber, edamame, avocado, seaweed salad, scallions, and pickled ginger equally to the bowls.

Sprinkle bowls with black sesame seeds. Serve with lime wedges and reserved teriyaki sauce.

Nutrition Facts per Serving **Calories:** 736 / **Total fat:** 27g (35% DV) / **Saturated fat:** 5g (26% DV) / **Trans fat:** 0g / **Cholesterol:** 96mg (32% DV) / **Sodium:** 690mg (30% DV) / **Total carbohydrate:** 67g (24% DV) / **Dietary fiber:** 11.5g (42% DV) / **Total sugars:** 9.5g / **Added sugar:** 4g (8% DV) / **Protein:** 56g / **Vitamin D:** 38mcg (189% DV) / **Calcium:** 208g (16% DV) / **Iron:** 5mg (30% DV) / **Potassium:** 1,806mg (38% DV)

Salmon Nutrition Highlights

In addition to those omega-3 fats, salmon (both farmed and wild) is rich in protein and is an excellent source of vitamin D, vitamin B3, vitamin B6, vitamin B12, and selenium.

Salmon Poke Bowls

Serves: 2
Course: Main course
Total time: 20 minutes

INGREDIENTS

For the salmon:

1 tbsp	reduced-sodium soy sauce
1 tbsp	unseasoned rice vinegar
1 tbsp	mirin
1 tsp	freshly grated ginger
	Juice of ½ lime
½ tsp	honey
¼ tsp	toasted sesame oil
¼ tsp	sriracha
½ lb	sushi-grade raw salmon, cut into ¼-inch cubes

Assembly:

1 cup	cooked warm brown short-grain rice
1 cup	edamame
½ cup	seaweed salad (we use Atlantic Sea Farms)
1	avocado, thinly sliced
1 small	cucumber, cut into bite-sized chunks
2	radishes, thinly sliced

For topping:

4	scallions (green parts only), sliced
	Black sesame seeds (optional)
	Crushed seaweed snacks (optional)
2 tsp	pickled ginger, more if desired
	Sriracha mayo (2 tbsp mayo + ½ tsp sriracha; adjust amount of sriracha based on desired level of heat)

For serving:

1	lime, cut into wedges

Cubed sushi-grade salmon marinated in a soy ginger dressing and served over warm brown rice, edamame, seaweed salad, avocado, cucumber, and radish. I would eat these poke bowls daily if I could! Feel free to swap the salmon for sushi-grade tuna, or even tofu, if preferred.

INSTRUCTIONS

Combine soy sauce, rice vinegar, mirin, ginger, lime juice, honey, sesame oil, and sriracha in a medium bowl. Whisk well. Add cubes of salmon and toss gently to combine.

Place brown rice into two bowls. Add edamame, seaweed salad, avocado, cucumber, radishes, and salmon with its sauce. Top with scallions, sesame seeds, and crushed seaweed snacks. Add pickled ginger and sriracha mayo to the bowls and serve with lime wedges.

Nutrition Facts per Serving **Calories:** 639 / **Total fat:** 27g (35% DV) / **Saturated fat:** 4g (19% DV) / **Trans fat:** 0g / **Cholesterol:** 68mg (23% DV) / **Sodium:** 781mg (34% DV) / **Total carbohydrate:** 59g (21% DV) / **Dietary fiber:** 13g (47% DV) / **Total sugars:** 11.5g / **Added sugar:** 4g (8% DV) / **Protein:** 42g / **Vitamin D:** 1mcg (4% DV) / **Calcium:** 204mg (16% DV) / **Iron:** 5mg (29% DV) / **Potassium:** 1,704mg (36% DV)

Those with compromised immune systems, as well as those who are pregnant, infants, young children, and older adults, should not consume raw or undercooked fish and shellfish.

Easy Salmon Burgers with Tzatziki

These salmon burgers can be whipped up in minutes, so they are perfect for a busy weeknight meal. They use canned salmon and a few other pantry staples that you probably already have on hand. These burgers freeze well, so make a big batch and freeze some for a healthy future fish dinner.

Serves: 4
Course: Main course
Total time: 15 minutes

INGREDIENTS

For the salmon burgers:

2 (5-oz) cans	salmon, skinless and boneless
½ cup	panko crumbs
1	egg, beaten
3 tbsp	chopped fresh dill
1 tbsp	lemon juice
¼ tsp	garlic powder
¼ tsp	kosher salt
⅛ tsp	ground black pepper
1 tsp	olive oil

Assembly:

¼ cup	tzatziki (see page 211)
4	whole-wheat slider buns
4	Bibb lettuce leaves
4 thin slices	red onion

For serving:

Lemon wedges

INSTRUCTIONS

In a medium mixing bowl combine salmon, panko, egg, dill, lemon juice, garlic powder, salt, and pepper. Shape into 4 patties.

Heat a sauté pan on medium high with 1 teaspoon olive oil. When oil is hot, add patties. Cook 2–3 minutes until lightly browned on the underside, then flip and cook an additional 2–3 minutes. Remove from heat.

Spread tzatziki on the top half of each bun or directly on burger. Add a lettuce leaf to each bottom bun and top with a salmon slider and a slice of red onion. Serve with lemon wedges.

Nutrition Facts per Serving **Calories:** 278 / **Total fat:** 8g (10% DV) / **Saturated fat:** 1.5g (9% DV) / **Trans fat:** 0g / **Cholesterol:** 101mg (34% DV) / **Sodium:** 465mg (20% DV) / **Total carbohydrate:** 25.5g (9% DV) / **Dietary fiber:** 3g (11% DV) / **Total sugars:** 3.5g / **Added sugar:** 2g (5% DV) / **Protein:** 26g / **Vitamin D:** 10.5mcg (53% DV) / **Calcium:** 311mg (24% DV) / **Iron:** 2mg (12% DV) / **Potassium:** 435mg (9% DV)

Sweet Citrus and Spice Salmon

Salmon rubbed with a simple blend of brown sugar, dried orange peel, dried mustard powder, garlic powder, dried onion, paprika, and salt, then baked until flaky. This is an easy, healthy, and ridiculously delicious way to serve salmon.

Serves: 4
Course: Main course
Total time: 20 minutes

INGREDIENTS

1½ lb	salmon fillet, cut into 4 pieces
1 tbsp	dark brown sugar
1 tsp	dried ground mustard
1 tsp	paprika
1 tsp	dried minced onion
1 tsp	garlic powder
1 tsp	dried orange peel
½ tsp	kosher salt

For serving:

	Any citrus wedges— orange, lemon, or lime

INSTRUCTIONS

Preheat oven to 425°F.

Place salmon on an aluminum foil–lined baking sheet. Pat dry with a paper towel. Combine spices together. Sprinkle generously over fish and let sit 10 minutes. If you have leftover rub, store it for next time in a sealed glass container in your spice cabinet.

Bake salmon for 9–12 minutes, until it flakes easily with a fork or until desired doneness (we like ours a bit rosy in the middle). Cooking time will vary depending on the thickness of the fillets and your individual oven. Broil for the last minute, if desired, to develop a crust on top of the fish.

Serve with your choice of citrus wedges.

RECIPE NOTE: Find dried orange peel in the spice aisle of your local grocery store.

Nutrition Facts per Serving **Calories:** 295 / **Total fat:** 13g (16% DV) / **Saturated fat:** 3g (15% DV) / **Trans fat:** 0g / **Cholesterol:** 96mg (32% DV) / **Sodium:** 388mg (17% DV) / **Total carbohydrate:** 6g (2% DV) / **Dietary fiber:** 0.5g (3% DV) / **Total sugars:** 4g / **Added sugar:** 3g (7% DV) / **Protein:** 37.5g / **Vitamin D:** 38mcg (189% DV) / **Calcium:** 29mg (2% DV) / **Iron:** 1mg (5% DV) / **Potassium:** 755mg (16% DV)

Honey Garlic Butter Salmon with Herbs

A beautiful salmon fillet topped with a honey, garlic, parsley, rosemary, thyme, and lemon zest honey butter, then roasted until the fish is perfectly rosy and flaky. The salmon is then topped with flaky sea salt and served with lemon wedges. This autumn fish dinner is perfect for sharing–with guests this fall, or serve it as a stunning main course for a holiday dinner.

Serves: 6
Course: Main course
Total time: 25 minutes

INGREDIENTS

2½ lb	salmon fillet, skin on (kept whole)
4 tbsp	butter, softened
3 tbsp	honey
	Zest of 1 lemon plus juice of ½ the lemon
½ cup	loosely packed Italian parsley, finely chopped
1 tbsp	fresh rosemary leaves, finely chopped
1 tbsp	fresh thyme, finely chopped
3 cloves	garlic, finely minced
½ tsp	kosher salt
¼ tsp	ground black pepper

For serving:

Flaky sea salt

Lemon wedges

INSTRUCTIONS

Preheat oven to 425°F. Prepare a baking sheet with aluminum foil or parchment paper and place the salmon on the baking sheet, skin side down. Blot the salmon dry with paper towels.

Combine softened butter, honey, lemon zest, lemon juice, parsley, rosemary, thyme, garlic, salt, and pepper.

Spread the butter mixture over top of the salmon fillet.

Bake salmon for 15–18 minutes or until the salmon is cooked to your preference. We like to broil the fish for the last few minutes to form a bit of a crust on top, but this is optional. Cooking time will vary depending on thickness of the salmon fillet, oven variation, and preferred doneness. This large salmon side will take longer to cook than if it were cut up into smaller fillets.

Remove salmon from oven and sprinkle with flaky sea salt. Either keep salmon on the baking sheet and place on the table for serving, or transfer carefully to a serving platter. Serve with lemon wedges.

Nutrition Facts per Serving **Calories:** 413 / **Total fat:** 22g (28% DV) / **Saturated fat:** 8g (41% DV) / **Trans fat:** 0.5g / **Cholesterol:** 127mg (42% DV) / **Sodium:** 372mg (16% DV) / **Total carbohydrate:** 11g (4% DV) / **Dietary fiber:** 1g (3% DV) / **Total sugars:** 9g / **Added sugar:** 8.5g (17% DV) / **Protein:** 42g / **Vitamin D:** 42mcg (210% DV) / **Calcium:** 41g (3% DV) / **Iron:** 1mg (7% DV) / **Potassium:** 853mg (18% DV)

Mediterranean Salmon

Simply pan-seared salmon topped with a fresh and vibrant Mediterranean salad of parsley, tomatoes, red onion, capers, and feta in a red wine and extra-virgin olive oil vinaigrette. This is a healthy, flavor-packed, and satisfying salmon recipe that's quick to prepare (ready in 15 minutes!) and simple enough for a weeknight.

Serves: 4
Course: Main course
Total time: 15 minutes

INGREDIENTS

For the salmon:

1½ lb	salmon fillet, skin on, cut into 4 pieces
¼ tsp	kosher salt
¼ tsp	ground black pepper
1 tsp	avocado or canola oil

For the Mediterranean salad:

1 cup	grape tomatoes, halved
½ cup	parsley, leaves only, roughly chopped
½ medium	red onion, diced
¼ cup	capers, drained
¼ cup	extra-virgin olive oil
2 tbsp	red wine vinegar
¼ tsp	kosher salt
⅛ tsp	ground black pepper

For serving:

¼ cup	feta cheese crumbles

INSTRUCTIONS

For the salmon: Pat salmon dry with a paper towel. Season with salt and pepper.

Heat a large cast-iron skillet over medium high heat. Add oil. When oil is hot, add salmon fillets to the skillet, skin side up. Cook 4–5 minutes. Flip salmon and cook an additional 4–5 minutes, or until salmon is just cooked through and begins to flake easily with a fork, or until desired doneness. Fish usually takes about 10 minutes per inch of thickness.

For the Mediterranean salad: While the salmon is cooking, combine all salad ingredients in a medium-sized bowl. Mix well.

Place salmon onto 4 plates and top with Mediterranean salad. Sprinkle with feta cheese. Serve.

Nutrition Facts per Serving **Calories:** 447 / **Total fat:** 29.5g (38% DV) / **Saturated fat:** 6g (31% DV) / **Trans fat:** 0g / **Cholesterol:** 105mg (35% DV) / **Sodium:** 689mg (30% DV) / **Total carbohydrate:** 4.5g (2% DV) / **Dietary fiber:** 1g (5% DV) / **Total sugars:** 2g / **Added sugar:** 0g (0% DV) / **Protein:** 39.5g / **Vitamin D:** 38mcg (189% DV) / **Calcium:** 88mg (7% DV) / **Iron:** 1.5mg (9% DV) / **Potassium:** 888mg (19% DV)

Soy Ginger Salmon in Foil

Salmon fillets, baby spinach, shiitake mushrooms, and scallions in a ginger, soy, and sesame sauce wrapped in foil packets and grilled (or baked). A healthy, flavor-packed dinner that'll easily become a favorite in your house, as it did in ours. And the best part about this recipe is that cleanup is a breeze!

Serves: 4
Course: Main course
Total time: 25 minutes

INGREDIENTS

For the salmon packets:

¼ cup	reduced-sodium soy sauce
2 tbsp	seasoned rice vinegar
2 tbsp	honey
1 tsp	toasted sesame oil
1 tsp	sriracha
1 tbsp	fresh grated ginger
¼ tsp	garlic powder
8 cups	packed baby spinach
1½ lb	salmon fillet, cut into 4 equal fillets, skin removed if desired
3½ oz	shiitake mushrooms, trimmed, sliced
1 bunch	scallions, thinly sliced, white and green parts, divided

For serving:

2 cups	cooked short-grain brown rice, warmed
	Scallions, reserved from above
1 tbsp	toasted sesame seeds
1	lime, cut into wedges

INSTRUCTIONS

Preheat grill to high heat.

Whisk together soy sauce, rice vinegar, honey, sesame oil, sriracha, ginger, and garlic powder until well combined.

Prepare 4 pieces of foil (about dinner-plate size). Place 2 cups of baby spinach in the center of each piece of foil. Top spinach with salmon, shiitake mushrooms, and half of the scallions. Pour marinade equally over top of each salmon packet. Fold over the foil to seal each packet tightly (you don't want heat to escape).

Reduce grill heat to medium high. Place packets on grill and cook for about 10–15 minutes, depending on thickness of salmon fillets. Cook until fish flakes easily with a fork and is opaque throughout (check salmon by removing one packet from the grill and opening very carefully to avoid the hot steam).

Remove packets from grill. Open packets carefully. Using tongs, place salmon fillets, veggies, and sauce over top of brown rice. Top with remaining scallions and toasted sesame seeds.

Serve with lime wedges.

RECIPE NOTES:

• If you'd prefer to make this salmon dish in the oven, place the packets on a baking sheet and place into a 400°F oven for 10-15 minutes (cooking time will vary depending on thickness of the fillets and your individual oven), checking for doneness after 10 minutes. When checking for doneness, do so carefully, as the packets are full of hot steam.

• The skin on the salmon will not crisp up, so feel free to remove it after cooking and prior to serving.

• The salmon fillets will likely not stay intact when transferring them from foil packet to plate. This is fine–just garnish the fillets and the dish will look and taste great, even if they are not perfect!

Nutrition Facts per Serving **Calories:** 501 / **Total fat:** 16g (21% DV) / **Saturated fat:** 3.5g (18% DV) / **Trans fat:** 0g / **Cholesterol:** 96mg (32% DV) / **Sodium:** 746mg (32% DV) / **Total carbohydrate:** 44.5g (16% DV) / **Dietary fiber:** 5g (19% DV) / **Total sugars:** 11g / **Added sugar:** 9g (18% DV) / **Protein:** 44.5g / **Vitamin D:** 38mcg (190% DV) / **Calcium:** 111mg (9% DV) / **Iron:** 4mg (22% DV) / **Potassium:** 1,365mg (29% DV)

Salmon Bites

Tender chunks of salmon fillet are marinated in ginger, soy, and sesame oil and grilled to juicy perfection. Perfect for feeding a crowd! Also, this recipe is one of the best for converting non-fish lovers into fish fans. I mean, how could anyone resist that glaze?!

Serves: 6
Course: Main course
Total time: 30 minutes

INGREDIENTS

½ cup	reduced-sodium soy sauce
¼ cup	seasoned rice vinegar
¼ cup	brown sugar
1 tbsp	minced fresh ginger, or use bottled minced ginger as a shortcut
½ tsp	toasted sesame oil
2 cloves	garlic, minced
1½ lb	salmon fillet, cut into 1–2-inch chunks (you can keep the skin on or remove, your choice)

For serving:

Black sesame seeds

Lemon wedges

INSTRUCTIONS

Whisk together soy sauce, rice vinegar, brown sugar, ginger, sesame oil, and garlic. Reserve a few tablespoons in a small bowl for serving (never use marinade that has been in contact with raw fish, meat, or poultry on a finished dish). Pour the rest of the marinade into a resealable plastic bag. Add salmon to the bag and let sit for 20 minutes at room temperature.

Preheat grill to high heat. Clean and oil grates.

Place salmon cubes onto the grill and reduce heat to medium high. Grill until salmon is cooked through or reaches desired doneness, turning 1 or 2 times during grilling time. Cooking time will be a few short minutes, as these are small chunks of fish. Remove from grill.

Sprinkle with sesame seeds. Drizzle with reserved marinade. Serve with lemon wedges.

Nutrition Facts per Serving **Calories:** 201 / **Total fat:** 8.5g (11% DV) / **Saturated fat:** 2g (10% DV) / **Trans fat:** 0g / **Cholesterol:** 64mg (21% DV) / **Sodium:** 309mg (13% DV) / **Total carbohydrate:** 4g (1% DV) / **Dietary fiber:** 0g (0% DV) / **Total sugars:** 3.5g / **Added sugar:** 3g (7% DV) / **Protein:** 25.5g / **Vitamin D:** 25mcg (126% DV) / **Calcium:** 18mg (1% DV) / **Iron:** 0.5mg (3% DV) / **Potassium:** 503mg (11% DV)

Teriyaki Salmon Kebabs

No summer grill-out is complete without kebabs! These teriyaki salmon kebabs are packed with flavor, crunch, color, and nutrition–and are guaranteed to convert anyone into a salmon lover! Salmon, broccoli, and red onion marinated in a quick homemade teriyaki sauce, skewered on kebabs, and then grilled until smoky and delicious. These salmon skewers are so easy and quick to make, and they're guaranteed to be a big hit among kids and adults alike.

Serves: 4
Course: Main course
Total time: 25 minutes

INGREDIENTS

For the marinade:

½ cup	reduced-sodium soy sauce
¼ cup	seasoned rice vinegar
¼ cup	brown sugar
¼ tsp	toasted sesame oil
1 finger	fresh ginger grated or finely minced (just over 1 tbsp minced)
2 cloves	garlic, minced

For the kebabs:

1 lb	salmon fillet, skin removed, cut into 1-inch cubes
1 head	broccoli, broken into bite-sized florets
1	red onion, cut into bite-sized chunks

For serving:

	Black sesame seeds (optional)
1	lime, cut into wedges
2 cups	cooked brown rice, warmed

INSTRUCTIONS

Preheat grill to high heat. Clean and oil grates.

Whisk together marinade ingredients. Reserve a few tablespoons in a small bowl for serving. Pour the rest of the marinade into a resealable plastic bag.

Add salmon, broccoli, and red onion to the marinade. Let sit 10 minutes.

Discard marinade. Skewer salmon, broccoli, and red onion onto metal skewers. (If using wooden skewers, soak in water for 30 minutes prior to using so they don't burn on the grill.)

Place skewers onto the grill and reduce heat to medium high. Grill, turning skewers after a few minutes to cook evenly. Grill until salmon reaches desired doneness, turning 1 or 2 times during grilling time. Remove from grill.

Sprinkle skewers with black sesame seeds. Serve with reserved sauce, lime wedges, and brown rice.

Nutrition Facts per Serving **Calories:** 361 / **Total fat:** 9.5g (12% DV) / **Saturated fat:** 2g (12% DV) / **Trans fat:** 0g / **Cholesterol:** 64mg (21% DV) / **Sodium:** 454mg (20% DV) / **Total carbohydrate:** 38g (14% DV) / **Dietary fiber:** 3.5g (12% DV) / **Total sugars:** 7g / **Added sugar:** 5g (10% DV) / **Protein:** 30g / **Vitamin D:** 25mcg (126% DV) / **Calcium:** 51mg (4% DV) / **Iron:** 1.5mg (9% DV) / **Potassium:** 766mg (16% DV)

Roasted Salmon with Herbs and Pomegranate

Salmon roasted to perfection, then topped with fresh chopped herbs in extra-virgin olive oil and sprinkled with pomegranate arils. This is a beautiful, simple, and festive addition to your holiday table.

Serves: 4
Course: Main course
Total time: 20 minutes

INGREDIENTS

For the fresh herbs in olive oil:

½ cup	extra-virgin olive oil
¼ cup	red wine vinegar
¼ cup	roughly chopped parsley leaves
2 tbsp	roughly chopped cilantro
½ oz	chives (1 small clamshell), thinly sliced
¼ tsp	kosher salt
⅛ tsp	ground black pepper

For the salmon:

1½ lb	salmon fillet (kept whole)
¼ tsp	garlic salt
⅛ tsp	ground black pepper

For serving:

½ cup	pomegranate arils
1	lemon, cut into wedges

INSTRUCTIONS

Preheat oven to 425°F.

Line a baking sheet with parchment paper or aluminum foil.

Combine all ingredients for fresh herbs in olive oil in a small bowl. Stir well. Set aside.

Place the salmon fillet on the baking sheet. Pat dry with paper towel and sprinkle with garlic salt and pepper.

Bake the salmon for 13–15 minutes, or until salmon flakes easily with a fork and is cooked through. This large salmon fillet will take longer to cook than if it were to be cut up into 4 smaller fillets. Broil the salmon for the last 1–2 minutes so it gets a bit crispy on the outside. Cooking time will vary depending on individual ovens and thickness of your fillet. Remove from oven.

Top salmon with fresh herbs in olive oil. Sprinkle salmon with pomegranate arils.

Serve with lemon wedges.

Nutrition Facts per Serving **Calories:** 539 / **Total fat:** 40g (51% DV) / **Saturated fat:** 6.5g (34% DV) / **Trans fat:** 0g / **Cholesterol:** 96mg (32% DV) / **Sodium:** 291mg (13% DV) / **Total carbohydrate:** 6g (2% DV) / **Dietary fiber:** 1.5g (6% DV) / **Total sugars:** 3.5g / **Added sugar:** 0g (0% DV) / **Protein:** 38g / **Vitamin D:** 38mcg (189% DV) / **Calcium:** 36mg (3% DV) / **Iron:** 1mg (7% DV) / **Potassium:** 818mg (17% DV)

Baked Salmon with Cranberry Relish

Simply roasted salmon topped with an easy, tart, and savory relish made with fresh cranberries, tangy red onion, red wine vinegar, and extra-virgin olive oil. This is an elegant yet simple dinner that's perfect for the holidays.

Serves: 4
Course: Main course
Total time: 20 minutes

INGREDIENTS

For the salmon:

1½ lb	salmon fillet, skin on, cut into 4 portions
½ tsp	extra-virgin olive oil
¼ tsp	kosher salt
⅛ tsp	ground black pepper

For the cranberry relish:

1 cup	fresh cranberries, washed and picked over
½ medium	red onion
¼ cup	extra-virgin olive oil
2 tbsp	fresh parsley
2 tbsp	red wine vinegar
1 tsp	sugar
¼ tsp	salt kosher
⅛ tsp	ground black pepper

For serving:

1	lime, cut into wedges

INSTRUCTIONS

Preheat oven to 425°F. Prepare a baking sheet with aluminum foil.

Pat salmon dry. Drizzle with extra-virgin olive oil. Sprinkle with salt and pepper.

Add all relish ingredients to a food processor. Pulse a few times to chop. Add more salt to taste, if needed.

Bake the salmon for 9–12 minutes, or until salmon flakes easily with a fork and is cooked through (time will vary, but a good rule of thumb is to cook the fish about 10 minutes per inch of thickness). Broil the salmon for the last 1–2 minutes so it gets a bit crispy on the outside. Remove from oven.

Plate salmon and top with cranberry relish. Serve with lime wedges.

RECIPE NOTE: Store any remaining cranberry relish in a sealed container in the fridge. It will keep for a few days.

Nutrition Facts per Serving **Calories:** 426 / **Total fat:** 27g (34% DV) / **Saturated fat:** 5g (25% DV) / **Trans fat:** 0g / **Cholesterol:** 96mg (32% DV) / **Sodium:** 376mg (16% DV) / **Total carbohydrate:** 7.5g (3% DV) / **Dietary fiber:** 1.5g (6% DV) / **Total sugars:** 3g / **Added sugar:** 1g (2% DV) / **Protein:** 37.5g / **Vitamin D:** 38mcg (189% DV) / **Calcium:** 34mg (3% DV) / **Iron:** 1mg (6% DV) / **Potassium:** 778g (17% DV)

Smoked Salmon Dip

This smoked salmon dip is smoky, slightly sweet, and oh so addictive! It's a great addition to any brunch spread, or served as an appetizer along with whole-grain crackers, thinly sliced red onion, and lemon wedges.

Serves: 4
Course: Appetizer
Total time: 5 minutes

INGREDIENTS

1 (3.5-oz)	can	smoked salmon, skin removed, flaked (we love Fishwife)
½ cup		reduced-fat whipped cream cheese
2 tbsp		chopped fresh dill
1 tbsp		minced red onion
1 tsp		fresh lemon juice
⅛ tsp		freshly ground black pepper

For serving:

12–16	whole-grain crackers
¼	red onion, thinly sliced
1	lemon, cut into wedges

INSTRUCTIONS

Place smoked salmon, whipped cream cheese, dill, red onion, lemon juice, and black pepper in a mixing bowl. Mix to combine. Refrigerate.

Serve with whole-grain crackers, red onion slices, and lemon wedges.

Nutrition Facts per Serving **Calories:** 146 / **Total fat:** 7g (9% DV) / **Saturated fat:** 2.5g (12% DV) / **Trans fat:** 0g / **Cholesterol:** 18mg (6% DV) / **Sodium:** 423mg (18% DV) / **Total carbohydrate:** 13g (5% DV) / **Dietary fiber:** 2g (8% DV) / **Total sugars:** 1.5g / **Added sugar:** 0g (0% DV) / **Protein:** 9g / **Vitamin D:** 0.5mcg (2% DV) / **Calcium:** 56mg (4% DV) / **Iron:** 1mg (6% DV) / **Potassium:** 191mg (4% DV)

Kelp

Kelp is large brown algae and a type of seaweed. Kelp is gaining in popularity as the new (sea) vegetable on the block that requires zero input (no water, no food, no fertilizer), can help improve water quality, and helps lessen the effects of ocean acidification. According to NOAA (National Oceanic and Atmospheric Administration), seaweed is the fastest-growing aquaculture sector—there are seaweed farms in New England (especially Maine), Alaska, and the Pacific Northwest growing sugar kelp, ribbon kelp, bull kelp, dulse, and more. I love that the interest in domestic kelp is growing, because currently the vast majority of seaweed on the market is imported. Kelp is tasty (briny, bright, and fresh) and good for you.

The first kelp products I ever tried (aside from the fluorescent green imported seaweed salad I had at sushi restaurants) were from the fermented kelp line by Atlantic Sea Farms. Many of the recipes in this chapter use these products—they are wonderfully flavorful and briny and serve as a nice complement to tacos, eggs, grain bowls, sashimi, pizza, and seacuterie boards (i.e., seafood charcuterie boards—find these on page 185.)

Lexi, Jenny's daughter, in Camden, Maine

We have now tried handfuls of different seaweed products, some better tasting than others. Products include kelp seasonings, kelp pastas, kelp jerky, seaweed salad, kimchi made with kelp, kraut made with kelp, kelp pickles, kelp burgers, kelp hot sauce, and more. I encourage you to seek out some of these domestic kelp products—you can find them online, at some grocers, and in fish markets. You can find a list of some of our favorite seaweed products in my kitchen staples list on page 249.

Kelp Nutrition Highlights

Kelp provides an excellent source of iodine and contains a source of other vitamins and minerals, including calcium, magnesium, vitamin K, folate, iron, and health-promoting antioxidants.

Loaded Breakfast Tacos

Warm flour tortillas packed with spinach, scrambled eggs, cheddar cheese, black beans, avocado slices, and Sea-Chi (kimchi made with kelp).

Serves: 4
Course: Breakfast
Total time: 15 minutes

INGREDIENTS

½ tsp	olive oil
8	eggs, beaten
8 street-taco-sized	flour tortillas, warmed (or sub corn tortillas)
2 cups	baby spinach
2 oz	shredded cheddar cheese
1 (15.5-oz)	can black beans, drained and rinsed
1	avocado, thinly sliced
½ cup	Atlantic Sea Farms Sea-Chi, plus more for serving
	Freshly ground black pepper

INSTRUCTIONS

Add olive oil to a medium skillet over medium high heat. When oil is hot, add eggs into pan, reduce heat, and stir until cooked through and fluffy.

Assemble tacos by adding spinach, eggs, cheese, black beans, avocado, and Sea-Chi to each warmed tortilla. Top with black pepper. Serve tacos with additional Sea-Chi, if desired.

RECIPE NOTE: If you can't find Sea-Chi, use your favorite store-bought or homemade kimchi.

Nutrition Facts per Serving **Calories:** 491 / **Total fat:** 22.5g (29% DV) / **Saturated fat:** 7g (36% DV) / **Trans fat:** 0g / **Cholesterol:** 342mg (114% DV) / **Sodium:** 430mg (19% DV) / **Total carbohydrate:** 46g (17% DV) / **Dietary fiber:** 15g (54% DV) / **Total sugars:** 3g / **Added sugar:** 0g (0% DV) / **Protein:** 27g / **Vitamin D:** 2mcg (10% DV) / **Calcium:** 289mg (22% DV) / **Iron:** 5.3mg (29% DV) / **Potassium:** 876mg (19% DV)

Kelp Vinaigrette

This simple vinaigrette is bright, briny, and perfect for any of your leafy green or grain salads.

Makes: ¾ cup
Serves: 6
Serving size: 2 tablespoons
Course: Sauces and dressings
Total time: 5 minutes

INGREDIENTS

½ cup	extra-virgin olive oil
¼ cup	red wine vinegar
3	Atlantic Sea Farms Kelp Cubes
1 tsp	Dijon mustard
1 clove	garlic
¼ tsp	kosher salt
⅛ tsp	ground black pepper

INSTRUCTIONS

Combine extra-virgin olive oil, vinegar, kelp, mustard, garlic, salt, and black pepper in a small food processor. Process until smooth and combined.

RECIPE NOTE: Dressing will keep in the fridge in a covered container for up to a week.

Nutrition Facts per Serving **Calories:** 166 / **Total fat:** 18g (23% DV) / **Saturated fat:** 2.5g (13% DV) / **Trans fat:** 0g / **Cholesterol:** 0mg (0% DV) / **Sodium:** 138mg (6% DV) / **Total carbohydrate:** 1g (0% DV) / **Dietary fiber:** 0g (1% DV) / **Total sugars:** 0g / **Added sugar:** 0g (0% DV) / **Protein:** 0g / **Vitamin D:** 0mcg (0% DV) / **Calcium:** 17mg (1% DV) / **Iron:** 0.5mg (2% DV) / **Potassium:** 16mg (0% DV)

Wild Blueberry PB Kelp Smoothie

This vibrant smoothie is blended up a few times a week in our house. It's packed with all the good stuff to fuel your morning–protein, fiber, healthy fats, antioxidants–and, most importantly, great flavor! We love that the nutrient-dense wild blueberries and umami-rich kelp both come from one of our favorite places in the world: Maine.

Serves: 2
Course: Breakfast
Total time: 5 minutes

INGREDIENTS

1 cup	unsweetened soy milk or any milk or milk alternative
1 cup	vanilla whole-milk yogurt
1 cup	frozen wild blueberries
1	frozen banana
2	Atlantic Sea Farms Kelp Cubes
2 tbsp	salted unsweetened peanut butter
2 tbsp	old-fashioned rolled oats

INSTRUCTIONS

Combine all ingredients in a high-speed blender and blend until smooth. Pour into two glasses and enjoy.

Nutrition Facts per Serving **Calories:** 363 / **Total fat:** 15.5g (20% DV) / **Saturated fat:** 4.5g (23% DV) / **Trans fat:** 0g / **Cholesterol:** 14mg (5% DV) / **Sodium:** 227mg (10% DV) / **Total carbohydrate:** 46g (17% DV) / **Dietary fiber:** 6.5g (24% DV) / **Total sugars:** 29g / **Added sugar:** 7g (14% DV) / **Protein:** 14g / **Vitamin D:** 1.5mcg (8% DV) / **Calcium:** 367mg (28% DV) / **Iron:** 2mg (12% DV) / **Potassium:** 738mg (16% DV)

Reese's Easy Guacamole with Kelp Chips

This kid-friendly guacamole couldn't be simpler to make and is guaranteed to be a hit among little ones. This is my 9-year-old niece Reese's recipe. She loves making this guacamole as an afternoon snack served with kelp chips (they are so tasty!) and veggies, because "it makes the veggies taste better." Guacamole is one of her favorite foods, and she likes this one because it has only "the stuff she likes" in it. Thanks for sharing with us, Reese!

Serves: 4
Course: Snack and appetizer
Total time: 5 minutes

INGREDIENTS

2	avocados, halved
	Juice of 1 lime
⅛ tsp	salt
⅛ tsp	garlic powder
⅛ tsp	black pepper

For serving:

1–2 oz	12 Tides Puffed Kelp Chips (sea salt flavor)
3	carrots, cut into sticks
3 stalks	celery, cut into sticks

INSTRUCTIONS

Scoop avocado from skin and place into a medium-sized bowl. Using a fork, mash the mixture into desired consistency.

Add lime juice, salt, garlic powder, and black pepper. Mix gently to combine.

Serve with kelp chips and veggie sticks.

RECIPE NOTE: If a simple kid-friendly guacamole isn't what you're after, check out the guacamole served over mahimahi on page 143.

Nutrition Facts per Serving **Calories:** 161 / **Total fat:** 11g (14% DV) / **Saturated fat:** 1.5g (7% DV) / **Trans fat:** 0g / **Cholesterol:** 0mg (0% DV) / **Sodium:** 173mg (8% DV) / **Total carbohydrate:** 16g (6% DV) / **Dietary fiber:** 6.5g (23% DV) / **Total sugars:** 2.5g / **Added sugar:** 0g (0% DV) / **Protein:** 2g / **Vitamin D:** 0mcg (0% DV) / **Calcium:** 27mg (2% DV) / **Iron:** 0.5mg (3% DV) / **Potassium:** 514mg (11% DV)

Seacuterie Boards

Seacuterie boards (a.k.a. seafood charcuterie boards) are a star in the entertaining arena. They are perfect for serving a crowd and can be assembled using any seafood and accoutrements you have on hand. Seacuterie will wow seafood lovers but will also entice seafood novices to try something new. Everyone can enjoy as little (or as much!) as they would like, and variety is key here. We like to mix and match tinned, fresh, cooked, seared, raw, or dried seafood—and don't forget the kelp. Add a few different seaweed items to your board for flavor, nutrition, and variety! There are some great kelp condiments and accoutrements that go perfectly with a seafood spread.

Try one of these fabulous boards, or create your own using your favorite seafood. Most important, seacuterie is meant to be fun and casual, so gather your favorite ingredients and people and indulge in your beautiful seafood creation.

Grilled Surf and Turf Platter

Strip sirloin steak, lobster tails, littlenecks, and veggies grilled to perfection, then served with herb butter, sea salt, and lemons. This celebratory summer platter is a sure party-pleaser!

Serves: 4-6
Course: Main course
Total time: 40 minutes

INGREDIENTS

1 lb	strip sirloin steak
¼ tsp	kosher salt
¼ tsp	freshly ground black pepper
2	lobster tails
1 tsp	olive oil, divided
1½ lb	littleneck clams
2 small heads	broccoli, cut into spears
1	red onion, cut into chunks
1	lemon, halved

For the compound butter:

6 tbsp	salted butter, softened
¼ cup	cilantro, chopped
¼ cup	basil, chopped
¼ cup	parsley, chopped
¼ tsp	kosher salt

For serving (optional):

Sea salt

Fresh herbs

Baguette chunks

INSTRUCTIONS

Sprinkle meat liberally with salt and freshly ground pepper on all sides and let sit for at least 30 minutes to come to room temperature.

Make compound butter by combining butter, herbs, and kosher salt.

Preheat grill to high heat. Clean and oil grates well—the oil will prevent the items from sticking.

Cut lobster tails in half and brush lightly with ½ teaspoon olive oil.

Rinse clams and discard any that are cracked or damaged, as they are likely dead. If any clams are open, gently tap them—if they close, keep them. If they stay open, toss them.

Toss broccoli, red onion, and halved lemon with remaining olive oil.

Place steak onto the grill and reduce heat to medium high. Grill until desired doneness, flipping halfway through cooking time. *USDA Food Safety states that steaks should be cooked to a minimum of 145°F with a 3-minute rest.* Just before (or just after) removing from the grill, top with a tablespoon of compound butter. Be careful: If you're doing it on the grill, it could cause flare-ups. Let steak rest for 5–10 minutes.

Place veggies, lemon halves, lobster tails (shell side down), and clams on the grill—you can do this while the steak is cooking if you have space. Flip the veggies after about 5 minutes and grill the veggies and lemon until lightly charred. No need to flip the lobster tails or clams. Just prior to removing from the grill, place a smear of compound butter on the lobster tails. Remove lobster tails once meat is opaque. Remove the clams after they've opened, being careful not to spill their liquor. If any don't open, discard them.

Slice steak against the grain and place on a serving platter. Melt t 2 tablespoons compound butter in the microwave in a small microwave-safe dish. Place clams on the serving platter and drizzle with the butter. Place lobster tails, veggies, and lemon halves on the platter. Sprinkle with sea salt and fresh herbs. Serve with remaining compound butter and hunks of baguette.

Nutrition Facts per Serving **Calories:** 419 / **Total fat:** 22g (28% DV) / **Saturated fat:** 11g (55% DV) / **Trans fat:** 1g / **Cholesterol:** 178mg (59% DV) / **Sodium:** 1264mg (55% DV) / **Total carbohydrate:** 12g (4% DV) / **Dietary fiber:** 2.5g (9% DV) / **Total sugars:** 2g / **Added sugar:** 0g (0% DV) / **Protein:** 43g / **Vitamin D:** 0.5mcg (2% DV) / **Calcium:** 155mg (12% DV) / **Iron:** 3.5mg (21% DV) / **Potassium:** 649mg (14% DV)

Serves: 4-6
Course: Breakfast or brunch
Total time: 45 minutes

INGREDIENTS

For the crab deviled eggs:

6	eggs
4 oz	lump crabmeat, picked over for shell fragments
3 tbsp	chopped chives, divided
2 tbsp	reduced-fat mayonnaise
1 tsp	stone-ground mustard
1 tsp	Old Bay Seasoning
	Juice and zest of ½ lemon
¼ tsp	freshly ground black pepper

For the smoked salmon dip:

1 (3.5-oz) can	smoked salmon, skin removed, flaked
½ cup	reduced-fat whipped cream cheese
2 tbsp	chopped fresh dill
1 tbsp	minced red onion
1 tsp	fresh lemon juice
⅛ tsp	freshly ground black pepper

For assembly:

½ cup	tzatziki (see page 211)
3 mini	bagels, halved and toasted
6	carrots
6 spears	asparagus
1 tin	sardines in preserved lemon (or plain)
6	radishes, thinly sliced
¼	red onion, thinly sliced
1	lemon, sliced into rounds or wedges
2 tbsp	capers
	Dill for garnish

Spring Seacuterie Board

Smoked salmon dip, crab-stuffed deviled eggs, tinned sardines, mini bagels, carrots, radishes, asparagus, tzatziki, red onion, capers, dill, and lots of lemon make up this stunning spring seacuterie board. Perfect for breakfast or brunch on Easter, Mother's Day, or any spring celebration.

INSTRUCTIONS

For the crab deviled eggs: Add eggs to a large pot in a single layer. Cover with 1 inch of water. Bring to a boil. Turn off heat and cover the eggs with a lid. Let sit for 10–12 minutes. Prepare an ice bath.

Drain water, remove eggs, and place in ice bath to stop the cooking process. Let sit in the ice bath for 12–14 more minutes. Peel eggs and slice in half. Remove yolk and place into mixing bowl, smash lightly with a fork.

Add crab, 2 tablespoons chives, mayonnaise, mustard, Old Bay Seasoning, lemon juice and zest, and pepper to the yolks. Mix well. Spoon mixture into egg whites. Top with remaining tablespoon chives.

Refrigerate until ready to serve. (If you have extra filling, place it in a small bowl for serving with the seacuterie board.)

For the smoked salmon dip: Add smoked salmon, cream cheese, dill, red onion, lemon juice, and pepper to a mixing bowl. Mix well until combined.

Assembly: Place deviled eggs, smoked salmon dip, and tzatziki in a triangle formation on a large platter (they should be spaced away from each other). Place the mini bagels near the smoked salmon dip. Place the carrots and asparagus near the tzatziki. Place the tinned sardines in any open spot.

Add radishes, red onion, and lemons to any open area of the platter. Place the capers in a small bowl and nestle anywhere on the platter. Add dill in any open spots.

RECIPE NOTE: Feel free to make this platter your own! Swap ingredients in and out. And assemble in any way you prefer; the board will be beautiful and tasty no matter how you arrange the ingredients.

Nutrition Facts per Serving **Calories:** 246 / **Total fat:** 12.5g (16% DV) / **Saturated fat:** 4g (22% DV) / **Trans fat:** 0g / **Cholesterol:** 219mg (73% DV) / **Sodium:** 542mg (24% DV) / **Total carbohydrate:** 12.5g (5% DV) / **Dietary fiber:** 3g (10% DV) / **Total sugars:** 6g / **Added sugar:** 0.5g (1% DV) / **Protein:** 21.5g / **Vitamin D:** 5mcg (27% DV) / **Calcium:** 192mg (15% DV) / **Iron:** 2mg (10% DV) / **Potassium:** 572mg (12% DV)

Lobster BLT Brunch Board

Sweet fresh lobster meat, toasted baguette, tomatoes, crisp lettuce, avocado, bacon, basil, mayo, capers, and lemon wedges–all displayed beautifully on a seacuterie board for guests to assemble their own lobster BLT creations.

Serves: 4-6
Course: Brunch or main course
Total time: 10 minutes

INGREDIENTS

1	baguette, sliced, toasted
1	heirloom tomato, sliced
2 oz	baby leaf lettuce
1	avocado, thinly sliced
½ lb	cooked lobster meat, chopped
4 strips	reduced-sodium bacon, cooked until crisp, halved
12	basil leaves
¼ cup	reduced-fat mayonnaise
2 tbsp	capers
1	lemon, cut into wedges

INSTRUCTIONS

Arrange toast, tomato, lettuce, avocado, lobster, bacon, and basil in rows on a large platter or wooden board.

Place mayo and capers in small bowls with spoons on the platter. Add lemon wedges. Serve.

Nutrition Facts per Serving **Calories:** 203 / **Total fat:** 9g (11% DV) / **Saturated fat:** 1.5g (8% DV) / **Trans fat:** 0g / **Cholesterol:** 62mg (21% DV) / **Sodium:** 528mg (23% DV) / **Total carbohydrate:** 19g (7% DV) / **Dietary fiber:** 3g (11% DV) / **Total sugars:** 3g / **Added sugar:** 0.5g (1% DV) / **Protein:** 13g / **Vitamin D:** 0mcg (0% DV) / **Calcium:** 65mg (5% DV) / **Iron:** 1.5mg (9% DV) / **Potassium:** 370mg (8% DV)

Fall Seacuterie Board

A beautiful seafood board with sautéed jumbo shrimp, tuna jerky, smoked salmon, Sea-Chi (kimchi made with seaweed), olives, capers, Boursin cheese, and crackers. This fall charcuterie board full of seafood goodness is the perfect fall appetizer!

Serves: 6
Course: Appetizer
Total time: 10 minutes

INGREDIENTS

½ lb	raw jumbo shrimp (21/25), peeled and deveined
¼ tsp	kosher salt
⅛ tsp	ground black pepper
½ tsp	olive oil
4 oz	tuna jerky (we love Pescavore)
1 (3.5-oz) tin	smoked salmon (we like Fishwife)
½ cup	Atlantic Sea Farms Sea-Chi or any kimchi
¼ cup	Castelvetrano olives
2 tbsp	capers, drained
5 oz	garlic-and-herb cheese spread (or any cheese spread), such as Boursin
2 oz	rice crackers

INSTRUCTIONS

Gather a large circular serving platter or board.

Pat the shrimp very dry and sprinkle with kosher salt and pepper.

Heat a skillet with olive oil over medium heat.

Once pan is hot, add the shrimp and sauté a few minutes on each side until shrimp are no longer translucent and are cooked through. Remove shrimp from heat.

Add shrimp to the serving platter in two separate sections.

Add tuna jerky to the platter. Add the can of smoked salmon to the platter.

Place Sea-Chi, olives, and capers in separate small bowls and add to the platter.

Remove cheese spread from packaging and add to platter or place onto a small plate or in a small bowl. Surround with crackers.

Add additional crackers to any empty spots on seacuterie board. Add serving utensils to the platter. Serve.

Nutrition Facts per Serving **Calories:** 229 / **Total fat:** 13g (17% DV) / **Saturated fat:** 6.5g (33% DV) / **Trans fat:** 0g / **Cholesterol:** 91mg (30% DV) / **Sodium:** 638mg (28% DV) / **Total carbohydrate:** 10g (4% DV) / **Dietary fiber:** 0.5g (2% DV) / **Total sugars:** 1g / **Added sugar:** 0g (0% DV) / **Protein:** 18.5g / **Vitamin D:** 2.5mcg (13% DV) / **Calcium:** 65mg (5% DV) / **Iron:** 1mg (6% DV) / **Potassium:** 256.5mg (5% DV)

Serves: 6
Course: Appetizer
Total time: 30 minutes

INGREDIENTS

For the cranberry mignonette:

2 tbsp	white wine vinegar
2 tbsp	prosecco, or cava dry sparkling wine
1 tbsp	minced shallot
1 tbsp	finely chopped cranberries
¼ tsp	sugar
¼ tsp	ground black pepper

For the cranberry cocktail sauce:

½ cup	cocktail sauce
¼ cup	frozen cranberries
½	lime, juice of
¼ tsp	kosher salt
¼ tsp	ground black pepper

For the seared scallops:

½ lb	sea scallops
⅛ tsp	ground black pepper
1 tsp	salted butter
½ tsp	olive oil

Assembly:

½ lb	cooked shrimp, chilled
6–8	raw oysters, shucked, kept very cold on ice
½ cup	cranberry chutney
¼ cup	olives (we like Castelvetrano olives)
2 tbsp	capers, drained
½ cup	herb-and-garlic cheese spread
3 oz	crackers of your choice
1	lime, cut into wedges
	Rosemary sprigs (for decoration)

Cranberry Seacuterie Board

Oysters on the half shell with a cranberry mignonette, shrimp cocktail with a cranberry cocktail sauce, seared sea scallops with a cranberry chutney, olives, capers, a garlic-and-herb cheese spread, and an assortment of crackers make up this beautiful seacuterie board. This seafood platter would be a stunning appetizer at any of your autumn or holiday gatherings.

INSTRUCTIONS

For the cranberry mignonette: Whisk together the white wine vinegar, sparkling wine, shallot, cranberries, sugar, and black pepper. Pour into a small serving bowl.

For the cranberry cocktail sauce: Add cocktail sauce, cranberries, lime juice, salt, and black pepper to a food processor. Pulse a few times until combined but still a bit chunky. Pour into a small serving bowl.

For the seared scallops: Make sure scallops are patted dry and their tough side muscles are removed. Season them with pepper on both sides. Heat a nonstick pan over medium high heat. Add the butter and oil. Once hot, add the scallops. Sear for 1–2 minutes on each side until desired doneness.

Assembly: Place Himalayan salt (or crushed ice) on a large serving platter. Add the seared scallops, oysters, and shrimp onto the platter in three separate sections. If using ice, place cooked scallops onto a small plate atop the platter to prevent them from cooling quickly.

Place the cranberry chutney in a small serving bowl and nestle next to the scallops. Place the mignonette next to the oysters and nestle the cranberry cocktail sauce next to the shrimp.

Place the olives and capers into small bowls and nestle onto the platter in an open spot. Place the cheese spread into a small bowl and nestle in any free space. Add crackers where room allows.

Add lime wedges around the platter. Fill any openings with rosemary sprigs. Add small spoons and knives as needed for serving.

Serve platter with glasses of dry sparkling wine or rosé.

Nutrition Facts per Serving **Calories:** 296 / **Total fat:** 10.5g (14% DV) / **Saturated fat:** 4g (19% DV) / **Trans fat:** 0g / **Cholesterol:** 100mg (33% DV) / **Sodium:** 1,024mg (45% DV) / **Total carbohydrate:** 31g (11% DV) / **Dietary fiber:** 2g (6% DV) / **Total sugars:** 16g / **Added sugar:** 11.5g (23% DV) / **Protein:** 19.5g / **Vitamin D:** 0mcg (0% DV) / **Calcium:** 259mg (20% DV) / **Iron:** 2mg (12% DV) / **Potassium:** 364mg (8% DV)

Christmas Seafood Platter

This seafood tree's shape is created with sprigs of fresh rosemary. Then it's filled (starting at the bottom) with oysters on the half shell, cranberries, lemon rings (or wedges), cooked shrimp, seaweed salad, Cape bay scallops, canned smoked salmon, and cooked lobster. The tree trunk is made of tuna jerky. Capers fill in some of the holes in the tree. Alongside this seafood board is melted butter (for the lobster), cocktail sauce (for the shrimp), and flaky sea salt.

Serves: 6
Course: Appetizer
Total time: 10 minutes

INGREDIENTS

	Rosemary sprigs (decor)
1 stick	tuna jerky (we love Pescavore)
12	oysters, shucked
	Cranberries (decor)
1	lemon, cut into rings or wedges
½ lb	cooked shrimp, any size
½ cup	seaweed salad (we prefer Atlantic Sea Farms Seaweed Salad)
½ lb	Cape bay scallops
1 (3.5-oz) can	smoked salmon
½ lb	cooked lobster meat
¼ cup	capers
2 tbsp	salted butter, melted
¼ cup	cocktail sauce
	Sea salt

INSTRUCTIONS

Using rosemary sprigs, create a tree shape on a large platter or baking sheet. Place tuna jerky at the base and layer the other ingredients up the tree.

Place butter and cocktail sauce on the platter outside the tree.

Add serving utensils and serve immediately.

RECIPE NOTES:

• When shucking the oysters, inspect for any damaged shells or off smells.

• Replenish ice-cold oysters as needed (they may not all fit at the bottom of your tree).

• Adjust amounts of seafood depending on the number of guests, and replenish platter as needed.

Nutrition Facts per Serving **Calories:** 210 / **Total fat:** 7.5g (9% DV) / **Saturated fat:** 3.5g (18% DV) / **Trans fat:** 0g / **Cholesterol:** 160mg (53% DV) / **Sodium:** 909.5mg (40% DV) / **Total carbohydrate:** 7g (3% DV) / **Dietary fiber:** 1g (4% DV) / **Total sugars:** 3g / **Added sugar:** 2g (5% DV) / **Protein:** 29g / **Vitamin D:** 1.5mcg (7% DV) / **Calcium:** 98mg (8% DV) / **Iron:** 2.5mg (14% DV) / **Potassium:** 444mg (9% DV)

Seafood Wreath

A festive holiday seafood wreath made with a base of crispy lettuce, sautéed sea scallops, sautéed bay scallops, cooked shrimp, cooked fresh lobster meat, seaweed salad, melted butter, cocktail sauce, and lemon wedges. This wreath is the perfect holiday appetizer–or serve it for dinner alongside a festive salad and warm crusty bread.

Serves: 4-6
Course: Appetizer
Total time: 10 minutes

INGREDIENTS

2 cups	crispy green little-leaf lettuce
½ lb	cooked lobster meat
½ lb	cooked shrimp (any size)
¼ lb	seared bay scallops
¼ lb	seared sea scallops
½ cup	seaweed salad (we prefer Atlantic Sea Farms Seaweed Salad), placed in a small bowl
¼ cup	salted butter, melted, placed in a small bowl
¼ cup	cocktail sauce, placed in a small bowl
1	lemon, cut into wedges
	Salt
	Freshly ground black pepper

For decoration (optional):

Rosemary sprigs or any green herbs—thyme, sage, oregano, or parsley would all work well

INSTRUCTIONS

Arrange lettuce leaves in a circle on the outer part of a circular serving plate, leaving the center of the circle open.

Arrange seafood on the lettuce, leaving four small spaces to fit the seaweed salad, melted butter, cocktail sauce, and lemon wedges.

Place seaweed salad, butter, cocktail sauce, and lemon in the open spaces.

Add fresh herbs around the outside of the seafood wreath.

Sprinkle seafood with salt and freshly ground black pepper. Serve.

Nutrition Facts per Serving **Calories:** 209 / **Total fat:** 9g (12% DV) / **Saturated fat:** 5g (26% DV) / **Trans fat:** 0g / **Cholesterol:** 162mg (54% DV) / **Sodium:** 754mg (33% DV) / **Total carbohydrate:** 7.5g (3% DV) / **Dietary fiber:** 1g (4% DV) / **Total sugars:** 3g / **Added sugar:** 2g (5% DV) / **Protein:** 25g / **Vitamin D:** 0mcg (0% DV) / **Calcium:** 84mg (6% DV) / **Iron:** 1mg (6% DV) / **Potassium:** 413mg (9% DV)

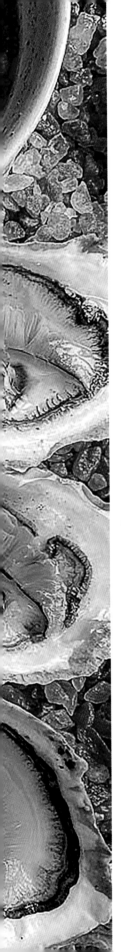

Seafood Sauces and Condiments

In this chapter you'll find some fantastic sauces and condiments that we love using on seafood—from mignonettes to butters to cocktail sauce to tzatziki—some traditional and others a bit more unexpected. All are simple to make and elevate any seafood dish.

Tartar Sauce

This homemade tartar sauce can be whipped up in minutes and goes really nicely with most any crunchy baked fish–especially our Baked Fish Bites (see page 144). We use kelp pickles in this recipe (which are fun to eat and so tasty!), but you can use any dill or bread-and-butter pickles of your choosing. Also, modify the level of spiciness here to your liking by adjusting the amount of hot sauce.

Makes: About ¾ cup
Serves: 6
Serving size: 2 tablespoons
Course: Condiments
Total time: 5 minutes

INGREDIENTS

½ cup	reduced-fat mayonnaise
¼ cup	kelp pickles (we love Barnacle Foods Kelp Dill Pickles), chopped, or use regular dill pickles
1 tbsp	chopped fresh dill
1 tsp	fresh lemon juice
½–1 tsp	kelp hot sauce (we love Barnacle Foods Kelp Hot Sauce), or your favorite hot sauce
⅛ tsp	garlic powder
¼ tsp	freshly ground black pepper

INSTRUCTIONS

Combine all ingredients in a small bowl. Mix well. Add additional hot sauce, if desired, and season with salt and pepper, if needed.

Nutrition Facts per Serving **Calories:** 45 / **Total fat:** 3.6g (5% DV) / **Saturated fat:** 0.6g (3% DV) / **Trans fat:** 0.0g / **Cholesterol:** 4mg (1% DV) / **Sodium:** 32mg (1% DV) / **Total carbohydrate:** 3.4g (1% DV) / **Dietary fiber:** 0.1g (0% DV) / **Total sugars:** 0.9g / **Added sugar:** 0.8g (2% DV) / **Protein:** 0.1g / **Vitamin D:** 0.0mcg (0% DV) / **Calcium:** 4mg (0% DV) / **Iron:** 0.0mg (0% DV) / **Potassium:** 14mg (0% DV)

Cocktail Sauce

There are many great bottled cocktail sauces available on your grocer's shelves, but if you have a few minutes to spare, try this homemade version–you'll be glad you did. And you can adjust the ingredients to your liking.

Makes: About ¾ cup
Serves: 6
Serving size: 2 tablespoons
Course: Condiments
Total time: 5 minutes

INGREDIENTS

½ cup	ketchup
3 tbsp	prepared horseradish
2 tbsp	fresh lemon juice
1 tbsp	Worcestershire sauce
½ tsp	kelp hot sauce (we love Barnacle Foods Kelp Hot Sauce), or any hot sauce
½ tsp	garlic powder
¼ tsp	freshly ground black pepper

INSTRUCTIONS

Combine ketchup, horseradish, lemon juice, Worcestershire sauce, kelp hot sauce, garlic powder, and black pepper. Stir well to combine. Add more hot sauce, to taste, if desired.

Nutrition Facts per Serving **Calories:** 28 / **Total fat:** 0.1g (0% DV) / **Saturated fat:** 0.0g (0% DV) / **Trans fat:** 0.0g / **Cholesterol:** 0mg (0% DV) / **Sodium:** 261mg (11% DV) / **Total carbohydrate:** 7.4g (3% DV) / **Dietary fiber:** 0.3g (1% DV) / **Total sugars:** 5.0g / **Added sugar:** 4.2g (8% DV) / **Protein:** 0.4g / **Vitamin D:** 0.0mcg (0% DV) / **Calcium:** 11mg (1% DV) / **Iron:** 0.3mg (2% DV) / **Potassium:** 107mg (2% DV)

Compound Butter for Seafood Three Ways

Garlic-and-herb butter. Citrus butter. Old Bay butter. All three of these simple compound butters elevate any fish or shellfish dish into something fancier, more luxurious, and more flavorful. A little bit of this butter goes a long way and adds a ton of flavor.

After preparing your fish or shellfish with minimal seasoning, try:

- Adding a pat of compound butter atop hot sautéed, grilled, or baked fish fillets
- Melting and drizzling over clams or mussels
- Melting and serving with lobster, shrimp, scallops, crab, and more
- Placing small dollops on grilled oysters

And don't stop at seafood–these butters are great spread on veggies, bread, and potatoes too!

Garlic Herb Butter

Makes: 1 stick compound butter
Serves: 8
Serving size: 1 tablespoon
Course: Condiments
Total time: 5 minutes

INGREDIENTS

1 stick	unsalted butter, softened
¼ cup	loosely packed fresh basil leaves, finely chopped
¼ cup	loosely packed fresh parsley leaves, finely chopped
1 clove	garlic, minced
½ tsp	kosher salt

INSTRUCTIONS

Mix all ingredients together until well combined. Place on a piece of parchment paper in a log shape. Roll up parchment (as you would a burrito), securing the ends by twisting parchment together. Refrigerate until ready to serve/use.

Nutrition Facts per Serving **Calories:** 103 / **Total fat:** 11.5g (15% DV) / **Saturated fat:** 7.2g (36% DV) / **Trans fat:** 0.5g / **Cholesterol:** 31mg (10% DV) / **Sodium:** 149mg (6% DV) / **Total carbohydrate:** 0.3g (0% DV) / **Dietary fiber:** 0.1g (0% DV) / **Total sugars:** 0.0g / **Added sugar:** 0.0g (0% DV) / **Protein:** 0.2g / **Vitamin D:** 0.0mcg (0% DV) / **Calcium:** 9mg (1% DV) / **Iron:** 0.2mg (1% DV) / **Potassium:** 19mg (0% DV)

Citrus Butter

Makes: 1 stick compound butter
Serves: 8
Serving size: 1 tablespoon
Course: Condiments
Total time: 5 minutes

INGREDIENTS

1 stick	unsalted butter, softened
	Zest of 1 lime (or lemon), plus juice of ½ the lime (or lemon)
½ tsp	kosher salt

INSTRUCTIONS

Mix all ingredients together until well combined. Place on a piece of parchment paper in a log shape. Roll up parchment (as you would a burrito), securing the ends by twisting parchment together. Refrigerate until ready to serve/use.

RECIPE NOTE: If you prefer less of a citrus kick and want a subtler flavor, use less citrus juice, or even omit it and just use the zest.

Nutrition Facts per Serving **Calories:** 102 / **Total fat:** 11.5g (15% DV) / **Saturated fat:** 7.2g (36% DV) / **Trans fat:** 0.5g / **Cholesterol:** 31mg (10% DV) / **Sodium:** 148mg (6% DV) / **Total carbohydrate:** 0.2g (0% DV) / **Dietary fiber:** 0.0g (0% DV) / **Total sugars:** 0.1g / **Added sugar:** 0.0g (0% DV) / **Protein:** 0.1g / **Vitamin D:** 0.0mcg (0% DV) / **Calcium:** 4mg (0% DV) / **Iron:** 0.0mg (0% DV) / **Potassium:** 7mg (0% DV)

Old Bay Butter

Makes: 1 stick compound butter
Serves: 8
Serving size: 1 tablespoon
Course: Condiments
Total time: 5 minutes

INGREDIENTS

1 stick   unsalted butter, softened

1½ tsp   Old Bay Seasoning

INSTRUCTIONS

Mix all ingredients together until well combined. Place on a piece of parchment paper in a log shape. Roll up parchment (as you would a burrito), securing the ends by twisting parchment together. Refrigerate until ready to serve/use.

Nutrition Facts per Serving **Calories:** 102 / **Total fat:** 11.5g (15% DV) / **Saturated fat:** 7.2g (36% DV) / **Trans fat:** 0.5g / **Cholesterol:** 31mg (10% DV) / **Sodium:** 133mg (6% DV) / **Total carbohydrate:** 0.0g (0% DV) / **Dietary fiber:** 0.0g (0% DV) / **Total sugars:** 0.0g / **Added sugar:** 0.0g (0% DV) / **Protein:** 0.1g / **Vitamin D:** 0.0mcg (0% DV) / **Calcium:** 4mg (0% DV) / **Iron:** 0.0mg (0% DV) / **Potassium:** 3mg (0% DV)

Sparkling Mignonette

We love oysters with lemon wedges and a mignonette. A mignonette sounds fancy, but it's not. Traditional mignonettes combine vinegar, shallots, and black pepper. This champagne mignonette combines white wine vinegar, a splash of champagne (getting a tad bit fancy here!), shallot, parsley, and black pepper.

Makes: ¼ cup, enough for 1 dozen oysters
Serves: 4
Course: Sauces and dressings
Total time: 5 minutes

INGREDIENTS

2 tbsp	white wine or prosecco vinegar
2 tbsp	dry champagne, prosecco, or cava sparkling wine
1 tbsp	minced shallot
1 tsp	chopped fresh parsley
¼ tsp	freshly ground black pepper

INSTRUCTIONS

Combine vinegar, sparkling wine, shallot, parsley, and pepper in a small bowl. Serve with freshly shucked oysters.

RECIPE NOTE: To make a basic mignonette, omit the sparkling wine and add 2 additional tablespoons white wine vinegar.

Nutrition Facts per Serving **Calories:** 9 / **Total fat:** 0.0g (0% DV) / **Saturated fat:** 0.0g (0% DV) / **Trans fat:** 0.0g / **Cholesterol:** 0mg (0% DV) / **Sodium:** 1mg (0% DV) / **Total carbohydrate:** 0.7g (0% DV) / **Dietary fiber:** 0.1g (0% DV) / **Total sugars:** 0.3g / **Added sugar:** 0.0g (0% DV) / **Protein:** 0.1g / **Vitamin D:** 0.0mcg (0% DV) / **Calcium:** 2mg (0% DV) / **Iron:** 0.1mg (1% DV) / **Potassium:** 18mg (0% DV)

Cranberry Mignonette

This gorgeous, tart, and slightly sweet mignonette is perfect for serving with oysters any time of year, but especially during the holiday season. The addition of sparkling wine and cranberry makes this mignonette truly celebratory.

Makes: ¼ cup, enough for 1 dozen oysters
Serves: 4
Course: Sauces and dressings
Total time: 5 minutes

INGREDIENTS

2 tbsp	white wine vinegar
2 tbsp	champagne, prosecco, or cava dry sparkling wine
1 tbsp	minced shallot
1 tbsp	finely chopped cranberries
¼ tsp	sugar
¼ tsp	freshly ground black pepper

INSTRUCTIONS

Whisk together the white wine vinegar, sparkling wine, shallot, cranberries, sugar, and black pepper. Pour into a small serving bowl. Serve with oysters on the half shell.

Nutrition Facts per Serving **Calories:** 11 / **Total fat:** 0.0g (0% DV) / **Saturated fat:** 0.0g (0% DV) / **Trans fat:** 0.0g / **Cholesterol:** 0mg (0% DV) / **Sodium:** 1mg (0% DV) / **Total carbohydrate:** 1.1g (0% DV) / **Dietary fiber:** 0.1g (1% DV) / **Total sugars:** 0.6g / **Added sugar:** 0.3g (1% DV) / **Protein:** 0.1g / **Vitamin D:** 0.0mcg (0% DV) / **Calcium:** 2mg (0% DV) / **Iron:** 0.1mg (0% DV) / **Potassium:** 18mg (0% DV)

Cranberry Cocktail Sauce

This unique cranberry cocktail sauce is tart and tangy–perfect for serving as part of your favorite seafood platter or just swapped out for regular cocktail sauce on a shrimp cocktail platter. Whip it up in minutes in your food processor.

Makes: Approximately ¾ cup
Serves: 6
Serving size: 2 tablespoons
Course: Sauces and dressings
Total time: 5 minutes

INGREDIENTS

½ **cup**	cocktail sauce
¼ **cup**	frozen cranberries
	Juice of ½ lime
⅛ **tsp**	kosher salt
¼ **tsp**	freshly ground black pepper

INSTRUCTIONS

Add cocktail sauce, cranberries, lime juice, salt, and black pepper to a food processor. Pulse a few times until combined but still a bit chunky. Pour into a small serving bowl.

Nutrition Facts per Serving **Calories:** 28 / **Total fat:** 0.0g (0% DV) / **Saturated fat:** 0.0g (0% DV) / **Trans fat:** 0.0g / **Cholesterol:** 0mg (0% DV) / **Sodium:** 272mg (12% DV) / **Total carbohydrate:** 7.2g (2% DV) / **Dietary fiber:** 0.4g (1% DV) / **Total sugars:** 5.4g / **Added sugar:** 4.4g (8% DV) / **Protein:** 0.2g / **Vitamin D:** 0.0mcg (0% DV) / **Calcium:** 6mg (0% DV) / **Iron:** 0.2mg (1% DV) / **Potassium:** 70mg (2% DV)

Chimichurri Sauce

Chimichurri is an oil-based Argentinean sauce made with lots of fresh herbs, shallots, and garlic. It's typically served with grilled meats and is fresh, bright, and tangy. We love it on seafood (scallops, salmon, white fish, and shrimp), grilled veggies–and I love to soak up the sauce with bread or rice.

Makes: Approximately 1½ cups
Serves: 12
Serving size: 2 tablespoons
Total time: 5 minutes

INGREDIENTS

2 cups	loosely packed flat-leaf parsley
¼ cup	loosely packed oregano leaves
¼ cup	red wine vinegar
1	shallot, finely minced
2 cloves	garlic, finely minced
½ tsp	red pepper flakes
¼ tsp	kosher salt
⅛ tsp	freshly ground black pepper
¾ cup	extra-virgin olive oil

INSTRUCTIONS

Finely chop parsley and oregano. Add to a small bowl.

Add red wine vinegar, shallot, garlic, red pepper flakes, salt, and pepper. Whisk together. Slowly whisk in olive oil. Season with additional salt and pepper, if needed. Serve.

RECIPE NOTES:

• Chimichurri will keep in a tightly sealed container in the fridge for at least three days.

• If you don't have shallot, use ¹⁄₄ of a red onion.

Nutrition Facts per Serving **Calories:** 130 /
Total fat: 13.7g (18% DV) / **Saturated fat:** 1.9g (10% DV) / **Trans fat:** 0.0g / **Cholesterol:** 0mg (0% DV) / **Sodium:** 56mg (2% DV) / **Total carbohydrate:** 2.1g (1% DV) / **Dietary fiber:** 1.1g (4% DV) / **Total sugars:** 0.2g / **Added sugar:** 0.0g (0% DV) / **Protein:** 0.5g / **Vitamin D:** 0.0mcg (0% DV) / **Calcium:** 44mg (3% DV) / **Iron:** 1.4mg (8% DV) / **Potassium:** 85mg (2% DV)

Quick Pickled Red Onions

These easy pickled onions are a must on any fish tacos–they add crunch, tang, and brightness. We also love them on sandwiches, in power or poke bowls, and atop salads. They are a staple in our fridge, and we make a batch weekly so we are never without.

Makes: Approximately 2 cups
Serves: About 32
Serving size: 1 tablespoon
Course: Condiments
Chill time: 8 hours or overnight
Total time: 8 hours, 5 minutes

INGREDIENTS

1	red onion, thinly sliced
½ cup	seasoned rice vinegar
1 tsp	sugar
½ tsp	kosher salt

INSTRUCTIONS

Combine red onion, vinegar, sugar, and salt in a glass container. Mix well. Cover and refrigerate for at least 8 hours or overnight, stirring it a couple times over the course of the chill time (if you can and if you remember!). Keeps for at least 3 days in the fridge.

Nutrition Facts per Serving **Calories:** 3 / **Total fat:** 0.0g (0% DV) / **Saturated fat:** 0.0g (0% DV) / **Trans fat:** 0.0g / **Cholesterol:** 0mg (0% DV) / **Sodium:** 37mg (2% DV) / **Total carbohydrate:** 0.5g (0% DV) / **Dietary fiber:** 0.1g (0% DV) / **Total sugars:** 0.3g / **Added sugar:** 0.1g (0% DV) / **Protein:** 0.0g / **Vitamin D:** 0.0mcg (0% DV) / **Calcium:** 1mg (0% DV) / **Iron:** 0.0mg (0% DV) / **Potassium:** 5mg (0% DV)

Tzatziki Sauce

Tzatziki is a creamy yogurt sauce (or dip) made with cucumbers, garlic, and dill. It's fresh, tangy, garlicky, and delicious. We love spooning it atop our salmon burgers (see page 158) or any simply prepared fish, using it as a dip for veggies, or serving it with toasted pita bread.

Makes: Approximately 2 cups
Serves: About 16
Serving size: 2 tablespoons
Course: Sauces and dressings
Total time: 10 minutes

INGREDIENTS

1 medium	cucumber, peeled, halved, seeded
12 oz	plain whole-milk Greek yogurt
¼ cup	finely chopped fresh dill
4 cloves	garlic, finely minced
1 tsp	extra-virgin olive oil
	Juice of ½ lemon
¼ tsp	salt
¼ tsp	ground black pepper

INSTRUCTIONS

Grate the cucumber with a hand grater. Wrap cucumber in a cheesecloth, squeezing out as much liquid as possible. Alternatively, place cucumber into a fine mesh strainer to drain and press the liquid out.

In a medium mixing bowl, combine yogurt, dill, garlic, olive oil, lemon juice, salt, and black pepper. Mix well. Add cucumber. Mix gently to combine. Add more salt and pepper to taste, if needed. Chill until ready to serve.

RECIPE NOTE: Be sure to strain the cucumber well to remove as much liquid as possible so your tzatziki isn't watery.

Nutrition Facts per Serving **Calories:** 23 / **Total fat:** 1.2g (1% DV) / **Saturated fat:** 0.6g (3% DV) / **Trans fat:** 0.0g / **Cholesterol:** 3mg (1% DV) / **Sodium:** 45mg (2% DV) / **Total carbohydrate:** 1.3g (0% DV) / **Dietary fiber:** 0.1g (0% DV) / **Total sugars:** 0.9g / **Added sugar:** 0.0g (0% DV) / **Protein:** 2.0g / **Vitamin D:** 0.0mcg (0% DV) / **Calcium:** 27mg (2% DV) / **Iron:** 0.1mg (0% DV) / **Potassium:** 52mg (1% DV)

Non-Seafood Appetizers, Side Dishes, and Salads

In this chapter you'll find some of our favorite appetizers, side dishes, and salads that we've made throughout the years—many of them packed with nutrient-rich veggies. These recipes complement the many different seafood dishes throughout this book.

Summer Panzanella Salad with Burrata

Hearty chunks of crisp, buttery bread tossed with fresh juicy garden tomatoes, baby crisp green-leaf lettuce, tangy red onion, sweet basil, and a garlicky balsamic vinaigrette topped with burrata. This salad is pure summer bliss in a bowl. Once those summer tomatoes start ripening in your garden (or on your patio, or at the farmers' market), save this salad a spot at your table. You'll be very happy you did.

Serves: 4
Course: Salad
Total time: 50 minutes

INGREDIENTS

1	baguette torn into about 1-inch cubes
2 tbsp	extra-virgin olive oil
¼ tsp	kosher salt, divided
⅛ tsp	ground black pepper
1 pint	cherry or grape tomatoes, halved
½ small	red onion, thinly sliced
2 oz	baby green leaf lettuce
½ cup	basil leaves, slivered or torn
8 oz	burrata (we buy a container that has 4 2-oz balls of burrata)

For the dressing:

¼ cup	extra-virgin olive oil
¼ cup	balsamic vinegar or white balsamic
2 cloves	garlic, minced
¼ tsp	kosher salt
⅛ tsp	ground black pepper

INSTRUCTIONS

Preheat oven (or toaster oven) to 300°F. Toss bread cubes with 2 tablespoons extra-virgin olive oil, ⅛ teaspoon salt, and pepper. Place bread cubes onto a baking sheet. Bake for 20 minutes, until crisp but still light in color), flipping halfway through cooking time. Remove from oven and let cool.

Meanwhile, add tomatoes to a large mixing bowl and sprinkle with remaining ⅛ teaspoon salt. Whisk together salad dressing ingredients. Pour dressing over tomatoes, add red onion, and toss.

Add cooled bread cubes and toss again. Set aside for a few minutes, at room temperature, to let the flavors meld and for the bread to soak up some of the tomato juices and vinaigrette and soften a bit.

When ready to serve, add lettuce and basil. Toss gently. Season with salt and pepper, if needed.

Add panzanella to bowls or plates and top each serving with burrata. Serve.

RECIPE NOTE: Burrata is cream-filled mozzarella that you can find in the cheese section of your local grocery store, near the mozzarella.

Nutrition Facts per Serving **Calories:** 465 / **Total fat:** 33.5g (44% DV) / **Saturated fat:** 11g (55% DV) / **Trans fat:** 0.0g / **Cholesterol:** 40mg (14% DV) / **Sodium:** 801mg (36% DV) / **Total carbohydrate:** 30.4g (12% DV) / **Dietary fiber:** 2.5g (9% DV) / **Total sugars:** 7.4g / **Added sugar:** 0g (0% DV) / **Protein:** 8.6g / **Vitamin D:** 0mcg (0% DV) / **Calcium:** 215mg (16% DV) / **Iron:** 2.3mg (13% DV) / **Potassium:** 376mg (8% DV)

Black Lentils with Tomatoes

An incredibly simple yet delicious combination of black beluga lentils, roasted tomatoes with garlic, pesto, and creamy mozzarella. This flavorful, protein-packed dish is perfect as a vegetarian main dish or a side dish.

Serves: 6
Course: Side dish or main course
Total time: 1 hour, 5 minutes

INGREDIENTS

For the roasted tomatoes:

2 pints	multicolored grape or cherry tomatoes
5 cloves	garlic, smashed
¼ cup	extra-virgin olive oil
¼ tsp	ground black pepper

For the lentils:

1 cup	black beluga lentils, rinsed and picked over

For serving:

¼ cup	homemade or store-bought pesto
4 oz	mini mozzarella balls
¼ cup	chopped parsley (optional)

INSTRUCTIONS

Preheat oven to 375°F.

Add tomatoes, garlic, olive oil, and pepper to a large baking or roasting dish. Roast for 1 hour, stirring occasionally. Remove from oven.

Meanwhile, bring 4 cups of water to a boil over medium high heat in a medium pot. Once boiling, add lentils and reduce heat to a simmer. Simmer lentils until tender, about 20 minutes. Drain.

Add lentils to tomatoes and stir to combine. Top dish with pesto, mozzarella, and parsley. Serve.

Nutrition Facts per Serving **Calories:** 290 / **Total fat:** 17.5g (22% DV) / **Saturated fat:** 4.1g (20% DV) / **Trans fat:** 0.2g / **Cholesterol:** 13mg (4% DV) / **Sodium:** 232mg (10% DV) / **Total carbohydrate:** 21.5g (8% DV) / **Dietary fiber:** 5.8g (21% DV) / **Total sugars:** 1.8g / **Added sugar:** 0.0g (0% DV) / **Protein:** 13.5g / **Vitamin D:** 0.1mcg (0% DV) / **Calcium:** 175mg (13% DV) / **Iron:** 3.3mg (18% DV) / **Potassium:** 481mg (10% DV)

Creamy Burrata with Pesto and Tomatoes

Creamy burrata topped with pesto, halved multicolored cherry or grape tomatoes, freshly ground black pepper, sea salt, and a drizzle of balsamic glaze. A simple, gorgeous, and fresh appetizer to celebrate all the summer flavors. In fact, this might be the only summer appetizer you will ever need.

Serves: 6
Course: Appetizer
Total time: 5 minutes

INGREDIENTS

6–8 oz	burrata
¼ cup	pesto, prepared or homemade
2 cups	cherry or grape tomatoes, halved
	Sea salt, to taste
	Freshly ground black pepper, to taste
1 tbsp	balsamic glaze or balsamic vinegar (optional)

For serving:

½	baguette, sliced and toasted, or whole-grain crackers

INSTRUCTIONS

Place burrata on a small serving plate. Top with pesto and spread the rest of the pesto around the burrata. Add halved tomatoes, sea salt, and freshly ground pepper. Drizzle with balsamic vinegar or balsamic glaze, if desired. Serve with whole-grain crackers or toasted baguette slices.

RECIPE NOTES:

• Burrata is cream-filled mozzarella that you can find in the cheese section of your local grocery store, near the mozzarella.

• To make a quick pesto: Add a bunch of fresh basil, $^1/_4$ cup pine nuts, $^1/_4$ cup shaved Parmesan cheese, and 2 cloves garlic to a food processor. While blending, drizzle in about $^1/_4$-$^1/_2$ cup of extra-virgin olive oil, more if needed. Process until smooth. Add salt and pepper to taste.

Nutrition Facts per Serving **Calories:** 123 / **Total fat:** 10.4g (14% DV) / **Saturated fat:** 4.7g (23% DV) / **Trans fat:** 0.0g / **Cholesterol:** 21mg (7% DV) / **Sodium:** 165mg (8% DV) / **Total carbohydrate:** 3.8g (1% DV) / **Dietary fiber:** .8g (3% DV) / **Total sugars:** 1.7g / **Added sugar:** 0.0g (0% DV) / **Protein:** 4.1g / **Vitamin D:** 0.0mcg (0% DV) / **Calcium:** 104mg (8% DV) / **Iron:** 0.3mg (2% DV) / **Potassium:** 163mg (3% DV)

Panfried Chickpeas with Fresh Herbs

Chickpeas panfried until crispy then sprinkled with sea salt and fresh herbs, like cilantro, parsley, and mint—or whatever herbs you have on hand. This is a fun and flavorful way to jazz up a plain (and boring!) can of chickpeas.

Serves: 4
Course: Side dish
Total time: 10 minutes

INGREDIENTS

1 tsp	olive oil
1 (15.5-oz) can	chickpeas, drained and rinsed
½ tsp	sea salt
⅛ tsp	ground black pepper
2 tbsp	chopped parsley leaves
2 tbsp	chopped cilantro leaves
2 tbsp	chopped mint leaves
2	scallions, white and green parts, thinly sliced

INSTRUCTIONS

Heat olive oil in a skillet over medium high heat. When hot, add chickpeas and panfry, tossing often, for about 5 minutes until they begin to toast and get lightly browned. Remove from heat.

Toss immediately with sea salt and pepper. Place into serving bowl and toss with fresh herbs (dry the herbs well prior to tossing). Serve.

RECIPE NOTES:

• For this recipe, use any fresh herbs you have on hand. And if you only have one herb, use it (just parsley, just basil, just cilantro, just scallions or chives, etc.).

• Make sure to dry fresh herbs very well. This will ensure that the chickpeas stay crispy and don't get soggy.

Nutrition Facts per Serving **Calories:** 111 / **Total fat:** 3.1g (4% DV) / **Saturated fat:** 0.3g (2% DV) / **Trans fat:** 0.0g / **Cholesterol:** 0mg (0% DV) / **Sodium:** 298mg (13% DV) / **Total carbohydrate:** 16.6g (6% DV) / **Dietary fiber:** 4.8g (21% DV) / **Total sugars:** 3.1g / **Added sugar:** 0.0g (0% DV) / **Protein:** 5.2g / **Vitamin D:** 0.0mcg (0% DV) / **Calcium:** 42mg (3% DV) / **Iron:** 1.0mg (5% DV) / **Potassium:** 115mg (2% DV)

Roasted Cauliflower Caprese Casserole

Cauliflower is roasted with garlic and tomatoes, then tossed with fresh mozzarella and seasoned panko crumbs, then baked again for a few more minutes before being topped with fresh basil and parsley. This is a very simple but incredible side dish that the whole family will love.

Serves: 4
Course: Side dish
Total time: 55 minutes

INGREDIENTS

1 small head	cauliflower, broken into florets
2 tbsp	extra-virgin olive oil
¼ tsp	garlic salt
⅛ tsp	ground black pepper
1¼ pints	grape tomatoes
3 cloves	garlic, sliced
8 oz	mini mozzarella balls
¾ cup	seasoned panko crumbs
5 leaves	basil, torn
2 tbsp	chopped parsley

INSTRUCTIONS

Preheat oven to 425°F. Spray a casserole dish with cooking spray.

Toss cauliflower with extra-virgin olive oil, garlic salt, and black pepper and add to casserole dish. Roast for 25 minutes, turning veggies halfway through cooking time.

Remove from oven, add tomatoes and garlic, and stir. Roast for another 10 minutes.

Remove from oven, add mozzarella, and stir. Top with panko crumbs. Place back into oven for 5–10 more minutes, until cheese is melted and panko is lightly browned.

Remove from oven. Top with fresh basil and parsley. Serve.

Nutrition Facts per Serving **Calories:** 339 / **Total fat:** 19.4g (25% DV) / **Saturated fat:** 7.7g (38% DV) / **Trans fat:** 0.4g / **Cholesterol:** 36mg (12% DV) / **Sodium:** 611mg (27% DV) / **Total carbohydrate:** 24.3g (9% DV) / **Dietary fiber:** 3.1g (11% DV) / **Total sugars:** 5.3g / **Added sugar:** 1.3g (3% DV) / **Protein:** 18.2g / **Vitamin D:** 0.2mcg (1% DV) / **Calcium:** 461mg (35% DV) / **Iron:** 1.8mg (10% DV) / **Potassium:** 511mg (11% DV)

Jenny and Mimi on Nantucket

Mimi's Potato Salad

My mom has made this potato salad for as long as I can remember. It's the best. Baby gold potatoes tossed with dill, red onion, celery, and chives plus a creamy dressing of yogurt, mayo, white wine vinegar, seasoned salt, and black pepper. It's the perfect lightened-up potato salad addition to your summer picnics or cookouts.

Serves: 8
Course: Side dish
Total time: 2 hours, 35 minutes

INGREDIENTS

1½ lb	baby gold potatoes, scrubbed
¾ cup	whole-milk plain Greek yogurt
½ cup	reduced-fat mayonnaise
2–4 tbsp	white wine vinegar
¾ tsp	seasoned salt
¼ tsp	ground black pepper
½ head	celery, thinly sliced
½	red onion, finely diced
¼ cup	finely chopped dill fronds
3 tbsp	thinly sliced chives

INSTRUCTIONS

Place baby gold potatoes in a large saucepan with enough water to cover them by about 1 inch. Bring water to a simmer over medium heat and simmer potatoes until fork tender, 15–20 minutes. Drain.

While potatoes are cooking, whisk together yogurt, mayonnaise, vinegar, salt, and pepper in a large serving bowl. Adjust dressing to taste.

Once potatoes are cool enough to handle, halve or quarter potatoes (keep skin on) and place into the bowl with the dressing. Toss gently to combine.

Add celery, red onion, dill, and chives. Toss again. Season with salt and pepper, if needed.

Chill for at least 2 hours or overnight. Serve.

Nutrition Facts per Serving **Calories:** 123 / **Total fat:** 3.7g (5% DV) / **Saturated fat:** 1.1g (5% DV) / **Trans fat:** 0.0g / **Cholesterol:** 7mg (2% DV) / **Sodium:** 133mg (6% DV) / **Total carbohydrate:** 18.9g (7% DV) / **Dietary fiber:** 2.0g (7% DV) / **Total sugars:** 2.8g / **Added sugar:** 0.6g (1% DV) / **Protein:** 4.0g / **Vitamin D:** 0.0mcg (0% DV) / **Calcium:** 47mg (4% DV) / **Iron:** 0.9mg (5% DV) / **Potassium:** 471mg (10% DV)

Crispy Brussels Sprouts with Warm Blue Cheese and Bacon

Brussels sprouts tossed with olive oil then roasted until crispy, topped with crumbled blue cheese and crispy bacon, and drizzled with balsamic glaze. This is a hearty, comforting, and wonderfully flavorful winter side dish.

Serves: 4
Course: Side dish
Total time: 35 minutes

INGREDIENTS

1½ lb	brussels sprouts trimmed, halved
1 tbsp	extra-virgin olive oil
¼ tsp	garlic salt
¼ tsp	freshly ground pepper
4 oz	blue cheese, crumbled
3 strips	natural thick-cut reduced-sodium bacon, cooked until crispy, crumbled

For serving (optional):

Balsamic glaze

INSTRUCTIONS

Preheat oven to 425°F. Line a baking sheet with aluminum foil.

Toss brussels sprouts with olive oil, garlic salt, and pepper and place on baking sheet.

Place in oven and roast for 15 minutes, stir, then roast another 10–15 minutes until desired crispness. Remove from oven and place into an oven-safe serving dish. Sprinkle with blue cheese crumbles. Turn on oven broiler.

Place under broiler for 2–3 minutes until blue cheese melts.

Remove from oven, top with crispy bacon, drizzle with balsamic glaze. Serve.

Nutrition Facts per Serving **Calories:** 252 / **Total fat:** 15.8g (20% DV) / **Saturated fat:** 7.1g (36% DV) / **Trans fat:** 0.2g / **Cholesterol:** 31mg (10% DV) / **Sodium:** 521mg (23% DV) / **Total carbohydrate:** 16.1g (6% DV) / **Dietary fiber:** 6.5g (23% DV) / **Total sugars:** 4.0g / **Added sugar:** 0.1g (0% DV) / **Protein:** 15.2g / **Vitamin D:** 0.2mcg (1% DV) / **Calcium:** 222mg (17% DV) / **Iron:** 2.6mg (15% DV) / **Potassium:** 786mg (17% DV)

Smashed Potatoes with Herbs

Small new potatoes, roasted then smashed and tossed with extra-virgin olive oil, herbs, and salt and baked until crispy, golden, and delicious. These smashed potatoes are ridiculously delicious and go well with any fish dish.

Serves: 4
Course: Side dish or appetizer
Total time: 45 minutes

INGREDIENTS

1½ lb small	"peewee" new potatoes
2 tbsp	extra-virgin olive oil
1 tbsp	chopped fresh rosemary
1 tbsp	chopped fresh parsley
¼ tsp	kosher salt
¼ tsp	freshly ground black pepper

INSTRUCTIONS

Preheat oven to 425°F.

Place potatoes on a foil-lined sheet pan and bake for 15 minutes. Remove from oven and smash potatoes with the bottom of a coffee mug or flat-bottomed glass. Drizzle generously with olive oil. Sprinkle with rosemary, parsley, salt, and pepper. Place back into the oven for 20–25 minutes until crispy. Add more salt and pepper if needed.

Serve as a side dish or as an appetizer.

RECIPE NOTE: These potatoes are delicious as is or served with a feta- or yogurt-based dip.

Nutrition Facts per Serving **Calories:** 189 / **Total fat:** 7.0g (9% DV) / **Saturated fat:** 1.0g (5% DV) / **Trans fat:** 0.0g / **Cholesterol:** 0mg (0% DV) / **Sodium:** 161mg (7% DV) / **Total carbohydrate:** 28.3g (11% DV) / **Dietary fiber:** 3.1g (11% DV) / **Total sugars:** 1.6g / **Added sugar:** 0.0g (0% DV) / **Protein:** 3.5g / **Vitamin D:** 0.0mcg (0% DV) / **Calcium:** 24mg (24% DV) / **Iron:** 1.6mg (9% DV) / **Potassium:** 745mg (16% DV)

Easy Roasted Cabbage

This is the side dish we make most often during the cooler weather months. The recipe couldn't be easier–it requires just a few ingredients. The cabbage is completely transformed in the oven, turning buttery and oh-so delicious. Serve alongside any of your favorite fish dishes.

Serves: 4
Course: Side dish
Total time: 40 minutes

INGREDIENTS

1 head	green cabbage, cored, thinly sliced
2 tbsp	extra-virgin olive oil
½ tsp	garlic powder
¼ tsp	kosher salt
¼ tsp	freshly ground black pepper

INSTRUCTIONS

Preheat oven to 425°F. Line a baking sheet with aluminum foil. Add cabbage, drizzle with olive oil. Sprinkle with garlic, salt, and pepper. Toss the cabbage well with your hands or tongs.

Roast cabbage for 30–40 minutes, tossing halfway through cooking time. Remove from oven. Serve.

Nutrition Facts per Serving
Calories: 118 / **Total fat:** 7.0g (9% DV) / **Saturated fat:** 1.0g (5% DV) / **Trans fat:** 0.0g / **Cholesterol:** 0.0mg (0% DV) / **Sodium:** 187mg (8% DV) / **Total carbohydrate:** 13.5g (5% DV) / **Dietary fiber:** 5.1g (18% DV) / **Total sugars:** 7.3g / **Added sugar:** 0.0g (0% DV) / **Protein:** 3.0g / **Vitamin D:** 0.0mcg (0% DV) / **Calcium:** 92mg (7% DV) / **Iron:** 1.1mg (6% DV) / **Potassium:** 391mg (8% DV)

Auntie Lauren's Kale Salad with Roasted Chickpeas

Serves: 4
Course: Salad
Total time: 25 minutes

INGREDIENTS

1 (15.5-oz)

can	low-sodium chickpeas, drained and rinsed
¼ tsp	curry powder
⅛ tsp	kosher salt
10 cups	curly kale

For the dressing:

¼ cup +	
2 tbsp	extra-virgin olive oil
	Juice of 1 small lemon
1 tsp	honey
⅛ tsp	kosher salt
⅛ tsp	black pepper

For serving:

¼ cup	crumbled feta

This simple yet flavorful salad is a regular on my sister Lauren's table. She first served it to her girlfriends while hosting a book club meeting–everyone loved it. Lauren likes the unexpected and protein-packed crunch from the chickpeas, and how the thinly sliced, massaged kale holds the lemony flavor of the dressing so each bite is delicious. She likes to serve this salad alongside simply prepared fish.

INSTRUCTIONS

Preheat oven to 400°F.

Pat chickpeas dry with a paper towel to remove excess liquid. Coat a baking sheet with cooking spray. Put chickpeas in a single layer on the baking sheet.

Sprinkle ¼ teaspoon curry powder and ⅛ teaspoon salt over chickpeas. Stir to combine.

Place in oven and bake for 15–20 minutes, depending on the level of crispness desired, shaking pan halfway through to rotate chickpeas.

Meanwhile, remove thick stems from kale. With a sharp knife, cut the kale into thin ribbons or small pieces by gathering a bunch of kale tightly in one hand and, using the other hand, cutting the kale into thin strips. Place kale into a large bowl. Work in batches until all of the kale has been cut.

Combine olive oil, lemon juice, honey, ⅛ teaspoon salt, and pepper in a mason jar. Seal jar with lid and shake until combined.

Pour dressing over kale and massage the kale with your hands for a few minutes, coating the kale with the dressing.

Sprinkle chickpeas and crumbled feta over kale.

Toss to combine and serve.

Nutrition Facts per Serving **Calories:** 231 / **Total fat:** 23.1g (30% DV) / **Saturated fat:** 4.1g (21% DV) / **Trans fat:** 0.1g / **Cholesterol:** 8mg (3% DV) / **Sodium:** 282mg (12% DV) / **Total carbohydrate:** 5.2g (2% DV) / **Dietary fiber:** 2.5g (9% DV) / **Total sugars:** 2.6g / **Added sugar:** 1.5g (3% DV) / **Protein:** 3.0g / **Vitamin D:** 0.0mcg (0% DV) / **Calcium:** 184mg (14% DV) / **Iron:** 1.1mg (6% DV) / **Potassium:** 205mg (4% DV)

Lauren (left) and Jenny (right) on Cape Cod in the '80s

New England Desserts and Beyond

A great seafood meal should always be followed by an extra-special dessert, don't you think? In this chapter, I've included some longtime favorite recipes that highlight nutrient-rich cranberries, apples, pumpkin, and wild blueberries. You'll also find an easy, nourishing, and incredibly tasty overnight oats breakfast recipe using wild blueberries.

These stunning photos were taken at one of Cape Cod Select's cranberry bogs in southeastern Massachusetts. Cape Cod Select is owned by the Rhodes family, who have been harvesting cranberries for over seventy years.

Cranberry and Apple Baked Brie

Diced apples, tart cranberries, pure maple syrup, and cinnamon are warmed in the oven with a wedge of Brie cheese, until the Brie is melted and ooey-gooey and the fruit is softened and sweet. The perfect fall or holiday appetizer or dessert!

Serves: 4-6
Course: Appetizer or dessert
Total time: 30 minutes

INGREDIENTS

8 oz	Brie cheese
1 small	apple, diced
¾ cup	fresh cranberries, picked over
¼ cup	pure maple syrup
½ tsp	ground cinnamon
⅛ tsp	sea salt

For serving:

Apple slices

Whole-grain crackers

INSTRUCTIONS

Preheat oven to 350°F. Place Brie into a small cast-iron skillet and surround with diced apples and cranberries.

Drizzle with maple syrup and sprinkle cinnamon over top of fruit and cheese. Place skillet into oven and bake 25–30 minutes until bubbly.

Remove skillet carefully from oven. Sprinkle with sea salt. Serve hot (with the handle covered for safety) with apple slices and crackers.

Nutrition Facts per Serving **Calories:** 180 / **Total fat:** 10.5g (14% DV) / **Saturated fat:** 6.5g (33% DV) / **Trans fat:** 0g / **Cholesterol:** 38g (13% DV) / **Sodium:** 289mg (13% DV) / **Total carbohydrate:** 14g (5% DV) / **Dietary fiber:** 1g (4% DV) / **Total sugars:** 11g / **Added sugar:** 8g (16% DV) / **Protein:** 8g / **Vitamin D:** 0mcg (1% DV) / **Calcium:** 88mg (7% DV) / **Iron:** 0mg (2% DV) / **Potassium:** 124mg (3% DV)

Cranberry Pumpkin Butter

Pretty ruby-red cranberries simmered with earthy pumpkin, pumpkin pie spice, cinnamon, and vanilla, then blended until smooth. This is the perfect fall spread that highlights the warm flavors of harvest season. It's also the perfect hostess gift for your fall or holiday parties.

Cranberries are packed with health-promoting compounds called proanthocyanidins. These "PACs" help prevent bad bacteria from sticking in the urinary and digestive tracts.

Makes: Approximately 4 cups
Serves: 64
Serving size: 1 tablespoon
Course: Sauces and spreads
Total time: 40 minutes

INGREDIENTS

1 lb	fresh or frozen cranberries, picked over
1 (15-oz) can	pure pumpkin
¾ cup	dark brown sugar
½ cup	water
1 tbsp	pumpkin pie spice
1 tbsp	cinnamon
½ tbsp	vanilla extract
¼ tsp	salt

INSTRUCTIONS

Combine all ingredients in a medium pot over medium heat. Cover and bring to a low boil, then reduce heat and simmer.

Simmer for about 30 minutes, stirring occasionally. Remove from heat. Let cool completely.

Using an immersion blender, blend cranberry pumpkin butter until smooth. Spoon into mason jars or other glass storage containers.

Refrigerate. Cranberry pumpkin butter will keep in a sealed glass jar in the fridge for at least a week.

Nutrition Facts per Serving **Calories:** 16 / **Total fat:** 0g (0% DV) / **Saturated fat:** 0g (0% DV) / **Trans fat:** 0g / **Cholesterol:** 0mg (0% DV) / **Sodium:** 29mg (1% DV) / **Total carbohydrate:** 4g (1% DV) / **Dietary fiber:** 0.5g (2% DV) / **Total sugars:** 3g / **Added sugar:** 2.5g (5% DV) / **Protein:** 0g / **Vitamin D:** 0mcg (0% DV) / **Calcium:** 6mg (0% DV) / **Iron:** 0mg (1% DV) / **Potassium:** 24mg (1% DV)

Cranberry Pumpkin Upside Down Cake

Ruby-red fresh cranberries are drizzled in honey then topped with a spiced pumpkin batter and baked into a stunningly festive, dense, and delicious cake. This dessert will be a showstopper at any fall or holiday celebration.

Makes: Two 9-inch round cakes
Serves: 16
Course: Dessert
Total time: 35 minutes

INGREDIENTS

1½ lb	fresh cranberries, picked over
½ cup	honey
1 box	organic vanilla cake mix (mix only; not prepared)
1 (15-oz) can	pumpkin puree
1 stick	salted butter, melted
2	eggs, beaten
2 tbsp	pumpkin pie spice
1 tsp	cinnamon

For serving:

	Vanilla Greek yogurt, whipped cream, or ice cream

INSTRUCTIONS

Preheat oven to 350°F.

Grease (with butter or cooking spray) the bottom and sides of two 9-inch round cake pans. Place the cranberries evenly on the bottom of each pan; there will be some overlap. Drizzle honey evenly over pans of cranberries.

In a large mixing bowl, combine cake mix, pumpkin, butter, eggs, pumpkin pie spice, and cinnamon. Beat with a handheld mixer on low until well combined. Pour batter equally between the two pans, over top of the cranberries.

Bake for 25–30 minutes or until a toothpick inserted into the center comes out clean. Let cool completely.

Once cool, run a knife along the outer edges of the cakes. To remove the cakes, place a large plate over top of the cake and flip it over. Tap the bottom of each pan lightly then remove pan. If a few cranberries stick to the pan, replace onto the cake with your fingers.

Serve with vanilla Greek yogurt, homemade whipped cream, or vanilla ice cream. If not enjoying right away, store in the refrigerator.

RECIPE NOTE: This recipe makes two separate cakes–one for your family and one to share! It's not intended to be a double layer cake.

Nutrition Facts per Serving **Calories:** 220.5 / **Total fat:** 6.5g (8% DV) / **Saturated fat:** 4g (20% DV) / **Trans fat:** 0g / **Cholesterol:** 36g (12% DV) / **Sodium:** 257.5mg (11% DV) / **Total carbohydrate:** 40g (14% DV) / **Dietary fiber:** 3g (12% DV) / **Total sugars:** 23.5g / **Added sugar:** 12g (24% DV) / **Protein:** 3g / **Vitamin D:** 0mcg (0% DV) / **Calcium:** 21mg (2% DV) / **Iron:** 1mg (7% DV) / **Potassium:** 108mg (2% DV)

Baked Apples with Cheddar

Apples stuffed with walnuts, raisins, cinnamon, and Vermont sharp cheddar. A sweet, savory, and satisfying dessert for fall. These baked apples are a great way to use up all the fruit you've picked at your local orchard. Apples are rich in fiber and health-promoting antioxidants.

Serves: 5
Course: Dessert
Total time: 40 minutes

INGREDIENTS

5	apples (we used Honey Crisp and Cortland, but you can use any good baking apple)
⅓ cup	chopped walnuts
⅓ cup	raisins
1 tbsp	brown sugar
¼ tsp	ground cinnamon
⅛ tsp	kosher salt
3 oz	sharp cheddar cheese, sliced

INSTRUCTIONS

Preheat oven to 350°F.

Wash and core apples. Using a spoon or melon baller, hollow out the center of each apple a bit more to make room for the filling. Nest the apples snuggly into a 6- or 8-inch cast-iron skillet.

Combine walnuts, raisins, brown sugar, cinnamon, and salt. Stuff the apples with the walnut mixture and crumble the rest atop the apples. Don't worry if some of the crumble falls onto the skillet—you'll just spoon that out after cooking. Top each apple with a slice of cheddar.

Bake apples for 25 minutes, or until apples are just tender. We like ours a bit crisp, so if you prefer yours more tender, bake for longer. Remove from the oven and enjoy.

Nutrition Facts per Serving **Calories:** 268 / **Total fat:** 11g (14% DV) / **Saturated fat:** 3.5g (19% DV) / **Trans fat:** 0g / **Cholesterol:** 17mg (6% DV) / **Sodium:** 175mg (8% DV) / **Total carbohydrate:** 41g (15% DV) / **Dietary fiber:** 5.5g (19% DV) / **Total sugars:** 32g / **Added sugar:** 6.5g (13% DV) / **Protein:** 6g / **Vitamin D:** 0mcg (1% DV) / **Calcium:** 149mg (11% DV) / **Iron:** 0.5mg (4% DV) / **Potassium:** 314mg (7% DV)

Pumpkin Crème Brûlée

Pure pumpkin puree, Greek yogurt, egg yolks, brown sugar, and pumpkin pie spice come together for a creamy, luxurious dessert that celebrates all the warming flavors of fall. The best thing about this dessert is that you probably have all of these ingredients on hand. We love that this treat is packed with protein and also provides vitamin A, calcium, and fiber.

Serves: 2
Course: Dessert
Total time: 5 hours, 45 minutes (includes chill time)

INGREDIENTS

¾ cup	plain Greek whole-milk yogurt
½ cup	pumpkin puree (not pumpkin pie filling)
¼ cup + 2 tbsp	packed dark brown sugar, divided
2 large	egg yolks
1 tsp	pumpkin pie spice
1 tsp	vanilla extract
⅛ tsp	kosher salt

For serving:

¼ cup	pumpkin seeds
⅛ tsp	sea salt

INSTRUCTIONS

Preheat oven to 325°F.

Whisk together yogurt, pumpkin, ¼ cup dark brown sugar, egg yolks, pumpkin pie spice, vanilla, and salt in medium mixing bowl. Divide mixture between two 3.5-ounce ramekins.

Place ramekins in a roasting pan. Add hot water to the pan so it hits halfway up the ramekins. Bake for approximately 30–35 minutes, until custard starts to set. Remove from oven and let cool.

Cover ramekins tightly with plastic wrap and chill at least 5 hours.

When ready to serve, preheat the broiler or use a kitchen torch. Sprinkle each ramekin with 1 tablespoon brown sugar and put on a baking sheet. Broil for 1–2 minutes, keeping a close eye on the brûlées so that they don't burn. Alternatively, turn on the kitchen torch and place close to the brûlées, melting the sugar, burning just slightly. Refrigerate 10 minutes, just until sugar hardens.

Serve topped with pumpkin seeds and sprinkled with sea salt.

RECIPE NOTE: If you prefer a bit more sweetness, you can use vanilla Greek whole-milk yogurt instead of plain yogurt.

Nutrition Facts per Serving **Calories:** 381 / **Total fat:** 15g (19% DV) / **Saturated fat:** 4.5g (23% DV) / **Trans fat:** 0g / **Cholesterol:** 189mg (63% DV) / **Sodium:** 357mg (16% DV) / **Total carbohydrate:** 53.5g (19% DV) / **Dietary fiber:** 3g (10% DV) / **Total sugars:** 47g / **Added sugar:** 40g (80% DV) / **Protein:** 10.5g / **Vitamin D:** 2mcg (10% DV) / **Calcium:** 189mg (15% DV) / **Iron:** 3mg (17% DV) / **Potassium:** 445mg (9% DV)

Baked Brie with Pumpkin Butter and Walnuts

Creamy Brie cheese topped with sweet and earthy pumpkin butter and crunchy walnuts, baked until melted and delicious. It's sweet, savory, and full of the flavors of autumn–the perfect fall or winter appetizer or dessert.

Serves: 8
Course: Appetizer or dessert
Total time: 30 minutes

INGREDIENTS

8 oz	Brie cheese
¼ cup	pumpkin or cranberry pumpkin butter
¼ cup	chopped walnuts
½ tsp	cinnamon

For serving:

2	apples, thinly sliced
4 oz	whole-grain crackers

INSTRUCTIONS

Preheat oven to 350°F. Place Brie on a piece of parchment paper atop a baking sheet. Top Brie with pumpkin butter, walnuts, and cinnamon. Bake for 20–25 minutes or until cheese is melted but hasn't yet lost its form.

Remove Brie on the parchment from oven and place onto serving platter. Serve with sliced apples and/or whole-grain crackers.

RECIPE NOTE: You could also place the Brie onto a small cast-iron skillet and leave it in the skillet for serving (oven to table). Just warn guests that the skillet is very hot.

Nutrition Facts per Serving **Calories:** 212 / **Total fat:** 11.5g (15% DV) / **Saturated fat:** 5.5g (27% DV) / **Trans fat:** 0g / **Cholesterol:** 28mg (9% DV) / **Sodium:** 410mg (18% DV) / **Total carbohydrate:** 19.5g (7% DV) / **Dietary fiber:** 2g (8% DV) / **Total sugars:** 6.5g / **Added sugar:** 1g (3% DV) / **Protein:** 8g / **Vitamin D:** 0mcg (1% DV) / **Calcium:** 66mg (5% DV) / **Iron:** 1mg (6% DV) / **Potassium:** 142mg (3% DV)

Wild Blueberry Crisp

This sweet wild blueberry crisp is easy enough for the kids to make–so let them make dessert! This is a gorgeous dessert to serve any time of year because it uses frozen wild blueberries.

Serves: 8-10
Course: Dessert
Total time: 50 minutes

INGREDIENTS

For the filling:

½ cup	wild blueberry preserves
	Juice of ½ lemon
2 tbsp	cornstarch
5 cups	frozen wild blueberries (we prefer Wyman's)

For the topping:

1½ cups	old-fashioned oats
¼ cup	almond flour
½ cup	chopped walnuts
½ cup	dark brown sugar
6 tbsp	salted butter, melted
½ tsp	vanilla extract
¼ tsp	kosher salt

For serving:

	Zest of 1 lemon
	Vanilla ice cream or whipped cream

INSTRUCTIONS

Preheat oven to 350°F. Spray a pie dish with cooking spray.

In a large bowl, combine preserves, lemon juice, and cornstarch. Stir in blueberries, then pour into a 10-inch pie plate.

To the same bowl you used to mix the filling, add oats, flour, walnuts, brown sugar, melted butter, vanilla, and salt. Mix well to combine.

Scoop crisp topping over top of blueberries.

Place in oven for 40–50 minutes until bubbling throughout and golden brown. Remove from oven.

Let cool slightly, sprinkle with lemon zest, then scoop and serve with vanilla ice cream or whipped cream.

Nutrition Facts per Serving **Calories:** 263 / **Total fat:** 13.5g (17% DV) / **Saturated fat:** 5g (25% DV) / **Trans fat:** 0g / **Cholesterol:** 18mg (6% DV) / **Sodium:** 120mg (5% DV) / **Total carbohydrate:** 35g (13% DV) / **Dietary fiber:** 4.5g (16% DV) / **Total sugars:** 20g / **Added sugar:** 13g (27% DV) / **Protein:** 3.5g / **Vitamin D:** 0mcg (0% DV) / **Calcium:** 45mg (3% DV) / **Iron:** 1.5mg (9% DV) / **Potassium:** 165mg (4% DV)

Wild Blueberries

Wild blueberries are a staple in our freezer year-round. In fact, my kiddos have permanent purple mustaches from eating them every day for breakfast. Wild blueberries are convenient (flash-frozen and ready for use), packed with nutrition (including brain health–promoting anthocyanins), and have a more intense blueberry flavor than cultivated blueberries.

Britt's Wild Blueberry and Lemon Overnight Oats

My sister Brittany has always loved overnight oats. These oats are inspired by a trip to coastal Maine, where she stayed at a B&B that served incredible breakfasts, including lemon and blueberry overnight oats. Britt's version is loaded with wild blueberries, adds chia seeds for plant-based fiber and protein, and adds a creamy and crunchy topping (yogurt and toasted walnuts). This nutrient-packed breakfast is sure to give you the energy to power through your day.

Serves: 1
Course: Breakfast or brunch
Total time: 8 hours, 5 minutes

INGREDIENTS

½ cup	old-fashioned rolled oats
1 cup	oat milk, soy milk, or milk of your choice
½ cup	frozen wild blueberries (we prefer Wyman's)
1½ tbsp	lemon juice
1 tbsp	chia seeds

For topping:

1 tbsp	whole-milk vanilla yogurt
1 tbsp	toasted walnuts
1 tsp	honey

INSTRUCTIONS

Combine oats, milk, wild blueberries, lemon juice, and chia seeds in a bowl. Stir, cover, and refrigerate overnight.

When ready to serve, spoon into a bowl, mason jar, or to-go container. Top with yogurt, toasted walnuts, and honey. Serve.

Nutrition Facts per Serving **Calories:** 463 / **Total fat:** 15.5g (20% DV) / **Saturated fat:** 2g (11% DV) / **Trans fat:** 0g / **Cholesterol:** 2mg (1% DV) / **Sodium:** 215mg (9% DV) / **Total carbohydrate:** 69.5g (25% DV) / **Dietary fiber:** 14.5g (53% DV) / **Total sugars:** 27.5g / **Added sugar:** 16.5g (33% DV) / **Protein:** 17.5g / **Vitamin D:** 3mcg (15% DV) / **Calcium:** 450mg (35% DV) / **Iron:** 5.5mg (32% DV) / **Potassium:** 708mg (15% DV)

Seafood Extras

This chart from Seafood Nutrition Partnership is a great resource when looking to incorporate more omega-3–rich seafood into your diet.

WHICH FISH IS THE RICHEST IN OMEGA-3s? (PER 3 OUNCE COOKED PORTION)

Studies show omega-3s can reduce risk of heart disease, depression, dementia and arthritis, and improve overall happiness. Prominent health organizations suggest eating a variety of seafood at least twice a week, aiming to consume an average of 250 to 500 milligrams of omega-3s EPA and DHA per day.

> 1,000 milligrams ♥♥♥♥	500 - 1,000 milligrams ♥♥♥	250 - 500 milligrams ♥♥	< 250 milligrams ♥
Anchovies	Barramundi	Alaska Pollock	Catfish
Herring	Mussels	Crab	Clams
Mackerel (Atlantic & Pacific)	Salmon (Chum, Coho, Pink & Sockeye)	Flounder/Sole	Cod
Oysters (Pacific)	Sea Bass	Mackerel (King)	Crayfish
Sablefish (Black Cod)	Swordfish	Rockfish	Grouper
Salmon (Atlantic & Chinook)	Tilefish	Snapper	Haddock
Sardines	Trout	Tuna (Skipjack, canned)	Halibut
Tuna (Bluefin)	Tuna (Albacore)	Walleye	Lobster
Whitefish			Mahi Mahi
			Scallops
			Shrimp
			Tilapia
			Tuna (Yellowfin)

Source: U.S. Department of Agriculture, FoodData Central at fdc.nal.usda.gov

If you are not able to meet the omega-3 recommendation from seafood then consider supplementing with omega-3 EPA + DHA capsules.

SEAFOOD NUTRITION PARTNERSHIP®

seafoodnutrition.org

How to Choose Sustainable Seafood

Sustainable *wild-caught* seafood comes from a fishery that preserves and protects wild fish and shellfish stocks and allows them to replenish, while also protecting the surrounding ecosystems and environment for the long-term. Sustainable *farmed* seafood (aquaculture) comes from a farm following responsible practices that have little impact on the surrounding environment. Farmed seafood helps decrease the pressure on our wild fisheries and helps meet the global demand for seafood so more people across the world can enjoy fish and shellfish.

The majority of supermarkets in the United States have a seafood sustainability policy or program in place, so ask about it when you're shopping for fish and shellfish. It's also a good idea to ask where the seafood is from (the source) and how long it's been in the fish case (to help determine freshness).

Look for third-party certifications that indicate and identify sustainable seafood. You can find the logos on packaging and in some cases on signage right at the fish counter. Some of the logos include:

- Aquaculture Stewardship Council (ASC)—for farmed seafood
- Best Aquaculture Practices (BAP)—for farmed seafood
- Marine Stewardship Council (MSC)—for wild seafood
- Alaska Responsible Fisheries Management (RFM)—for wild seafood
- Fair Trade USA—farmed and wild

NOAA (National Oceanic and Atmospheric Administration) Fisheries has a great online resource at Fishwatch .gov, which allows you to enter a popular seafood species harvested or farmed in the United States to help you find sustainable seafood choices.

And if you're lucky enough to be buying local seafood, you're purchasing sustainable seafood. Supporting your local fishermen and women whose livelihood depends on those seafood sales helps support your community. And it means your seafood traveled minimal miles so you are getting the freshest seafood you can buy—unless you catch it yourself!

Lastly, domestic seafood is also sustainable seafood. According to NOAA, the United States is a recognized global leader in sustainable seafood. Our fisheries are strictly regulated by government agencies. So, when you can buy domestic seafood, I encourage you to do so to support our domestic fishermen and women and our local economies.

Wild or Farmed–How Do You Choose?

Both wild and farmed seafood can be sustainable seafood. Neither is "better" than the other, and I do not like to pit one against the other, because the answer is complicated and depends on how each is managed (see "How to Choose Sustainable Seafood" above). We need both wild and sustainably farmed and harvested seafood in order to fulfill the global demand for seafood. Aquaculture can help us meet the growing seafood demand, reduce the pressure on our wild fisheries, and reduce our dependence on seafood imports. According to NOAA, it is estimated that between 70 and 85 percent of seafood eaten in the United States is imported.

By buying sustainable wild-caught and responsibly farmed seafood, you are purchasing seafood that is nutrient-rich, delicious, and good for our planet and our oceans. Also, as mentioned in "How to Choose Sustainable Sea-food," if you are purchasing domestic seafood of either type, you can rest assured you are purchasing sustainable seafood. The United States is a recognized global leader in sustainable seafood, and all of our fish and shellfish are carefully regulated by government agencies.

In our household, we purchase both types of seafood—wild caught as well as farmed—and I feel good about that choice for our family. If you are concerned about either, I would encourage you to ask lots of questions at your fish market or seafood counter at your grocery store—as well as do your own research online to make purchasing decisions that you can feel good about.

Seafood Food Safety

- Always purchase seafood from a reputable source.
- If you are planning on eating your seafood undercooked or raw, make sure you trust your fishmonger and know that the seafood has been handled and stored properly. Consuming raw or undercooked seafood increases your risk of foodborne illness.
- Seafood should be cooked to a safe internal temperature of 145°F to minimize risk of foodborne illness.
- Those with compromised immune systems, as well as those who are pregnant, infants, young children, and older adults, should not consume raw or undercooked fish and shellfish.
- Raw fish and shellfish should be kept in the refrigerator at 40°F or less. Store it on the bottom shelf, in the back of the fridge, as this is typically the coldest spot. Keep a thermometer inside the refrigerator to assure it stays at temperature. Use fish and shellfish as soon as possible.
- If your raw or cooked seafood smells off—fishy, ammonia-like, rancid, or sour—don't eat it, as it's likely not safe to consume.
- Always wash your hands prior to and after handling raw seafood (or any raw meat product).
- Keep cooked and raw foods separate to avoid cross-contamination, and be sure to wash all surfaces, cooking equipment, and utensils after using them on raw seafood.
- Never use a marinade that has been used on raw seafood on your final cooked dish. If reusing marinade on cooked food, you need to rapidly boil it first to kill any harmful bacteria.
- Keep food out of the danger zone (between 40°F and 140°F) where bacteria can quickly multiply.
- Food should not be kept out of refrigeration for more than 2 hours (or 1 hour if temperatures are above 90°F).
- For EPA-FDA information on fish and shellfish consumption for those who might become pregnant, are pregnant, are breastfeeding, and for children, visit www.epa.gov/fish-tech/epa-fda-advice-about-eating-fish-and-shellfish.
- It's a good idea to keep a fire extinguisher easily accessible just outside the kitchen in case there's a kitchen fire. Nowadays fire extinguishers can be purchased with designs on them to match your kitchen decor—we have both a lobster and a vegetable extinguisher.

Cooking Seafood to a Safe Internal Temperature

According to FoodSafety.gov, the safe internal temperature for cooking fish is 145°F, as measured in the thickest part of the flesh with a meat thermometer. We typically pull our seafood off the heat around 140°F, knowing that the internal temperature will continue to rise a bit to the safe internal temperature of 145°F. If you don't have or use a meat thermometer, cook until the fish flakes easily when a fork is inserted in the thickest part. A fish fillet that is cooked through will lose its translucency and will be opaque.

Start with the 10-minute rule for cooking time. Measure or eyeball fish at its thickest section and cook it for approximately 10 minutes per inch of thickness, flipping halfway through cooking time.

All of this being said, there are certain fish that you may prefer to undercook. For us, that's sushi-grade salmon (we prefer it slightly undercooked in the center), sushi-grade tuna (if we don't eat it raw, we'll sear it), and fresh sea and bay scallops. White fish we will always cook through.

Seafood can become rubbery when overcooked, so take care to watch for signs of doneness, or use your meat thermometer.

For shellfish, in brief:

- Mussels, clams, and oysters will open when they're cooked. Discard any that don't open.
- Scallops will turn opaque and the flesh will firm up. Do not overcook these beauties; instead opt for slightly undercooking, and you can always put them back on the heat if needed. Take them off the heat before they become firm.
- Shrimp will become opaque, firm up, and curl.
- Lobsters will turn bright red and their antennae will pull out easily. The meat will be opaque and firm.
- Crabs will turn bright red and meat will become opaque.

Cooking Seafood from Frozen

- When thawing seafood, the best way to do so to preserve texture is to thaw it slowly. This is done by leaving it overnight in the refrigerator.
- If you have forgotten to do that, the next best method is to place the item in a resealable plastic bag and run cold (not warm, not hot) water over it, or place it in a bowl of cold water and change out the water every 30 minutes until the seafood is thawed.
- Never let seafood thaw on the counter at room temperature, as bacteria can multiply, increasing your chances of foodborne illness.
- I don't recommend cooking seafood directly from frozen. I find the texture suffers, and because of the liquid released during the cooking process, the fish or shellfish ends up steaming in that liquid (instead of roasting, pan searing, etc.).

Budget-Friendly Tips for Incorporating Seafood

Seafood can be an affordable, nutritious, and delicious addition to anyone's diet, regardless of budget. It shouldn't just be reserved for special occasions.

Here are a few tips for incorporating seafood on a tight budget:

- Shop canned and frozen options—these tend to be more affordable than fresh.
- Shop sales—this is an obvious one, but typically supermarkets will offer specials on a few seafood species at least once a week. Similarly, there is always a brand of frozen and canned seafood on sale.
- Buy frozen in bulk—if you have room in your freezer, stock up on individually frozen fish and shellfish in bulk, which tends to be more affordable than smaller packages.
- Buy local—if you live near the coast, you may be able to buy local direct from a fisherman at great prices.
- Think beyond the big fish by using smaller canned species like sardines and anchovies. And shellfish like mussels, clams, and oysters are inexpensive and packed with nutrition, making them a great addition to meals.
- Similar to the above, look for local underutilized species that tend to be more affordable—in New England, things like monkfish, skate wings, scup, striped bass, and more.

Tips to Get Kids to Eat More Seafood

Fish and shellfish are packed with vitamins, minerals, and nutrients essential for our kids' growing brains and bodies. Specifically, seafood contains omega-3 fatty acids, protein, B vitamins, vitamin D, zinc, selenium, and more. The amounts and mix of nutrients vary, depending on the species, so the goal is always to incorporate a wide variety of fish and shellfish into your family's diet. We know that the nutrients in fish and shellfish can help support growing brains (they're even beneficial for IQs!), healthy hearts, healthy eyes, strong bones, and a strong immune system.

They are not fail-safe, and my kids' love for seafood ebbs and flows, but below are a few tips that have worked for us over the years in raising little seafood lovers:

- Pair seafood with something familiar. Serve the seafood at a meal along with items they already know and love. Offer just a small portion of it.
- Prepare it in a familiar way. If your kids love seasoned and breaded chicken tenders, make seasoned and breaded fish fingers. Same recipe, just different protein.
- Don't fear the flavor. Our kiddos don't like spicy things, but they do like flavor. So I add flavor without going overboard. One thing my son doesn't like is green things (herbs) in his food, so I remove any fresh herbs in his portion. My daughter's favorite salmon recipe (included in the Salmon chapter), has a rub that combines brown sugar, cumin, garlic powder, and salt.
- Try it at lunch. Both of my kids are a lot more willing to try new foods at lunchtime vs. dinnertime, which tends to always be meltdown hour.
- Put it on your plate. Or in our case, Daddy's plate. My son will eat whatever Daddy eats, so be a role model by eating the foods you want your child to eat.
- Add a dipping sauce. Peanut sauce, tartar sauce, cocktail sauce, sour cream/Greek yogurt mixed with Old Bay Seasoning, citrus vinaigrette, even ranch dressing are great sauces to try with seafood. Or simply offer melted butter and lemon juice.
- Crust it and cake it. Add crunchy seasoned panko breadcrumbs. Or put fish or shellfish into a crispy patty or cake—like salmon or crab patties.
- Don't force it. If your kiddo doesn't want to try it, move on and try another day. Oftentimes it takes multiple exposures to a new flavor before a child begins to like it.

Fresh vs. Frozen, Canned, Tinned, or Dried Seafood

We buy all of these types of seafood and always will. We are lucky to live in New England, on Cape Cod, where we have access to local fresh seafood year-round. That's what we choose most often for dinner. That being said, you cannot beat frozen fish/shellfish, tinned/canned fish and shellfish, and dried fish (like tuna jerky) for convenience, affordability, and accessibility.

We always have frozen shrimp, homemade crab cakes, and often frozen tuna steaks in our freezer, canned crab and fermented kelp products in the fridge, and canned tuna, canned salmon, canned shellfish, seaweed snacks, and tuna jerky in the pantry.

The freezing process for fish and shellfish has improved drastically over recent years. Most fish are flash-frozen directly on the boat where it is caught, just minutes after being caught. That means the quality is preserved—freshness, nutrition, and flavor are locked in. And this flash-freezing process results in a much better texture than what you would get from freezing your own fish in a home freezer.

It's important to note that many of the "fresh" seafood options available at your local supermarket are actually previously frozen. So ask your fishmonger if the fish is actually fresh or if it's been frozen and thawed. If it's the latter, our recommendation is to go to the freezer case and buy the same fish frozen and thaw it yourself at home.

A well-stocked seafood kitchen contains all types of seafood.

Seafood Staples

Below is a list of some kitchen staples that we always have on hand for easy, quick seafood meals. I've only included brand names of items that are tried-and-true staples in our home.

FRIDGE:

- Fresh seafood from our local fish market
- Lump and jumbo lump crabmeat
- Atlantic Sea Farms Seaweed Salad, Sea-Chi, and Sea Beet Kraut
- Fresh ginger
- Ginger paste
- Pickled ginger
- The Ginger People products—pickled ginger, ginger juice, grated ginger
- Fresh herbs
- Fresh veggies
- Little Leaf Farms lettuce
- Lemons
- Limes
- Oranges
- Scallions
- Freeze-dried herbs
- Cocktail sauce
- Tartar sauce
- Wasabi mayo
- Ketchup
- Whole-grain and Dijon mustard
- Worcestershire sauce
- Reduced-sodium soy sauce
- Fish sauce
- Toasted sesame oil
- Butter—both salted and unsalted
- Greek and regular yogurt
- Mayonnaise
- Parmesan cheese
- Cheddar cheese (we prefer Cabot)
- Blue cheese (we prefer Bay Blue from Point Reyes Farmstead Cheese Company)
- Feta cheese
- Capers
- Dill and bread-and-butter pickles
- Barnacle Foods Kelp Pickles
- Barnacle Foods Kelp Hot Sauce
- Sriracha
- Miso paste
- Salsa
- Eggs
- Bacon
- White wine
- Rosé (we prefer Shea Wine Cellars and Two Mountain Winery)
- Beer

FREEZER:

- Frozen shrimp—look for those with a third-party sustainability certification
- Frozen tuna steaks
- Luke's Lobster frozen lobster meat
- Red's Best frozen fish and sushi
- North Coast Seafoods—Naked Seafood line
- Atlantic Sea Farms Ready-Cut Kelp and Kelp Cubes
- Frozen corn
- Frozen whole-grain rolls and bread
- Wyman's frozen wild blueberries
- Cape Cod Select frozen cranberries

PANTRY:

- Canned salmon
- Canned smoked salmon—we love Fishwife
- Canned tuna (we prefer tuna in olive oil)
- Tinned sardines and anchovies
- Pescavore Tuna Jerky
- Neptune Snacks Fish Jerky
- Canned beans
- Lentils
- Canned tomatoes
- Chicken broth
- Clam broth
- 12 Tides Puffed Kelp Chips
- Rice crackers
- Whole-grain crackers
- Seasoned panko crumbs
- Plain panko crumbs
- Rice vinegar
- Red wine vinegar
- Balsamic vinegar
- White wine vinegar
- Avocado oil
- Extra-virgin olive oil
- Cooking spray
- Canola oil
- Brown sugar
- Nature Nate's Honey
- Walnuts
- Peanut butter
- New potatoes
- Sushi rice
- Brown rice
- Long-grain white rice
- Flour tortillas
- Corn tortillas
- Pasta
- Farro
- Garlic
- Avocados
- Vidalia onions
- Red onions
- Shallots
- Tomatoes

SPICE DRAWER:

- Garlic powder
- Ground cumin
- Ground ginger
- Curry powder
- Onion powder
- Paprika and smoked paprika
- Crushed red pepper
- Dried orange peel
- Dried oregano
- Dried thyme
- Dried rosemary
- Black pepper
- Kosher salt
- Barnacle Foods Kelp Seasoning
- Old Bay Seasoning
- Cajun seasoning
- Italian seasoning
- Black and white sesame seeds
- Bay leaves

Seafood Resources

- **Eating with the Ecosystem** (eatingwiththeecosystem.org): Eating with the Ecosystem promotes a place-based approach to sustaining New England's wild seafood, through flourishing food webs, healthy habitats, and short, adaptive seafood supply chains. Using a mix of research, events, supply chain facilitation, and education, the organization engages seafood lovers in crafting a regional seafood system that supports New England's marine ecosystems and the people who depend on them.
- **Seafood Nutrition Partnership** (seafoodnutrition.org): Seafood Nutrition Partnership (SNP) is the leading 501(c)3 nonprofit organization in the United States building awareness of the health and nutritional benefits of seafood. SNP is addressing the country's public health crisis through education programs that inspire Americans to incorporate more seafood and omega-3s into their diets for improved health as per leading health organizations.
- **National Oceanic and Atmospheric Administration** (noaa.gov): NOAA is an agency that enriches life through science. Their reach goes from the surface of the sun to the depths of the ocean floor to keep the public informed of the changing environment around them. NOAA's mission is to understand and predict changes in climate, weather, ocean, and coasts; to share that knowledge and information with others; and to conserve and manage coastal and marine ecosystems and resources.
- **NOAA FishWatch U.S. Seafood Facts** (fishwatch.gov): Provides information on popular seafood harvested or farmed in the United States to help you make educated seafood choices.
- **Fishermen's Alliance** (capecodfishermen.org): The Cape Cod Commercial Fishermen's Alliance consists of fishermen, community members, public officials, and scientists working together to build creative strategies, advocate for improved marine policies, protect the ocean ecosystem, and ensure the viability and future of Cape Cod's fisheries.
- **Division of Marine Fisheries** (mass.gov): The Massachusetts Division of Marine Fisheries manages the state's commercial and recreational saltwater fisheries and oversees other services that support the marine environment and fishing communities.
- **Aquaculture Stewardship Council** (asc-aqua.org): The ASC is a certification program and label for farmed seafood that is helping to address some of the more pressing consumer, social, and environmental challenges of our time.
- **Marine Stewardship Council** (msc.org): MSC is an international nonprofit on a mission to end overfishing and ensure seafood is caught sustainably.
- **Global Seafood Alliance** (globalseafood.org): GSA advances responsible seafood practices worldwide through education, advocacy, and demonstration. GSA convenes seafood industry leaders, academia, and NGOs to collaborate on crosscutting issues like environmental and social responsibility, animal health and welfare, food safety, and more.
- **Best Aquaculture Practices** (bapcertification.org): As part of GSA (above), BAP ensures aquaculture is done responsibly through its third-party certification program.

Some of our favorite online markets to purchase high-quality seafood:

- Red's Best: redsbest.com
- North Coast Seafoods: northcoastseafoods.com
- Luke's Lobster: lukeslobster.com
- Island Creek Oysters: islandcreekoysters.com
- Pescavore: pescavoreseafood.com
- Atlantic Sea Farms: atlanticseafarms.com
- Barnacle Foods: barnaclefoods.com
- 12 Tides: 12tides.com
- Secret Island Salmon: secretislandsalmon.com

Sources and references:

- Eatright.org
- SeafoodNutrition.org
- NOAA.gov
- EatingwiththeEcosystem.org
- CapeCodFishermen.org
- BAPCertification.org
- GlobalSeafood.org
- MSC.org
- ASC-aqua.org
- FairTradeCertified.org
- Mass.gov
- SeafoodHealthFacts.org
- Seagrant.UMaine.edu
- LobsterFromMaine.com
- FishWatch.gov
- USDA.gov
- FDA.gov
- MyPlate.gov
- FoodSafety.gov
- DietaryGuidelines.gov
- EPA.gov
- WildBlueberries.com
- NewBedfordSeafood.org
- JennySheaRawn.com

Index

About the Author

Jenny Shea Rawn is a nationally recognized Registered Dietitian with master's degrees in Nutrition and Public Health from Tufts University. She spent almost a decade working at Shaw's Supermarkets/SUPERVALU as the regional health-and-wellness media spokesperson and nutrition expert, where she covered 450+ stores and was regularly featured in TV spots on news stations up and down the East Coast. After leaving the supermarket industry, she worked for a couple years at a global public relations firm. Jenny has been featured in hundreds of local and national media outlets, including the *Boston Globe*, Fox 25 News, the *Boston Herald*, FoodNetwork.com, *The Chef's Kitchen*, *Cape Cod & the Islands* magazine, NESN, NECN, WEEI, *Women's Health*, *Shape*, *Progressive Grocer*, the *Cape Cod Times*, and many more. She was a featured guest speaker for the Network of Executive Women, Go Red for Women Events with the American Heart Association, Harvest on the Harbor, the Women's Health Symposium, and others.

After saying goodbye to the corporate world, Jenny launched her own business, focusing on nutrition communications, recipe development, and food photography for healthy-food brands. Jenny also founded a seafood- and coastal cuisine–focused blog (JennySheaRawn.com), which focuses on simple yet elevated seafood recipes and coastal cuisine for the home cook and is a great resource for anyone looking to incorporate more seafood into their diet.

In Jenny's free time she enjoys spending time with her family, running, walking, gardening, going to the beach, and, of course, cooking and learning everything there is to know about seafood and coastal cuisine. Jenny has completed nine marathons and countless half-marathons around the New England area.

As a child, Jenny's family vacationed on Cape Cod (Chatham or Wellfleet) or Nantucket, and that's where her love of the Cape and Islands began. She's been a lobster and swordfish lover since birth, and as a young child she would request lobster for her birthday dinners. Jenny's love for the ocean runs deep—so deep, in fact, that one of the reasons she chose her college, Boston University, is because Boston was a "quick drive" to the Cape (although we all know that drive is never quick).

Jenny and her husband live on Cape Cod, in Falmouth, Massachusetts, with their two beach-loving kiddos.

Photos by Lee Geishecker, VagabondView Photography